D0776759

J. T. CHRISTIE:

A GREAT TEACHER

JTC in his early days at Westminster

J. T. CHRISTIE

A GREAT TEACHER

A selection of his own writings
with introductory memoirs by

DONALD LINDSAY

ROGER YOUNG

AND

HUGH LLOYD-JONES

The Plume Press

MALDON · ESSEX

1984

First published in 1984
by the Plume Press Ltd
West Bowers Hall, Woodham Walter,
Maldon, Essex CM9 6RZ

Designed and produced
by Janet Allan
Printed and bound in Great Britain by
Butler & Tanner Ltd, Frome and London

ISBN 0 947 656 00 6

British Library Cataloguing in Publication Data

Christie, John, *1899–1982*
J.T. Christie.
I. Title
082 PR6005, H68/
ISBN 0 947656 00 6

Contents

PART III: ON ENGLISH LITERATURE and selected jeux d'esprit

PART IV: ON RELIGION AND CHRISTIANITY

Prefatory

When John Christie died in 1980, there were many who mourned the passing of one of the great teachers of his generation. There was sadness too that John had never assembled his occasional writings into volume form and that the details of a distinguished career would soon pass into oblivion. For these reasons this book contains three biographical sketches and a small selection of John's own papers that reflect his work as a teacher, a classical scholar, a lover of literature and a devout Christian.

We are most grateful to those schools and colleges with whom JTC was associated who have made the publication of this book possible; in particular the Governing Bodies of Repton School, Rugby School, Winchester College, Westminster School, the Dragon School, Trinity College, Glenalmond, Jesus College, Oxford, and Trinity College, Oxford. Our cordial thanks are also due to Lucie Christie, her daughters Catherine Porteous and Jane Darwin, and to John's nephew, Henry Christie, who have given the staunchest support since the idea of the book was initiated. A particular tribute must go to Donald Lindsay, who had once worked under John Christie as an Assistant Master at Repton, for the enormous trouble he took over the completion of his long biographical sketch, and to Professor Hugh Lloyd-Jones and Sir Roger Young, both former pupils of JTC's, for their perceptive appreciations; also to W.R. LeFanu, JTC's brother-in-law, for his very considerable help in the editing of the volume.

The publishers would also like to thank the following who have given permission for the re-publication here of articles by JTC: Oxford University Press, the British Association for the Advancement of Science, the *Times Literary Supplement*, William Collins, Sons & Co, the BBC, the Dragon School and *The Spectator*.

Finally the family would like to record their gratitude for

the tireless efforts of Frank Herrmann who put the book together. Without his enthusiasm, good nature, determination and expertise, JTC's works would never have been collected, nor would the memoirs have been written.

Curriculum Vitae: John Traill Christie

Born 19 October 1899 at Ongar, Essex; fourth and youngest son of C.H.F. Christie, DL, JP, and Margaret Eleanor, daughter of the Rev C.S. Palmer, Canon of Hereford.

Educated at St David's School, Reigate, 1907–1913, and Winchester College (scholar), September 1913 to December 1917.

Training for war service in Coldstream Guards 1918–19.

Scholar of Trinity College, Oxford, May 1919 to July 1922: First Class in Honour Moderations 1920, First Class in Litterae Humaniores 1922; B.A. 1922.

Sixth Form Master, Rugby School, September 1922 to July 1928.

M.A. Oxford 1928.

Fellow and Tutor, Magdalen College, Oxford 1928–1932.

Head Master of Repton School, 1932–1937.

Married at Christ Church, Bray, Co Wicklow on 8 April 1933 Lucie Catherine, daughter of Thomas Philip LeFanu, CB, and Florence, daughter of the Rev James Sullivan.

Head Master of Westminster School, May 1937–December 1949, including wartime evacuation to Lancing, Sussex, 1939–1940 and Bromyard, Herefordshire, 1940–1945.

Principal of Jesus College, Oxford, 1950–1967; Honorary Fellow 1967.

Assistant Master, part-time, at Westminster School, 1967–1969.

Lived after retirement at Church Cottage, Great Henny, near Sudbury, Suffolk, 1970–1980.

Died on 8 September 1980, survived by his wife, his daughters Catherine Porteous and Jane Darwin, and six grand-children.

John Traill Christie 1899–1980: A MEMOIR

'It is the object of education through all its stages to release the imprisoned splendour.' W. W. VAUGHAN

John was born on 19 October 1899, the fourth son of Charles Henry Fehler Christie, in the pleasant, old-fashioned family house, known as The Wilderness, at Chipping Ongar in Essex. Scottish blood flowed in his veins for his great-great-grandfather, the Rev Alexander Christie, had been the episcopalian Dean of Aberdeen. Of greater interest to John was Alexander's second son, Jonathan Henry Christie, who from Glasgow University came to Oxford as a Snell Scholar at Balliol. He decided to remain in England and became a solicitor of repute. John's particular interest in his great-grandfather arose from Jonathan's friendship with John Gibson Lockhart, the son-in-law and biographer of Sir Walter Scott, of whose novels John had expert knowledge and lasting admiration. Apart from being the father of four sons and three daughters and one of the leading authorities on conveyancing, Jonathan's claim to fame lay in the duel which he fought one moonlit night near Chalk Pit Farm in 1821, with John Scott, editor of the *London Magazine*. He had seen fit to publish letters reflecting adversely on Lockhart's conduct of *Blackwood's Magazine* and also on Jonathan, who, on behalf of his friend, demanded an apology or satisfaction. Eventually Scott issued a challenge which led to the duel in which he was mortally wounded. In the subsequent trial at the Old Bailey Jonathan was acquitted, it being established that Scott had been entirely in the wrong and that Jonathan, in the words of Sir Walter Scott, had 'behaved with the utmost moderation and gallantry and had no mode of avoiding the sleeveless quarrel fixed on him'.

Jonathan's third son, Alexander Henry Christie, John's grandfather, was a member of the Stock Exchange, a great reader like his father and from 1837 a member of the Athenaeum. A love of books and of reading was from early days a marked characteristic of the Christie family and Alexander built up a vast, miscellaneous collection of books which became John's delight. In the library at Ongar John found not the shelves of carefully bound volumes on which eighteenth-century gentlemen prided themselves but hundreds and hundreds of books amassed for the sheer joy of reading.

John's father was born in 1857 and he became a highly trusted but unadventurous stockbroker, whose wise advice was widely sought but whose innate caution prevented him from making his own fortune. At heart he was happiest as a country gentleman, greatly respected in Essex where he was both a Deputy Lieutenant and a Justice of the Peace. He regularly read the lesson in Ongar Parish Church and as Colonel Christie he was for many years a distinguished Territorial Army Officer in the Essex Regiment. A touch of the old Scottish puritanical background could be detected in his love of bicycling, which earned him a Half-Blue at Oxford. At first he rode on a high machine but later on a 'safety' model. To cycle uphill and into the wind gave him special pleasure. In 1891 he married a very charming wife, Marjory Palmer, whose father was for many years vicar of the Herefordshire parish of Eardisley and later a Canon of Hereford Cathedral. He is immortalised by a carved stone head on the south side of the north door of the great West Front, just inside the Cathedral. From his mother John inherited his sense of fun and his gift of amusing talk. She never wrote even a short note without a witty turn of phrase. Four sons were born of this happy marriage.

The four brothers were, in different ways, a problem to their parents and their father never really understood any of them. Alec, the eldest, after Winchester and Christ Church, Oxford, studied as a barrister. He was never able to practise for after serving with the 8th Hussars in World War I he succumbed to sleepy sickness from which he never wholly recovered. He was able to be of use in various ill-paid social service posts but never to return to the Law. The second son, Charles, knew without a shadow of doubt that he wanted to be a Naval Officer. In an attempt either to test his vocation or to cure him of an aberration his father took him round the British Isles in a coaster. Charles thrived; his father was horribly sick. So Charles went to Dartmouth but the promising career which lay ahead of him was cut short in 1929 by his sudden death from appendicitis when a Lieutenant-Commander. Arthur, the third son, was a very delicate child who was thought not strong enough for Winchester but able to survive Shrewsbury, which he disliked. He was a musical boy, who wanted to learn the piano, but this was not permitted by his father who regarded playing the piano as an essentially feminine accomplishment. He had always been very good with his hands and on leaving Shrewsbury he showed great foresight by starting a garage. He possessed the first motor bicycle in Essex and clearly foresaw the development of motor transport. As a result, by the late thirties he was able to sell his garage at a great profit and could henceforth indulge his taste for small boat sailing, music and motor cars.

Last of the family came John, marked out from early days as being far cleverer than his parents or his brothers. The family were proud of him but also slightly in awe of him, for John lived in an intellectual world of his own. As he grew older they could not fail to notice the streak of ruthlessness which fine scholars so often possess when in pursuit of their particular discipline. John, however, loved Ongar and The Wilderness garden and he was devoted to his family. When his father died in 1924 and the house had to be sold – it was later knocked down to make a car park – John wrote from Rugby where he was teaching: 'I went home and said goodbye to rocks and stones and trees which had bedded themselves deeper in the heart than one knew'. His happy home life gave him a deep and lasting attachment to the undramatic Essex countryside and to the wide skies, the villages and the marvellous parish churches of East Anglia. It was to Essex that in old age he returned.

Shortly before his eighth birthday John went away to his preparatory school, St David's at Reigate. From here he won a scholarship to Winchester, entering College in September 1913 at the same time as Thomas (later Sir Arthur) Norrington, his life-long friend. Thanks to the library at Ongar John arrived at Winchester far more widely read in English literature than most clever boys of his age. Later in life he once said: 'There is always something dangerous as well as touching in an extreme devotion to the scenes of one's youth. Winchester has for me an immense *genius loci* but I don't wholly approve of all that it stands for'. However, a distinguished career there ended in December 1917 when he won a classical scholarship to Trinity College, Oxford.

The war was by no means over and there could be no question of going up to Oxford at once. So John enlisted in the Coldstream Guards. An attack of mumps while he was at the Cadet Camp at Bushey delayed his going to France until too late to take an active part in the final Allied advance, but he stayed on after the Armistice and was commissioned. This delighted his parents who realised that their youngest son was not such an impractical academic as they had feared. The barrack room was, in fact, John's only experience of living at close quarters with tough working class men, and his mother maintained that he would never have managed men as he did without the experience of the Bushey Camp. For such an unmilitary man he was unexpectedly proud of his brief army career. When years later his younger friends wore regimental ties after National Service John remarked: 'Damn it! Why shouldn't I wear a Brigade tie? At least I was in a real war'. So Catherine, his eldest daughter, presented him with a tie which he wore.

John went up to Trinity in May 1919. He was extremely fortunate in his Tutors: for two terms he was with Cyril Bailey in Balliol until T.F. Higham was released from the forces. Tommy Higham was a great Honour Mods: Tutor who later became Public Orator. In his brilliant skill at composing Latin and Greek verse and prose John revelled and came to emulate him. A 'First' in Mods: was followed by a 'First' in Greats for which he was tutored by a man whom he venerated, H.A. Pritchard, and a Fellowship seemed his inevitable reward. But Norrington – himself a Trinity man and later President of the College – felt sure that during these years at Oxford John became convinced that his vocation was that of a teacher. So in 1922 he accepted without hesitation an invitation to teach Classics to the Upper Bench at Rugby.

To invite John to take over the Upper Bench must have seemed a very controversial appointment by W.W. Vaughan, who had returned to his old school a year earlier as its first lay Headmaster. While John's academic qualifications could not be faulted, he was totally without experience. Even a teacher of genius, as John proved to be, has to learn by practice how to take a lesson and later in life John used to recall the pitfalls of his first year and his debt to senior colleagues who showed him how to arrange his time and teaching. Furthermore, he had to contend with two problems which an experienced teacher might have found daunting. To occupy the room where Arnold had once taught might have been an honour, but the Upper Bench room has six sides so that wherever the master's desk was placed, some boys were behind his back. More worrying was a much wider range of ability among the pupils than John would have experienced at Winchester. In addition to clever future scholars the Rugby tradition meant that the Upper Bench contained senior prefects, distinguished games players and the like whose love of the Classics was minimal. However, before long early difficulties were overcome and John's matchless skill in expounding a classical text and his ability to fire the imagination and to share his delight with his pupils are what remain in the minds of many, not all of them classical scholars, who became his lifelong friends. Memorable, also, were the hitherto unheard of visits to Greek plays at Bradfield and Oxford.

As a new master waiting with his colleagues to go into Chapel, John stood out with his striking but unusual appearance. His height, fair hair and searching eyes made him seem to boys very different from the usual run of masters. He looked absurdly young and there are many, probably legendary, stories of mothers visiting Rugby who mistook him for a prefect. It was an age of powerful Housemasters and John used to say that years later he was still subject to a recurrent nightmare in which he found himself chosen to referee the Cock House rugger final with rival Housemasters on opposite sides of the field, united solely in their condemnation of his decisions.

During his later years at Rugby John became House Tutor at School Field, a House run by the Rev E.F. Bonhote, a kindly but unimaginative Housemaster. This brought him into contact with boys of differing abilities and interests, whom he used to invite in batches to have tea in his lodgings. To stimulate conversation with younger boys and others with whom he had not much in common he relied upon a complete set of Ordnance Survey maps, finding that tongues were loosened as they talked about the places on the map near their homes. For a short period he had to run the House when Bonhote was ill. It was not a very happy time for it was impossible to conceal from boys that John's interests and his ideas on running a House contrasted markedly with those of the Housemaster. The House was not in good order and, in John's view, too concerned with athletic achievements, but a difficult month or two proved useful experience when in time he became a Headmaster. He was by no means opposed to games; he was a useful squash rackets player and while at Rugby learned to play Rackets under the guidance of Mark Hankey, a boy at Rugby though not his pupil.

Boys did not always find it easy to get to know John; his intellectual powers and slightly austere manner could be off-putting. His deep love of English literature revealed an emotional side to his nature which casual acquaintances did not suspect. Probably he would have enjoyed being allowed officially to teach English, not merely to bring it into his Classical lessons. Unfortunately senior boys were taught English - and if report be true, taught very badly - by the Headmaster. It was on holiday reading parties to which young former Rugbeians at Oxford and Cambridge were invited that they came to know him fully. George Allen recalls a bicycling holiday with John and another boy after their final term at Rugby. 'A long since vanished ferry boat at Kirk Hammerton; the first astonishing impact of Fountains Abbey; Evensong at Ripon Cathedral; the excitements of Upper Wensleydale and - not least - pedalling slowly up the Chevin in pouring rain. Nothing deterred him, least of all the sometimes primitive accommodation. He was never a physically robust man but he took it all in his long stride and, of course, we were all equals.' It was late in August 1926 that Edmund Compton joined John and Thomas Norrington and Donald Lucas (later to be a Fellow of Kings') on a reading party at Church Stretton. Never till then had Compton suspected the fun and frivolity which John could show, especially in verbal sparring with Norrington. Nor had he realised John's stamina as a fell walker. For in John's opinion every respectable scholar should also be a good walker, able to know his way across the countryside and appreciate all that he saw.

Life at Rugby was both demanding and satisfying. 'Delightful work,' he wrote, 'but it flows into spare time like the sea and fills every inlet. I enjoy teaching more and more ... I wouldn't be a don.' This prophecy was soon proved false. John's fame as a teacher could not for long be confined to Rugby and in 1928 he was enticed back to Oxford as Fellow and Tutor at Magdalen College.

John was at Magdalen for only four years. He quickly earned a reputation as a hardworking Tutor and an inspiring lecturer. But he did not find College life so demanding or so fulfilling as life at Rugby. In the 'twenties and early 'thirties Magdalen, like many another beautiful college, was something of a lotus-land and John's puritan conscience may have led to fears of self-indulgence. A man who shunned hot baths and soft beds, though in moderation he enjoyed good food and drink, at first gave the impression to more sybaritic colleagues of being self-righteous and something of a prig. He was neither. As a Tutor he regretted the lack of opportunity to do the kind of teaching which he had come to love and he was depressed at the poor quality of some of his pupils. However, when he was made Secretary to the Tutorial Board, a body responsible for keeping a strict eye on teaching standards in the College, he was in his element. He had a task which gave him much more to do within the College and earned him the respect of his fellow dons. Some of John's early dissatisfaction with life at Magdalen stemmed from not being engaged upon a major piece of research. This would have filled his time and made him more in line with a don's life. To many a don research came first; to John nothing was more important than teaching.

Early in 1932 a former Rugby pupil whose home was in Ireland, Hamon Dickie, dropped in to see John at Magdalen. In the course of casual conversation John mentioned that he felt that he would like to get married but had not so far met the right girl. As Dickie was leaving John said that he was coming to Ireland in the Easter vacation on a walking tour with his colleague, Adam Fox, and he wondered if he might spend the Easter weekend at Dickie's house at Bray in County Wicklow. Dickie assured him of a warm welcome and went away pondering on such of his Irish girlfriends as might suit John.

Living near the Dickies at Bray were the LeFanus, a family of Huguenot origin. By the nineteenth century several of the family had become people of consequence in Ireland. In 1826 Thomas

LeFanu, a nephew of R.B. Sheridan, the playwright, had become Dean of Emly and Rector of Abington; he was the father of Sheridan LeFanu, novelist and ghost story writer, and of William LeFanu, a civil engineer who became much involved in the development of the Irish railway system. William had eight sons and two daughters; the eldest son Thomas, a retiring and scholarly man, the possessor of a good library, was an official in the Chief Secretary's office in Dublin. For five years he was seconded to London, taking his family with him for much of each year. Then to his delight he was appointed Commissioner of Public Works in Ireland (the equivalent of Permanent Secretary of the Office of Works in England), the post which his father had held thirty years earlier, and was proud to remain head of the office, though due for retirement, when the Irish Free State was established. He shared with his wife, a good field botanist, a love of gardening, though not her delight in music which he considered to be one of the nastier noises. It was their daughter, Lucie, whom Dickie planned to introduce to John.

The world in which Lucie and her brother William grew up has largely vanished. It was an age when it was customary in Ireland for a married couple to live near the house of their parents. This gave children a feeling of security and permanence as well as supplying them with a bevy of uncles, aunts and cousins all living in the neighbourhood. Lucie went first to a local girls' school where she became proficient in French but regretted being taught Latin rather than Italian. She later went to Alexandra College in Dublin which had been founded before women were admitted to Trinity. One of her six uncles, Victor, kept open house for his nephews and nieces. He had formerly played rugger for Cambridge and Ireland and owned a house with bookshelves stocked with Stevenson, Shaw, Wells, Arnold Bennett, Anthony Hope, Kipling and O'Henry, all able to be borrowed by avid readers like Lucie. Her cousins and the children of old family friends came to know each other well through tennis parties and picnics in the summer and dances and parties at Christmas time. Lucie's mother encouraged her piano playing and urged her to learn to play ragtime, a useful accomplishment at local dances when the professional musicians were at supper.

A sister of Lucie's mother lived in Co. Wexford and her daughter became almost a sister to Lucie. Here was the attraction of farmyard and surrounding fields, while only four miles away was the sea, with a long stretch of sandy shore, to which they and their friends went on bicycles or by pony cart. Nearer home Lucie and her brother, or Lucie alone with her dog, walked the mountain paths, a mere half hour's bicycle ride away. Dublin was only a dozen miles off and for the price of 1s 6d in the Circle or 5s in the Stalls the plays of Synge, O'Casey and Shaw could be seen at the Abbey Theatre, then in its heyday. For music the Royal Dublin Society's thirteen Chamber Concerts each winter were available.

Of the cheerful company surrounding her Lucie was the central figure in every activity. She was recognised as the most intelligent and widely read member of the group with the ability – to be invaluable later in her life – to make a success of any gathering of whatever age in which she was involved. However idyllic in some respects Irish life was, permanent residence in rural Ireland would have proved too cramping and would have offered too little scope for her talents. She needed to move in a wider world and John was to make this possible.

John arrived at Bray on the Thursday before Easter. Next day Dickie and John were joined by Lucie and a friend for a rather wet picnic at Glendalough. John and Lucie clearly enjoyed each other's company and John found Lucie fully capable of holding her own in conversation and in capping his quotations. They met again next day but on Easter Monday John left for his walking tour. However, at Whitsun Lucie asked Dickie if he thought that she would enjoy Commem. at Oxford as John had invited her to come. Receiving unhesitating encouragement Lucie went to Oxford and from then onward the outcome was clear. John visited Bray again shortly after his appointment to Repton had been announced and he and Lucie became engaged. They were married at Bray on 8th April 1933. Lucie brought to the marriage complementary qualities of infinite value to John. The austere side of his nature and traditional outlook – 'I recognise I am a late-Victorian Evangelical in many of my likes and dislikes' – were now matched by an Irish wife who would always be unconventional and unpredictable and who, happily for them both, had a mind of her own. Shortly before the wedding John, in a lyrical outburst, told Dickie that he was marrying 'a wild swan'. After a honeymoon in the West of Ireland John brought his 'swan' to face the conventions and rigid outlook of an English public school in the 'thirties.

John became Headmaster of Repton in September 1932. During the two terms before his marriage his widowed mother kept house for him. For a young and rather shy man it was not easy to follow Geoffrey Fisher, who had come to Repton in 1914 and who over eighteen years had won the respect and affection of masters and boys alike. Unwittingly Fisher added to John's early difficulties by his habit of returning to Repton from his Chester bishopric, unannounced, and being found by his less self-assured successor in the dormitories of the Hall, the Headmaster's House, chatting happily to the boys. John bore no lasting ill will for this curiously insensitive behaviour for he and Fisher became close friends.

Fisher had been an outstandingly able administrator and John inherited from him a smooth-running and well organised school. John had no great love for administration, nor had he any wish to keep everything in his own hands. The administrative burden was heavy for he could at first call only on the assistance of an elderly clerk who also served the Bursar, and this encouraged him to delegate more than Fisher had done. John also believed that the masters needed to be more involved in helping to run the School than had hitherto been the practice.

As a Headmaster John was not by nature a great innovator and revolutionary changes were not needed. First Lesson and Chapel before breakfast disappeared unlamented, as did the Eton jacket for young boys – an inefficient garment in John's opinion 'leaving off where it ought to begin'. The antique washing rooms in the boys' boarding houses were brought up to date and the worst House, the Mitre, was replaced by a completely new building. Major changes in the running of boarding houses affected masters rather than boys. A Housemaster's tenure of his House was limited to fifteen years. Since this resulted in younger men becoming Housemasters John persuaded the Governors to end the practice whereby an incoming Housemaster had to buy all the furniture of the boys' side of the House from his predecessor. John, who was a victim of this in the Hall, knew what an impossible financial burden this was for a man with limited tenure. He himself was in debt for most of his time at Repton because of this. He also altered the per capita food allowance to a Housemaster. If a Housemaster overspent he had to meet the debt from his own resources; if he underspent the surplus went back to the School. John arranged that Houses which fed the boys well and yet kept within financial limits were rewarded by improvements to the House.

However, John's real interests did not lie in the material sphere. His contribution to Repton lay in the stimulus which he gave to the intellectual side of school life. Repton's need, as John perceived it, was a radical change of emphasis: mind and spirit must be recognised as being of greater importance than the body. He was no opponent of games or of athletic prowess. What worried him was the excessive deference paid to the athlete in comparison to the scholar and the obsessive interest in the results of inter-School and inter-House contests. These loomed too large in the eyes of boys, partly because they mattered far too much to many of his Staff. 'I hope, Headmaster, that you will be giving a half holiday so the School can watch the Derbyshire Friars' [cricket] match?', a Housemaster enquired at the end of a Staff meeting. 'Excellent idea! The only time a Repton boy ever reads a book', was John's swift reply. This sally, like many another tilt at the Establishment, delighted irreverent younger masters but did not always endear John to his more senior colleagues. He and Lucie long remembered the sight of another Housemaster sitting despondently alone on the edge of the cricket field long after the players had departed, unable to believe the impossible, that his House had been defeated. 'And on his birthday, too', said his equally heartbroken wife.

To change a school's values takes time: there can be no short cuts. John knew that the ultimate solution lay in the quality of the teaching staff. On arrival at Repton he was delighted to find a number of pleasant and clever boys at the top of the school and he was anxious to ensure that they were not only adequately instructed but were also excited and stretched intellectually. Like the great Victorian headmasters, whom he in some ways resembled, John believed that a headmaster's first duty was to set an example as a fine teacher. This side of his work came naturally to him and he took as big a share as time allowed in the teaching of Classics and English literature. To his young masters he made it abundantly clear that their primary task was to teach well. Other activities were valuable and were encouraged by him but they came second in his scale of values. 'Ah, my friend, for your first year your bride should be the school,' was his slightly daunting remark to a new master contemplating matrimony. New recruits to the profession were not left to their own devices. A knock on the form-room door and into the young man's lesson, without prior warning, John would come. 'Don't take any notice of me,' he would say as he took a seat at the back of the room – an impossible request to meet. Yet afterwards invaluable advice and encouragement always followed.

It was a much harder task to rekindle the fire in the belly among some of the older masters. By means of discussion groups, which he started, and by friendly and apparently casual conversation he nudged his more hidebound colleagues into thinking afresh about their teaching. His Rugby experience led him to introduce House Tutors into all the Houses, partly to give young men an insight into the problems of running a House and also as a means of infiltrating new ideas into the barons' castles. Lucie was amazed at how traditionally-minded one or two Housemasters could be. Coming away from a dinner party in one House she burst out to John about their host: 'He actually talked to me as if I were a Conservative'!

A former Rugby pupil visiting Repton in 1935 noticed the effect of what he called Lucie's 'benign influence' on John. He had seen John excited and thrilled and happy but until now he had never sensed the deep contentment which marriage had brought. The old critical outlook and quick wit were unchanged but John seemed to have grown more tolerant. This may well have been the result of becoming a father, for at the end of January 1935 Lucie's first child, Catherine, had been born. Almost exactly a year later a second daughter, Jane, arrived.

John was the first layman to be appointed Headmaster of Repton. Both on the platform and in the pulpit he was a most accomplished and compelling speaker. He could hold the rapt attention of audiences of any size from a small group of boys studying a Gospel to the unseen thousands who listened to his religious broadcasts. Yet he never forgot, in his own words, that 'fluency of speech will always impress boys but ultimately will influence them less than sincerity'. He was humbly aware that 'the last and perhaps most powerful weapon in any man's armoury is the unconscious example of his own life'.

In May 1937 John succeeded Dr Costley-White as Headmaster of Westminster. He had been at Repton for only five years and there were some who felt that he had not given the school the length of service which was its due. Others, and they were the majority, deeply regretted the departure of their lost leader. The truth is that John had never been wholly happy at Repton. It was not quite the ideal school for his particular genius but without doubt he had been the right man for Repton at that moment in its history. Moreover it was a physically tiring post. For apart from the normal duties of a headmaster, John was Housemaster to ninety boys. An excellent resident House Tutor could not relieve him of the final responsibility and housemastering also added to the burden of his correspondence – 'I have a heap of Fussiana from parents before me' – and parents claimed his supposedly free time on Sundays. He loved the Repton countryside which had a quietness akin to Essex, though his romantic sense insisted that the River Trent was too tempestuous to run through a pastoral landscape. Nevertheless, the invitation to move to a school steeped in history and with a great tradition of classical learning could not be resisted. He could not know that the next twelve years were to prove as stern a test as any headmaster has had to face.

John loved Westminster. Although a countryman, he enjoyed living in a beautiful house in the heart of London. A school with a great literary tradition, which numbered Dryden and Gibbon among its former pupils, which every year produced a Latin play and which regarded Westminster Abbey as its school chapel could not fail to appeal to him. The close connection with the Abbey meant that John found himself immediately involved in the ritual of the coronation of King George VI and Queen Elizabeth, as were the King's Scholars with their traditional cries of Vivat! Vivat! Soon afterwards the new King and Queen came to the school to see the Latin play. Unknown to John the invitation to Buckingham Palace had been sent by the College monitors who awaited John's reaction to the King's acceptance with some anxiety. As John's first Captain of the School later wrote: 'There is no doubt that after Costley's smooth and rather bumbly approach, John arrived with all the sharpness of vinegar'. However, all went well and John, in kindness to his royal guests, composed a very much shortened prologue to the play.

It was impossible for boys – and masters – not to be struck by and to be slightly in awe of that tall, slender figure, with its immensely long legs, walking at great speed across Little Dean's Yard. It was some time before he discovered that the nickname 'Legs' was his. His sandy hair and fair complexion were accentuated by the dark suit which he habitually wore. His voice, easy to imitate, was unmistakable with its incisiveness, its slightly nasal twang and the characteristic 'Ha!', which often ended a comment. When addressing the School he appeared to stand on one leg, like a stork, with head on one side, a sideways twist of the lips – especially when some quick rejoinder slipped out – and a trick of one hand grasping the other arm behind his back. He could be formidable – no bad thing for a new headmaster – and a trifle remote, which often concealed an innate shyness. From his Scottish forebears he had inherited a seriousness and a moral purpose which alarmed lesser mortals until they discovered the fun and bubbling sense of humour which were an essential part of him. The twinkle in his bright blue eyes and an almost puckish delight in the amusing side of people and events betrayed an intensely human person. His power of kindly mimicry was considerable. At a school like Repton in the countryside the Headmaster is always on duty: it is difficult for him to escape. Even on a country walk he is liable to be tackled by someone. Westminster was very different. Once outside Dean's Yard he can be an anonymous citizen. As John said to Lucie: 'No one is likely to stop me in St James's Park and say "One of your boys has been riding one of my sheep"!' This really had occurred at Repton.

A King's Scholar on his way to breakfast was waylaid by John with the curt command: 'Do up your button, boy'. (The curiously old-fashioned use of the word 'boy' was friendly and not intended to remind a pupil of his inferior position.) With the offending button firmly in its place, John added: 'That's better. Now come and have breakfast with me, will you?' Stories abound of private kindnesses shown to those needing help. On his first day as a headmaster a former Repton assistant master received a letter of good wishes. The letter pointed out how everyone would have written to congratulate him when the appointment was announced but – in the words of John's beloved Browning – it is 'when the blasts denote I am nearing the place' that a word of encouragement is needed. For his dealings with his colleagues John knew the value of a short letter of appreciation. When it came to a reprimand or the conveying of unpleasant tidings he believed that this should not be done by letter but face to face, however much he was tempted to shrink from doing this. John was as old-fashioned in his mode of addressing masters as he was with boys. He never used a master's Christian name in case there might come a moment when a master had to be dismissed. Even John Carleton, the Under Master with whom he worked so closely, was never called by his Christian name until John had left Westminster for Oxford.

Modern headmasters are sometimes judged by their powers of administration. As at Repton John admired administrative skill not for its own sake but because 'it will leave a headmaster time for what is, I believe, more lasting work'. He feared 'the standing danger that mere administration may absorb more time than it should'. He knew that most assistant masters, while appreciating a smooth-running school, valued more a headmaster capable of making firm decisions, even if unwelcome. As a sensitive and emotional man – though the scholar was mostly in control – John must often have agonised over some of the big decisions which he had to make, especially when they affected individual masters. When it came to wartime the decisions affected the very existence of the School. He never shrank from wielding authority, for that was a headmaster's work, but he was strengthened by knowing whence that authority must be derived. Years later when addressing the now extinct Conference of Schoolmasters and College Tutors – familiarly known as 'Dons and Beaks' – he spoke of how he had learned from his study of the Gospels 'that all power divorced from the source of supreme power, God, was in danger of failing ... if one's power and the right to command is treated as a trust from God, then authority becomes a true and precious form of divine obedience, while human obedience ceases to be felt as degradation'.

The Westminster Odyssey belongs to the history of the School and cannot be told in full here. Yet the bare outline is sufficient to show the magnitude of the problems which John and his Governors faced between 1938 and 1945.

Broadly speaking, the story falls into a prologue and two parts.

In face of the growing menace from Germany John had made an arrangement with Rossall School in Lancashire to share Rossall's buildings in the event of war. On returning with Lucie from a Hellenic cruise to Greece at the end of August 1938 he found that the situation had deteriorated to such an extent that before the September term began he felt it right to inform parents of the possible move to Rossall at short notice. The plan was short-lived. A Westminster parent high up in the Home Office secretly warned John that unknown to Rossall's headmaster his school was earmarked to receive a branch of the Civil Service. It was necessary to find another school sufficiently short of numbers – it was a time when many public schools needed more pupils – to accommodate Westminster. Lancing College, whose headmaster was an old Westminster, came to the rescue. In response to a telegram offering to help, John Carleton was sent off to investigate. On 29 September, thanks to meticulous preparation and rehearsal, a fleet of buses brought Westminster to Lancing. When he arrived John was greeted with the news of the Munich Agreement and he had to make a decision whether to turn round and go back to London or to remain and see if war had really been averted. He made the wise decision to remain in Sussex for a week. It proved a providential decision because of the valuable lessons learned in what proved to be a dress rehearsal for the long-term move a year later.

The week spent at Lancing had made clear the need for far more accommodation if the exile were to be prolonged. So during the Easter holidays of 1939 John and Lucie returned to Sussex and made provisional arrangements for day boys to be housed in two buildings in Shoreham, though they would be taught at Lancing, and for one third of the boarders to live at Hurstpierpoint, the neighbouring Woodard School. The School finally moved to Sussex in September 1939 but it was intended that this move would be a temporary measure until more spacious accommodation could be found or the School be able to return to London. This sojourn at Lancing ended abruptly, however, after the fall of France in June 1940 with the obvious danger of invasion in the Shoreham area and the enforced evacuation of Lancing to Ludlow. The West Country was clearly the safest area and Dr John Murray, Vice-Chancellor of Exeter University, made it possible for Westminster to settle in comparative comfort into Halls of Residence for the remainder of the Summer Term.

The second part of the story began in July 1940 when the Westminster Governors acting on the extraordinary belief of one of their number, highly placed in the Air Ministry, that London would not be bombed, decided to re-open the school in Dean's Yard in September. John had now to work out a detailed programme for life at Westminster under war time conditions. Black-out restrictions, transport difficulties, playing fields dug up for trenches, air raid warnings and safety precautions all had to be faced. On 7 September the last bed was back in place; on 8 September the Blitz on London began.

It rapidly became apparent that the School could not remain in London. Exeter University was no longer available. So John, with half-a-dozen colleagues, scoured the countryside. It was a frustrating task. One likely property was scheduled for the giraffes from the South Kensington Museum; another had an inadequate water supply; nearly all had long been requisitioned and their release would have to be fought for with the appropriate Whitehall department. By mid-October Herefordshire was in favour as the most promising area and by the beginning of November John established his headquarters at Bromyard with the school scattered in various houses over a distance of five or six miles.

In March 1941 John wrote a Letter to Old Westminsters: 'There was much negotiation before we could think of moving in: and when we did move in there was much to do. Two of the houses could not unfairly be described as derelict: one had not been lived in for twenty years and brambles were pushing into the drawing room. While pioneers were working down at Bromyard, a group of masters and School staff were packing up not merely what we wanted down in Herefordshire but the whole of Westminster School! ... Class-rooms, playing-fields, laboratories ... even windows and floors had to be made and made largely by our own efforts ... Gardening, house-painting, road-mending, tree-felling are only some of our many new "stations", and all the better education because they are not deliberately contrived for the boys' good but because, if they are not done, life could not continue'.

Here for nearly five years John held together a school which inevitably dwindled in number, a source of acute financial anxiety at a time of heavy expenses. 'Contract and carry on' was his determined motto even if, as he said, he were reduced to tramping the countryside with only the forty King's Scholars at his heels. Although the danger of invasion had receded it was always a possibility and at Christmas 1941 John sent a card to a friend in the Secret Service: 'If you have early advice on invasion send me a wire – code word Flat Bottoms'. Never for one moment did he allow boys or masters to forget that a school is primarily a place of learning and that somehow teaching must be carried on. John's loyal secretary had been killed by a bomb on Church House before the move to Bromyard began and it was John with John Carleton who had found her. Efficient replacements were difficult to find. One of these he described in a letter to John Carleton who was on war service. She 'looks like the nicest kind of water-rat in a Lewis Carroll world, sitting up and "taking letters" with busy paws from, say, a beaver, benign and efficient. I claim to be benign ... It is a lazy man's joy, this typing business. While I bicycle to Buckenhill in the rain the water-rat is busy'.

Catering and transport difficulties increased as petrol rationing became more severe. John cycled long distances to take his classes, resolutely refusing to claim a greater petrol allowance. In May 1941 he learned that School and College Dormitory, Westminster's two oldest buildings and the heart of the School, had been destroyed. Daily there were new worries to be shouldered and swift decisions to be made. Once he was established in Bromyard Lucie and their daughters joined him. As ever, her courage and gaiety helped to lighten the load of responsibility and to share in upholding morale. Nevertheless, in the last resort the final decisions and advice given to distant Governors could only be his, though he recognised to the full the debt which he acknowledged in his Letter to Old Westminsters: 'Can any School or any Head Master have been better served by the Masters, the men and the boys?' Years later Lucie added that she wished he had included the masters' wives on whom the burden of catering fell.

After John's death one of his Housemasters wrote: 'In Herefordshire he had to balance the claims and welfare of widely separated units of his school – the conflicting claims on time and energy of the School's primary purpose of education, the necessity for extensive self-help in rearing and growing food, and the need for the School to play its proper national part in the local Home Guard. Those who shared these days, during and just after the war, with John Christie enjoyed a sense of purpose and achievement and a great deal of fun as well ... in retrospect we can realise how very much we owed to his unswerving integrity as well as to his great skill in preserving unity among us. The right man in the right place at the right time'. John, writing to John Carleton shortly after VE Day 1945, looked back over the exhausting years, realising that problems of a different kind lay just ahead: 'Yes, "the tyranny is overpast". I fear that in material ways Westminster did worse than any school in England and under a more forceful lead might well have found a better wicket. But one is as one is: and we have had happiness and mild adventures and great co-operation. I rather quail at the opening of the next chapter'.

Shortly after the war ended John went to Italy to talk to the troops about the opportunities for becoming schoolmasters and he was amused that he had been temporarily gazetted a Major-General in order to fly back in time for term. However, it soon became apparent that the war years and the problems of resettlement in London had taken their toll and in 1946 John became seriously ill. It was typical of him that when he recovered there was no thought of accepting a less demanding post until he felt that Westminster's future was assured. Thus a suggestion made to him in 1946 that he should become Principal of Jesus College, Oxford, was declined. 'School' and 'College' had been destroyed and the urgent need to rebuild was hampered by the difficulties of obtaining the right materials. Loss of income and the heavy costs of exile posed serious financial problems. There was no shortage of boys but to fill up the school with too many young boys would have resulted in a recurrence of the problem with an abnormally heavy leave in five years time. Nor were suitable young masters readily available.

Furthermore, the role of a school like Westminster in the rapidly changing educational pattern of the post-war world needed careful thought and far-reaching decisions. 'What do I want Westminster to be post-bellum? Well, there's an airy little breakfast table topic.' More serious was his request to John

Carleton, who was not released from service until the autumn of 1945: 'Tell me how you think the School could be better run. Don't think of me at all – but of Westminster'.

When John declined to be a candidate for the post of Principal, the Fellows of Jesus College elected John's friend, Sir Frederick Ogilvie. Sadly he was only to serve the College for little more than three years as he died suddenly in 1949. John was again approached and invited to succeed him. By the end of 1949 he felt justified in leaving Westminster and returning to Oxford. A War Memorial Appeal with which he had helped enabled much of the war damage to be restored; he had also founded a flourishing Under School; and had been instrumental in acquiring No. 17 Dean's Yard for the School itself. The chief and lasting achievement of his twelve years as Head Master was to bring Westminster safely through the greatest crisis of its long history. 'Has the deep but modest consciousness of power entered into you?', he asked a friend. 'It never did to me.'

A happy married life is the greatest of blessings, especially for a headmaster. His wife, by being a friend to all on board, can tell him of any difficulties which members of his staff are facing domestically and by sharing his own worries, can often save him from doing the wrong thing or from doing the right thing in the wrong way. His children perform an invaluable service by puncturing his self-importance and thus cutting him down to size. Any picture of a headmaster, if it is to be complete, must therefore include some account of a side of his life largely unknown to his pupils – his relationship with his children.

'Poor little mites! Educate, educate, educate all day long!' was Catherine and Jane's much loved Nanny Boo's comment. Only in the sense that his daughters learned much from John was this true for he never deliberately set out to 'educate' them. He loved children and greatly enjoyed their company, fascinated by the way that their minds worked. He was a marvellous storyteller and on their walks together he would suddenly say: 'Did I ever tell you the adventure of . . .?'. Before he could finish the sentence he was stopped by cries of 'No, you didn't. Tell us, tell us'. His stories might be ready-made from the *Odyssey* or his own invention. Together the three of them used to make up tales based on some of their games. They possessed the Happy Families cards with the original drawings and they invented stories about the various characters, such as Hetty Chip, the carpenter's daughter, who wanted a hammer for her birthday, or Freddy Dip, the dyer's son, who got into trouble for playing with his father's dyes and who invented a dye which could change colour. The stories were usually kept for walks and Catherine and Jane each had a private series which were told when one sister was not there. To keep up with John's pace they had early to learn to walk fast, a lesson which in later life had sometimes to be unlearned if they were not to out-walk the young men of their acquaintance.

At home, rather than tell stories John preferred to read aloud, which he did superbly, skipping undetected anything too long-winded, or alarming, or, occasionally, improper. By using a different tone of voice for each character he made them come alive. He chose the books simply because he had himself enjoyed them – Andrew Lang's Fairy Stories or tales about Robin Hood. From these he went on to The Jungle Books, Stevenson, Dickens and Scott. He also read poetry to them, never trying to 'refine' their taste. He knew that *Horatius* or *The Charge of the Light Brigade* were right for young minds and that their limitations would become apparent in later years. If he were not reading to them he loved playing word games or paper games, but he never enjoyed formal card games. It was a delight when chess could be learned. 'Always play to win,' he used to say, but he was generous in warning about a rash move and allowing second thoughts.

'To be with a child you have got to be a child' is a nanny's saying and John kept much of a child's direct, absorbed interests and joys almost all his life. He retained his childhood delight in climbing trees. He was a child in his love of little expeditions to a tea or coffee shop in mid-morning. 'It always makes me feel it's really the holidays to do something pleasant and wholly unnecessary in the morning.' Expeditions were planned for Catherine and Jane's girl friends when they came to stay. They would be taken swimming in the Serpentine early in the morning, or in later years to go punting on the river at Oxford. Whenever Lucie was visiting her parents in Ireland special treats were arranged for he knew how much they missed her. When he bought the cottage at Great Henny on the Essex-Suffolk border, to which he eventually retired, he invented entertaining versions of croquet on the hilly lawn. In the summer he took the family to swim in the Stour or in the Bures' mill pond; in winter they would be taken to slide on nearby ponds.

John was a great remembrancer and marker of occasions. He used to produce presents and sometimes verses not only on birthdays but to mark any distinction won or to commemorate the day when they were confirmed, or had learned to ride a bicycle, or had said goodbye to Boo, or had left their wartime home in Herefordshire. He was one of the very few fathers of the girls at their boarding school who wrote to both of his daughters every week. They did, however, wish that he would not come to preach or lecture while they were at the school. He chose presents very seriously if rather erratically. When he found what he thought was a really good present he proudly showed it in secret to other people first and was upset if the recipient did not seem quite as excited by it as he was. He excelled as a recipient himself of presents from his grandchildren, spending time slowly opening the parcel and making wild guesses as to its contents.

The war years in Herefordshire meant long walks across the Downs to school. As soon as Catherine and Jane were old enough they rode on bicycles and a Welsh Mountain pony, Black Bess, was bought for them from a local farmer. As a boy John had enjoyed riding ponies and he always kept on his desk the hoof of his pony, Prince, made into a paperweight. On the weekly expedition to take the laundry basket to the house of Mrs Harris he lightened the task by recounting stories of the Scarlet Pimpernel, whose secret call 'the sea mew's cry thrice repeated' the family adopted and they used to pretend that within the laundry basket lay the Dauphin whom they were smuggling out of France. In later years London taxi drivers were surprised to be summoned by John with the sea-mew's cry.

As a deeply religious man John brought his daughters up to say their prayers and to go to church – though when young they were excused the sermon. Every evening there were family prayers and Bible reading which he kept up until about the time that Catherine and Jane went away to school. As children they found the routine good and reassuring but they might have been embarrassed by it in adolescence had it not been discontinued.

John had no sisters and his whole life had been spent in purely masculine institutions. It was not, therefore, surprising that his understanding of adolescent girls was less wide and sympathetic than of children. When he felt it necessary to express disapproval he could be severe, and reproof or the occasional punishment somehow left the girls resentful and often rather baffled. For a man who believed in educating girls as much as boys it was strange that the school chosen for them was so unacademic. It was even more surprising that he did not actively encourage Catherine to go to a university. All that she needed was a little assurance from him. Although he always tried to notice a new dress and to say something pleasant about it, he had an old-fashioned suspicion of their very natural interest in clothes, cosmetics and parties. 'I knew young men often discussed young ladies but I never knew young ladies discussed young men' – an odd remark from a devotee of Jane Austen. In fact, he sometimes gave the impression that he found even the most innocent forms of courtship rather vulgar. He could be curiously blind to the difficulties which a young girl might be facing and it was only when grown up that Jane realised with amazement that her father had had no suspicion of the miseries of shyness which she had experienced as a girl, probably as he had never himself been socially shy in this way.

Nevertheless, as they grew up they realised anew what good company their father was. When in high spirits his quick wit, turn of phrase and skill as a mimic were a delight. As the grand-children came John took the same interest in them as he had taken in his own children. At Oxford he was seen racing upstairs to carry down a tiny grand-daughter to see a circus procession passing down the Turl. Later she was heard chanting ecstatically under her breath: 'El-er-phants: Grand-fath-er! El-er-phants: Grand-fath-er!'

Oxford meant a very pleasant home-coming for John, and it was, as he said, delightful to be welcomed for himself and not for his office. However, he found Oxford in 1950 a very different place from the Oxford of his years at Trinity and Magdalen. In those happy days Colleges jealously guarded their independence against any serious attempt by the University to increase its control, and dons were able to pursue their researches and to teach largely untroubled by administrative tasks, save those which concerned their College. Increasing government grants and a sharp rise in the number of undergraduates inevitably led to less College autonomy, more committee work and a heavier teaching load for Tutors. John, as has been said, never loved administration and committees, though as Principal he conscientiously took his share. 'If committees increase,' he said, 'set not your heart upon them – with emphasis on the word *heart*.' For committees, he insisted, were no more than '*generally* necessary to salvation'.

John always regarded the growth of bureaucracy with distaste and some alarm. Thus he was not one to give a warm welcome to the Franks Commission on Oxford. He foresaw in its deliberations a threat to the Oxford which he understood and loved; an Oxford of autonomous Colleges in which learning and teaching flourished and were all-important. He got little enjoyment from sitting in front of 'Lord Franks and his fellow inquisitors', adding, 'As I took my chair at the table in the Schools it struck me that I was probably the oldest man in the room, but it was very like having a viva all over again. And as I walked home I said to a companion, "Thank goodness there isn't a Class List".' This was not to imply that John was reactionary. When, for example, in 1965 New College proposed to admit women undergraduates – one of the most profound challenges to tradition – he sympathised with a move which would reduce the disparity of women to men in the University and he reminded opponents of the plan that the admission of women had proved a success in the newer universities. At the same time he was perhaps glad that the change did not come to Jesus College in his day.

In the 1920s, Trinity and Magdalen, with most other Colleges, had largely confined their admission of Commoners to boys from the independent schools. These were the young men whom John had always taught and with whom he was most at ease; though he did once say to Lucie: 'I don't really like toffs'. With the increase in Local Education Authority grants, Oxford and Cambridge at once became more readily accessible to pupils from the maintained schools and John found the undergraduates – he was never heard to use the word 'students' – socially more mixed than he had hitherto experienced. Moreover, even in pre-war days, Jesus College, with its close Welsh connections and its ties with some of the ancient grammar schools in England rather than with the public schools, had never been as socially exclusive as many other colleges. This situation John hoped to modify. Indeed, before he arrived back in Oxford hints had been given him that the College would benefit from a wider intake. Once in office he felt it to be one of his tasks to attract more boys from the public schools to the College, a policy the reverse of what was happening elsewhere in the University though aimed at achieving the same result of a wider social mix among the undergraduates. It was not a policy which commended itself to most of the Fellows.

To be Head of a House at Oxford or Cambridge is to hold a position of great prestige but surprisingly little power. In a College meeting the vote of the most junior Fellow carries equal weight with that of the Head of House. This was a very different relationship from that of a headmaster to his staff. John was well aware that as Principal he was *primus inter pares* but in the matter of Commoner admissions he held that the College statutes gave him full power to pick and choose. He was prepared to make a stand in favour of choosing a man of character and general ability rather than one whose claim a Tutor pressed by virtue of his showing in the entrance examination. It was a stand which inevitably led to clashes of policy with a Tutor for Admissions and dons primarily interested in securing a promising pupil.

Differences with the Governing Body did not prevent John from enjoying good talk at High Table. He was always a fascinating conversationalist and he entered fully into the task of entertaining not only his own guests but any whom the Fellows had invited. Young dons were helped in their teaching by his advice and his love of literature was irresistible. No colleague could fail to be aware of his civilising influence which in subtle ways affected the whole College. Reading a paper on Browning to a literary club, or translating Virgil with one or two scholars, delighted him. Outside the College he belonged to various small groups whose members ate together and discussed a paper. He especially loved meetings of the 'Comp. Club' at which, over tea and crumpets, scholarly members criticised each other's Latin and Greek compositions.

John had always loved the company of the young, especially those prepared to make an attempt to keep up with him intellectually and physically on a rapid afternoon walk. He was always available to help any man needing advice. Many an undergraduate found in his outwardly aloof Principal a warm-hearted counsellor and friend. John was scornful of the horror with which one or two dons looked on undergraduate pranks. He was severe with miscreants but refused to send men down for wildness with no vice in it. 'If their spirits rise, mine can rise further.' He was particularly tender-hearted towards misdemeanours committed by an amusing character or by a man who showed promise as a creative spirit. A College poet of some distinction, Dom Moraes, faced rustication until John saved him on the grounds that much allowance had to be made for poets. He reminded his colleagues of the lasting reproach incurred by University College for sending down the young Shelley and of how the kind of marble monument raised in expiation by that College would be beyond the financial resources of a relatively poor College like Jesus. When late at night the quadrangle was noisy with talk and laughter John would fling open a window in the Lodgings: 'Gentlemen, it's time you went to bed'. He always addressed undergraduates collectively as 'gentlemen', though, as one of them once said to Jane Christie: 'He treats us as gentlemen, which we aren't'. However, when faced with the crisis of a young man's sudden death or a man in serious trouble with the Law, John acted swiftly, decisively and with great wisdom, as his colleagues readily acknowledged.

John and Lucie believed that it was an important part of their task to foster a feeling of unity among the Fellows and their wives. This was all the more important as the College's Governing Body increased in John's time from 14 to 23, with a corresponding increase in Research Fellows and Lecturers. When she arrived at Jesus with John, Lucie was amazed at the lack of cohesion among the dons' wives, so very different from the close-knit community of Westminster in war time. She did not at first realise how far apart many of them lived for it was only when houses became dear to buy that the College began to buy houses for dons. She also found it odd that on the morning after a pleasant dinner party with good conversation in another College where she and John had been guests, dons, who had been very forthcoming the previous evening, would pass her unacknowledged in the street in what they hoped looked like deep abstraction. Later, however, the widow of a recent Provost of Worcester told her that she never bowed to dons.

Lucie did her utmost to break down this isolation and she made the Principal's Lodgings the centre of good entertaining and friendly meetings. She had much to do with the formation of the Newcomers' Club. A group of the wives of Heads of Houses, with the wife of the Rector of Exeter College as prime mover, realised the need for a club to help the wives of graduate students especially those from overseas who were lonely and neglected, particularly when tied by young children. On the night of the annual College Gaudy, Lucie instituted a dinner for the wives of the Jesus dons, who later in the evening shared in the entertaining of old members of the College.

Hospitality was not confined to dons and their wives. Lucie and John saw as much as possible of undergraduates and six came to lunch each week. The Literary Club sometimes met in their drawing room and mulled their wine in the kitchen. The Jesus and St Anne's Music Club often met in the house. Each February John and Lucie gave a dance to which undergraduates brought their own partners and in the big dining room there was space for some two dozen couples. At a time when there were a number of Scots in the College there were reel parties. Unlike some Heads of Houses who annoyed their undergraduates by going out of College on the night of a Commem. Ball, John and Lucie always took a party to their Commems. and an extra floor was laid down in their garden.

John might dislike committee meetings but this did not prevent him from accepting membership of a number of school Governing Bodies. It was one way to attract good men to the College. He was pleased to be asked to be the Masters' representative at Rugby and he also governed Christ College, Brecon, Glenalmond, Haileybury, the Dragon School at Oxford, and one girls' school, St Mary's, Calne. In addition he greatly enjoyed governing St Deiniol's library for scholars at Hawarden. The College was generous about leave of absence and permitted him to spend seven months in India as a member of the Government Education Commission on Secondary Education, accompanied for part of the time by Lucie and Catherine. When on his own he reported to her his doings in characteristic style. 'The real old-fashioned snobbery lingers on here. I really do prefer Indians to any but the nicest commercial gentlemen from Marlborough or Malvern.' He also spent a long vacation going round South

America on behalf of the British Council to report on schools to which they sent teachers of English.

As an after-dinner speaker at Gaudies and Old Members Association dinners John was unsurpassed. Here his wit, his nice choice of words and his incisive manner of talking delighted his audiences. On these occasions it was incumbent on him to list Collegiate successes and achievements, which he prefaced on one occasion by saying that he spoke '*with a certain sober pride* – a phrase used by headmasters on speech days who intend to boast without incurring the charge of boastfulness'. Unlike many an after-dinner speaker John knew the value of brevity. At his final Gaudy he referred to a dinner at Magdalen when the retiring President spoke until 11.0 p.m. 'He had much to recall', commented John, 'and as I remember he recalled it.'

In one sense John was a war casualty. The long strain of Westminster's years in exile had undermined his health. At Oxford he was again seriously ill with an internal ulcer and had to undergo two major operations. This not only sapped his energy and made long meetings of the College Governing Body exhausting, but it also caused his one great disappointment. He was invited to succeed T.F. Higham, his old Tutor, as Public Orator, a post which he coveted and which he would have filled with distinction. He turned it down not on the grounds of health but because he was due to become Vice-Chancellor; he did not greatly relish the prospect but he thought that it would be good for the College to accept. However, after his illness his doctors advised him not to undertake the strain of the heavy duties involved. By the time that he had decided to take his doctors' advice the post of Public Orator had been filled.

John had refused the Vice-Chancellorship largely because he felt that it would be unfair to the College if thereby he further impaired his health. Equally self-sacrificing was his decision to retire in 1967, three years before he need. The quatercentenary of the College would be celebrated in 1971 and he thought that his successor should be firmly settled in office before then. In his final Gaudy speech he referred to his impending retirement as 'a move – what shall I say? – not universally lamented'. He felt sad that much of what he had hoped to achieve had not come to completion. His sense of failure was really the expression of a very tired man, who had struggled courageously against illness for much of his time at Jesus. At Jesus College today what his former colleagues recall is his fine scholarship, his personal kindness and the civilising influence which powerfully altered the cultural ethos of the College.

On leaving Oxford John returned for a time to London in order to do some part-time teaching at Westminster. He used to say that he divided his friends into two groups: those who thought him mad to return as an assistant master in the school of which he had once been Head Master; and those who understood that teaching mattered more to him than any other activity. While teaching at Westminster John and Lucie lived in the basement flat of Catherine's house in Elgin Crescent. The cottage at Great Henny near Sudbury had been bought just after the war as a holiday home and a place for eventual retirement. A temporary home was all that they needed in London while John was teaching. Moreover, John was never a wealthy man and he could not have afforded to keep Henny and rent a London house at the same time. Throughout his life he tended not to worry overmuch about money, maintaining that his financial principles were a matter of Rouge et Noir. 'Pass-book Noir, OK. Rouge, beware!' Each move that he had made since his appointment to Repton – to Westminster and then to Jesus College – had involved a drop in salary. At that time Westminster offered its Head Master no pension. Luckily, after his mother's death in 1943, he inherited his share of her estate.

John's return to Westminster, although welcomed by John Carleton, now Head Master, presented one delicate problem. John expected to be given a good share of the top classical teaching, an expectation which the Senior Classical Master could hardly have welcomed. John Carleton had to explain gently that John could not have all the clever boys to teach, however well he would have taught them. John understood this and found enjoyment in teaching, among other groups, what he called his 'wicked Virgilians' in a middle school form. In the autumn of 1968 John fell and seriously injured his back while sprinting for a bus, which started as he boarded it and threw him into the street. Over the next two-and-a-half years he suffered frequent bouts of acute pain which no treatment relieved. He continued his teaching until the end of 1969 by which time his back had become so painful that he could no longer carry on. So John and Lucie settled at Great Henny with his books housed in the former local school building which he bought, and which also provided much needed accommodation for the growing family of grand-children when they came to stay. During 1971 for no ascertainable reason the back pain suddenly ceased and he was well enough in the next year or so to have a holiday in France and one in Ireland.

After this the tragic, slow decline began. Very gradually his fine mind became increasingly confused though until near the end he could enjoy hearing favourite books by Scott or Jane Austen read aloud. In 1978 he broke his femur and though it was successfully mended the shock accelerated his decline. He and Lucie greatly valued the kindness of their local doctor at Henny who, knowing that no treatment had been of any avail, used to drop in late in the evening after his day's work to chat to John and cheer him up. Occasionally the mists of confusion were blown away. A young man staying at Henny mentioned to John that he had been reading *Alice in Wonderland*. For a moment the old fire was alive. 'Marvellous work', said John. 'Almost as full of quotations as *Hamlet*.' He lingered on until on 8 September 1980 death came to him as a friend. He was buried in the quiet churchyard at Great Henny.

The concluding lines of a poem which John loved to read to his pupils – Browning's *A Grammarian's Funeral* – are not inapplicable to this great teacher:

> Peace let the dew send!
> Lofty designs must close in like effects:
> Loftily lying
> Leave him – still greater than the world suspects,
> Living and dying.

DONALD LINDSAY

John Christie: Christian, Preacher, Teacher, Headmaster

Among the 'Memories of John Christie by former pupils' published in *The Elizabethan*[1] in February, 1981 I was particularly struck by the following two quotations:

> The great passion in JTC's life was literature – and primarily the plays of Sophocles. (Robin Denniston)

> He was, quite simply, the best teacher, and I think the best preacher, that I have ever come across ... I remember a sermon on Charity in Exeter Cathedral that was the most moving I have ever heard. (Richard Faber)

If I had not re-read some of John Christie's sermons and radio talks, I think I should have agreed with Robin Denniston's view that the great passion in his life was literature – and primarily the plays of Sophocles. The sermons made me change my mind. I now believe that the great passion of his life, its central source of conviction and energy, was Christian Love.[2] He saw it 'as evident all through Jesus' ministry in Galilee and in his death on Calvary' and found it brilliantly expounded in 'St Paul's famous chapter in Corinthians 13 – one can't know that chapter too well'. This certainly bears out Richard Faber's memory of the sermon on Charity (Agape) which he preached in Exeter Cathedral, and of John Christie himself as 'the best preacher that I have ever come across'.

Nevertheless if this was his great passion, some explanation is required to show why almost all his life was spent in teaching; why, for all that he was a great preacher, he was never ordained; and why, even granted that, as a school-master, he had 'few

[1] The Westminster School magazine.

[2] I use hereafter the word John Christie most often used – AGAPE.
'What was this new spirit? Love ... it was a new word then; and it's a great pity we use for this wonderful new thing a word which has to do duty for so much else besides. The new word in Greek was Agape.'

equals and no superiors this century', it was his teaching rather than his preaching which left the deepest mark on some of his pupils. Studying some of the inspiring sermons and religious broadcasts of this remarkably gifted, complex and often very private Headmaster has challenged me to try to answer these questions. Whether the answers are right or wrong, the quest has thrown new light on someone whom I mistakenly thought I already knew quite well.

What puzzles as much as impresses me about the sermons is their directness and simplicity of style. 'Le style c'est l'homme', John was fond of quoting. Yet in this case it did not quite appear so. Certainly as a skilful teacher he knew that the message he had to give must be clear and forceful if it was to have its proper effect. Nevertheless, the style is so down-to-earth and is formed from such simple straightforward words that no-one who did not know would have guessed that this speaker was one of the outstanding classical scholars of his time. There is nothing in them to suggest the clever young don or the scholarly writer of sophisticated Latin and Greek verses or the student of Plato who got a First in Greats. Nor is there any real evidence in them of his abundant knowledge and deep understanding of English and Classical literature; the simplicity is not exactly what one would associate with the wide-ranging mind of one of the best teachers in England. Of course it has to be remembered that apparently 'simple' English, especially if it has the mark of eloquence rightly associated with John Christie's style, is probably the most difficult thing of all to achieve in formal writing or speech; Max Beerbohm and C.S. Lewis come to mind as comparable modern masters of the art.

I feel that the solution is itself curiously simple: not only does he himself say that

> One's religion must ... stand the test of everyday language and everyday living. It must not be kept as a respectable extra like a Sunday suit;

but also the passion and intensity with which he speaks of the centrality of Agape is such that everything else has to be put aside to reveal it in its stark power. It is that mixture of starkness and power which convinces me that this was indeed the most important thing in his whole life.

Agape is not only the most important, it is also the most frequently recurring theme in his sermons. There are a few other themes, notably Authority and Truth; but they are not numerous, and it is to Agape that he returns again and again. Can it be that in this lies the reason for his having been a great preacher and yet not ordained? He announced one day in Latin prayers up School that there was no truth whatever in the Daily Telegraph rumour that he was likely to take holy orders; he was not. Why not? Was it because, while nothing was more important in his life than that central theme, it did not have sufficient range and variety of theological interest to justify ordination? Preaching freed him to lay bare the heart of the matter, narrowed to one main point. Yet to satisfy his intellectually quick, diversely gifted and well-stocked mind, he needed more than one central message. If he was to harness all his talents to his life's work, he must have a vocation which would offer wide-ranging scope and variety of interest. The answer lay in teaching: it was not too far removed from preaching, yet out of the pulpit; in direct contact with his pupils he could deploy his gifts to the full, and find all the intellectual challenge and excitement to which his breadth of learning and scholarly riches entitled him.

It is also surprising that there should be so little theology in the sermons. This cannot have arisen from ignorance; he was far too well and widely read for that. It would be amazing if it arose from a lack of interest in ideas, theological or philosophical; he had plenty of capacity for them if he chose to exercise it. No; the strongest impression given by the sermons is that his commitment to Agape – his loyalty to Christ – stems, not from argument nor from thinking out his position intellectually, but from direct experience. One series of radio talks makes it quite clear that the claims of Agape arose from his struggle to come to terms with other people – particularly those other people whom 'he could not bear'[1] or who 'could not bear him'. How could he cope with such people, particularly in a position of authority, without being

[1]There is an illuminating little comment of self-revelation in one talk where he speaks of:

> 'the deplorable Galilean accent of Jesus and most of his disciples. Let us not forget that; oh dear, let me not forget it with my sad prejudice in favour of an educated voice.'

in danger of losing his temper or his dignity? Reading the Gospels with a mind fully capable of a new and fresh approach, and no doubt also observing that some others whom he admired seemed to be able to cope precisely because they were Christians, he experienced Agape as the answer. Practising it and praying for it reinforced the initial experience. He realised that he had discovered 'the new thing which had begun to run its glorious course in the world that first Easter morning', 'the biggest, deepest, newest force in my own life', 'a force not generated by me but coming from outside'. 'You discover something else as well: there spring up all around you more and more fields for Agape. It never lets you rest, this great new power you have let into your life'. 'I wanted to share it with you', he goes on, and because he was a good teacher he shared it with his audience in the most direct and down-to-earth way he could – in simple words with simple illustrations based on real life, which would mean something direct and forceful to his listeners whoever they might be, clever or foolish, young or old, educated or not, provided that they could respond to fundamental experiences like 'falling in love in the ordinary sense of the phrase' ('How much more attractive our everyday neighbours suddenly seem to our eyes when we are in love!') or realising that 'you can't be fully a member of the family if you refuse to get on with Jack and Dick and Mary' or knowing 'the grumbler in the daily morning train to London; the clumsy char-woman with no manners; one of your brothers or sisters-in-law'. Such experiences, illuminated by the vision and inner conviction of Agape, need very little in the way of theology to make their message clearer. Heart speaks to heart in that style of preaching and with that one message to preach.

Yet there is another paradox inherent in this. I suggested that JTC was 'a private person'. To many he was a somewhat distant, austere figure, whom they admired greatly, whose voice they delighted to hear and whose pleasing humour and scholarly skills impressed them, but whose inner character and human individuality they found it difficult to make contact with. How did such a person come to choose Agape as his central theme (even if it 'isn't primarily a feeling at all'), and how did he come to speak so directly from the heart about it in public? I believe that, paradoxically, it was precisely the public nature of the pulpit which made it possible. His friend C.S. Lewis[1], whom he much admired, and who was himself not given to 'wearing his heart on his sleeve', gives us a clue to the answer. He speaks of the anonymity conferred upon us by certain forms of ceremonial dress; the same is true of certain forms of public performance. The pulpit gave JTC just the context he needed in which he could at one and the same time remain distantly semi-anonymous and yet speak personally and passionately from the heart.

I doubt if more than a privileged few ever got inside the defences which protected his inner self. That of course had the effect of making the rare glimpses of that inner self all the more powerful in their impact on the beholder. There is a passage in a private paper about his childhood, and in particular about his older brother, Charles, in which one catches just such a glimpse. While it purports to speak of his brother, one feels it tells one more about himself; for there is a touch of natural and understandable envy in his description of Charles' open-hearted, easy, relaxed capacity to get on close and intimate terms with other people. That kind of intimacy did not come naturally to John. Instead he had to be content with other gifts, often more dazzling and apparently attractive, which nevertheless sometimes prevented the open-hearted exchange of comradeship.

As a boy, I always ascribed his habit of directing and controlling a conversation to the fact that he was a Headmaster; later in life I realised that this was part of the man – a device which protected him from others' coming too dangerously close, and which was then transferred to his style as a Headmaster. Not for him the open-ended dialogue, the exchange of ideas on equal terms, the welcoming of colleagues' views and suggestions before he himself had declared his hand. Rather he led from the front, determining the agenda and very often foreshadowing the conclusion before the discussion had begun. It was hard to imagine him sitting waiting for a boy, particularly a shy boy, to come out with his problems. And so it often proved: he would look up

[1] It is interesting to note the similarity between the two men and also their differences: C.S. Lewis used a great variety of topics for his books, talks and sermons; John Christie hardly more than one. C.S. Lewis spoke and wrote with an amazing range of imaginative imagery and ingenuity of illustration; John Christie much more plainly and earthily. Yet, as I have already said, both shared a simple directness of style.

from his desk, ask 'what is it, boy?' and then, like some impatient competitor in a quiz competition, give you the answer to your question before it had been fully put. He was apt to run the conversation and assume he knew where it was going, so that it was even possible to find oneself outside the room again before realising that a vital part of the business on which one had gone to see him had been omitted. Nevertheless, he was often extraordinarily good at understanding intuitively what was in a boy's mind, despite appearing to impose his own solution to the problem.

His strong, sometimes formidable, style of leadership ('he was not very good at running committees or getting a consensus among, say, housemasters; he tended to steam-roller his way through with his ideas - often very good ideas') may or may not be correctly explained in the way I have suggested. It did nevertheless create a moral dilemma - or so it seemed to me as I read the sermons: how could he reconcile that single-minded capacity to drive ahead on his own steam with his commitment to Agape? How could he practise Agape and yet treat other people as less than his equals? It is, as I know, a dilemma which has faced other Headmasters who profess a Christian commitment; so JTC was not exceptional in that. Nevertheless with typical honesty he grappled with it and tried to solve it head on. I have mentioned that two other themes besides Agape recur in his sermons - namely, Authority and Truth. He used both to resolve the problems created by his position and by his personality. He was a man 'in authority' and 'under authority'. He was accountable and at the same time must be decisive. He did not believe that the authority he wielded came from his title, even if his responsibility to wield it did. Authority, he believed, is derived, first, 'from the only true source of effective authority - from [a man's] personality'; secondly,

> [because] the only authority which Jesus brings to bear is the authority of his own constant, loving, God-directed personality, ... I came to learn from ... the Gospels the message of our religion to one whose duty it was to command others, however small the scale might be - that all power divorced from the source of supreme power, God, was in danger of failing.

In support of this view he speaks of Churchill, whose 'many hundreds of commands ... were carried out with cheerfulness, goodwill and initiative not because of his official power but because he was the man we saw, the man we knew him to be'. Again he cites Kent in *King Lear*, who

> says to the unrecognised King Lear 'you have that in your countenance I would fain call Master'. 'What's that?' asks the other, and Kent replies 'authority'.

Yet again JTC says 'what you are – thence alone comes the true, the only authority worth having'. Yet, as a Headmaster, he also had to exercise the authority he had been given, given both by the temporal power of his Governors and by the divine power of God; and in exercising it he had to put his trust in God that what he was would reveal in his countenance what others would fain call master. Judging by what his pupils and colleagues said of him, I cannot but believe that his trust was well founded. At the same time it was not something that was easily achieved or maintained. The call to exercise authority, like the call continuously to practise Agape, demands endless prayer, endless wrestling. I am sure I am not alone in recalling JTC as he wrestled in prayer; indeed the image of him in Bromyard Church at my last school service is vividly etched on my memory. He 'struggled'; he 'agonised', using that word, as he himself would have pointed out, in its proper sense, derived from the Greek word 'ἀγων' meaning 'a contest'.

He was not a meek and mild man; he was strong and he had strong feelings, not least anger and a sense of obligation to censure others when his keen mind saw that they were at fault. How were these feelings in their turn to be reconciled with Agape? Here St Paul provided him with the key idea – namely, 'speaking the truth in love'. This essential, demanding and difficult skill, so crucial to human and professional relationships, JTC understood full well and explained with great force and clarity:

> Love is not always tender; there are times when it must be stern ... A colleague seems to us to be wrong: we tell him the truth; he resents it, and the friendship is broken. We decide regretfully not to try again. But our mistake was not that we told him the truth, but that we did not tell him it in love. If

> we can speak the truth, not with ... any touch of malice, but reluctantly and ... with a passionate desire to help him, ... there will be no permanent breach ... To maintain the truth in love is ... to rejoice that we have even a partial vision of the truth ..., to disagree generously, to oppose without rancour; and it means – not easy for one who commands the attention and admiration of his class – to rejoice when another can join his truth to ours, correct our truth by his.

The apparent contrast I have drawn between John Christie the preacher and John Christie the teacher should not lead us to suppose that they were in opposition or represented two different people. Quite the contrary. On the one hand, his literary interests could, on occasion, be the inspiration of his preaching. 'A sermon of his at the Dragon School', the Oxford Society Journal reported, 'which had to be based, by tradition, on the play performed the day before was a memorable tour de force. The play had been Henry IV part I.' On the other hand, the effect of his teaching in the classroom could be as electrifying as his preaching from the pulpit. Even his subject matter did not stray too far from the lodestone of Agape, though it drew on an infinite variety of literary sources – mainly and most lovingly from Sophocles, but also from Browning, Sir Walter Scott, Catullus, Cicero, Thucydides, St Paul and Shakespeare. As William Barnes said of him:

> One of the three great teachers in my life. We read *King Lear* together and from then on dates a life-long love of Shakespeare. Even more memorable ... is the afternoon when he sat down and read to us *My Last Duchess* by Browning.

Such memories could be echoed by every one of his pupils, some of my own favourites being my introduction to Browning's *An Epistle to Karshish, the Arab Physician* and *A Death in the Desert*, to Thompson's *Hound of Heaven* and to Sophocles' *Philoctetes* and *Antigone*. The latter particularly appealed to him – and to me – because it spoke so eloquently of love and suffering more than four hundred years before the supreme example of love and suffering was to be revealed to the world. Herein, I am sure, lies the contrast between John Christie and other great teachers of literature, as has been pointed out to me by one of his pupils –

> JTC had a strong sense of drama: he used words beautifully and effectively. But his audience never had any doubt that what he said came from the heart and stayed in the mind. With others the appeal, however strong, was just that of a splendid actor's performance.

In conclusion, while I may be wrong about much that I have tried to explain, of one thing I am certain: the influence of his 'great passion for Agape' was and has been incalculable. In one of his radio talks, speaking of Jesus as a teacher, he said

> Jesus sowed seeds in their hearts; seed-sowing is the root meaning of the word to educate. Sowing seeds, first of curiosity, then wonder, then interest and at length of a passionate desire for a new life less unworthy of their master.

And in another passage he said

> what will dwell with our pupils and influence them is their impression of our own genuine, deeply hidden, humbly held ideals; what we really and truly live by. For these there is no substitute and ultimately no disguise because they are largely unconscious.

Judged by these criteria, no less than by the criterion of leading and teaching by example, JTC was undoubtedly a great teacher. If you look at what his former pupils say, it is soon apparent that what happened to them was in fact the sowing of seeds, the seeds of curiosity, wonder, interest and even of some passion which came to direct or rule their lives.

In reading his sermons and talks I have been astonished to discover how many of the ideas I have constantly used and lived by came from him. In many cases their origin had previously been obscure to me; they were part of the furniture of my mind and my life. Had I been asked to recall from memory some of the phrases and quotations which JTC used to illustrate his lessons or his preaching, I should probably have picked out several which I have re-discovered in his sermons and talks; nevertheless many of them would not have occurred to me as first sown by him. But sown they were, taking root and growing into some of the most richly illuminating ideas and precepts of my life –

Don't look at me; look the way I am looking.

I can't hear what you are saying. My ears are deafened by what you are.

St Paul's 'speaking the truth in love'.

Men glibly say 'we needs must love the highest when we see it'. But that's not true. Remember how Jesus speaking of some of the Jews said 'they have seen and hated both me and my Father'.

Iago's bitter self-revelation when speaking of Cassio: 'He hath a daily beauty in his life which makes mine ugly'.

That paradoxical saying of Jesus: 'To him that hath shall be given; and from him that hath not shall be taken away even that which he hath'.

Browning's 'A man's reach should exceed his grasp Or what's a heaven for?'.

Sophocles': 'ἐρως ἀνικατε μαχην'.

These and many other memorable lines have enlightened and enriched and strengthened my own and other pupils' lives – just as some lighter moments will often have made us smile in reminiscence. How many other teachers besides myself have heard themselves say to a pupil, 'ingenious but wrong', with its precisely judged apportionment of praise and blame? And how few preachers would dare to break off in the middle of a sermon to say to an inattentive listener below the pulpit, 'Er – don't jingle your money in your pocket, boy'!

'No true teacher has proved his worth until his pupils are no longer under his eye and out in the world'. It is clear from the memories by former pupils in *The Elizabethan* that others besides myself have had the experience of a life profoundly influenced by his personality and by the force of his teaching and preaching. Today we should say that he had charisma. He antedated and anticipated the word. The 'charm' of which so many spoke who knew or heard him at the height of his powers was no easy-going, elegant blandness; it was compounded of supremely professional competence, intensity of vision and eloquence, and a deep understanding of pupils and their parents. He cut out trivial, social small-talk – he was at once too serious and too civilised for that. Rather he spoke with great moral force of the things which gave him delight and satisfaction, mostly in literature, and of the things on which the deepest part of himself was grounded, mostly in the Gospels and St Paul's letters. As Richard Faber put it so felicitously –

> On the one hand there was, evidently, a tough, moral fibre, almost puritanical and sometimes a bit alarming in its intensity. On the other hand he was extremely cultivated, with a graceful and easy appreciation of elegance and humour. The contrast between these two was never jarring; they fused into a unified personality; but they would not have done so in a less remarkable man.

To try to determine the relative importance of John Christie the Headmaster, the teacher, the preacher or the Christian would be quite unprofitable. What has dwelt with us and influenced us is our conscious or unconscious recognition of those moments when what he said and did and was were one. Those were moments of revelation whose impression on us has been lifelong precisely because we could see at the heart of the Headmaster and the teacher and the preacher genuine, deeply hidden, passionately held beliefs – what he really and truly lived by – centring on his commitment to Christian love and the love of Christ.

ROGER YOUNG

J.T. Christie as a Teacher

Early in 1937, when I was in my second year at Westminster, the news that our Head Master, the Reverend Harold Costley-White, was retiring and would be replaced by Mr J.T. Christie, then Head Master of Repton, caused me to feel both sadness and alarm. Sir Angus Wilson in a memoir of his schooldays has compared Costley – that was how we all used to refer to him – with Archdeacon Grantly, and like him he retained something of the eighteenth century. His finely chiselled features, his mane of white hair, his silvery and melodious voice made him seem the pattern of a dignified clerical head master of the old school; and his genial and imposing manner, while in the highest degree elaborate, could not justly be written off as pompous, revealing as it did from time to time touches of a humour and detachment that indicated no small degree of knowledge and understanding of the world. Being low in the school while Costley was there, I cannot claim to have experience of his teaching in the way that older persons must have known it.

But he would occasionally come to our form room, send away the master and take the period himself. Sometimes it was to read a few chapters of the Old Testament in the convenient selection which he had edited with a colleague; my only memory of its editorial technique is that in the account of how the children of Israel mutilated their fallen enemies, the word *foreskins* was replaced by *trophies*. At other times Costley would read with us that strange poem, written in an unusual and perplexing metre, in which Catullus recounts how Attis, the favourite and adorer of the great Asiatic mother goddess Cybele, 'dismembered himself', to use the translation which the Head Master recommended, in order to gratify the goddess. On either topic Costley gave us an impressive *tour de force*, a splendid performance by an accomplished actor.

The element of the eighteenth century which Costley, though in many ways a Victorian, conserved made him a most appropriate Head Master for Westminster. The school passed through difficult years at the beginning of the nineteenth century; but one result of its refusal to abandon its metropolitan situation was that it escaped many of the changes which came over the public schools during that period, partly as a result of the influence of Thomas Arnold. Westminster produced fewer lawyers and civil servants than other schools, and despite its situation fewer politicians; it produced more actors, journalists and men of letters. The school list contained many exotic names, done full justice to by Costley when he read it through at the beginning of each term. We were more sophisticated than boys in most public schools, something that became very clear when in 1939 we were evacuated to Lancing and Hurstpierpoint. Some of my contemporaries seemed surprisingly well informed about women, or about finance; one was said to have replied to Costley's inquiry whether we knew the facts of life by saying 'Yes, sir, but I should like to hear your version'. Costley was an appropriate person to preside over such a school; and though I think some of us were conscious that his magnificent exterior concealed no great profundity, we were grateful for this deficiency and we appreciated his performance.

Several of us were thus somewhat alarmed by the paragraphs about the new Head Master which were published in the newspapers. It was clear that his academic qualifications were superior to those of Costley or any member of the existing staff. People who anticipated a tightening up of academic standards were right; under the new regime, a number of the less gifted or less industrious boys decided to call it a day. But the only fact that seemed to throw any light on the personality of the Head Master designate was that at Repton he had made the Officers' Training Corps compulsory. Was he then a patriotic militarist? I had had the misfortune to spend four years as a boarder at a preparatory school designed to prepare boys to enter the Navy by passing into Dartmouth College; I loathed this place, and still detest its memory. Would the new Head Master try to make the atmosphere of Westminster resemble this?

When J.T. Christie visited the school as Head Master designate, his appearance struck me as formidable, even alarming. His great height, his pale blue eyes and light-coloured hair, his springy and athletic gait made his appearance highly distinctive and most unlike that of his predecessor; his manner seemed severe, and my fear that he would turn out to be a militaristic martinet was not diminished.

When the new Head Master actually arrived, it became clear at once that he was a believing Christian, and one whose religion had a larger element of enthusiasm, in the old-fashioned sense, than Costley's had. He retained a good deal that was Victorian, and was indeed in some ways not wholly suited to the prevailing ethos of Westminster. But though some of my gifted contemporaries were alienated by this difference, not one of them denied that as a teacher he had extraordinary qualities, and since in his first term I entered the Sixth Form, which he taught for two periods a week, I very soon discovered this. I had taken two years to get there, instead of the one year normally required by a King's Scholar, and intended to spend only one year studying classics before going over to the history side, then flourishing under a celebrated teacher, John Bowle. But Christie's teaching was to cause me to change my plan.

In that Michaelmas term of 1937 we read with Christie Caesar's Civil War. At my prep school I had read sections of the Gallic War; as the master did nothing to explain what Caesar and his men were doing in Gaul, I had not found this author entertaining. The first period of that term made it clear to me that John Christie was a teacher utterly unlike any other I had encountered, and incomparably more interesting. He began with a short sketch of the career of Julius Caesar, pausing every now and then to ask one of us to supply some necessary fact. He asked me for what activity Caesar was particularly noted, and since I knew that Caesar was over forty before he commanded an army, and felt anxious to impress, I replied 'As a statesman'. This turned out to be the wrong answer, and I wished the earth would swallow me. But I soon forgot this incident, as I listened with increasing interest to Christie's account of the political events which led to the crossing of the Rubicon, wishing to learn all about the Civil War and to make a favourable impression on this extraordinary person.

When we came to the actual translation of the text, Christie was just as effective as he was when teaching us the history. He was not less but more systematic than the other masters, and demanded a higher standard of accuracy, taking great trouble over grammar and syntax; but when he was discussing them, these things no longer seemed to be a dry collection of quasi-mathematical rules but something intimately connected with the language of a text that was potentially full of life, and having something of the exciting irregularity of life itself.

But Caesar, fascinating as Christie made him, was less engrossing than the book we read during the following term, the *Philoctetes* of Sophocles. Sophocles was a favourite author of Christie's, who had lectured on him as a don at Magdalen; the Oxford text of AC Pearson had then been a comparatively new book, and Christie had studied the divergencies between this and Sir Richard Jebb's celebrated edition with special care. Despite the passage of time and certain obvious limitations, Jebb's Sophocles is still an incomparable instrument for anyone who wants to learn Greek, written by a scholar who, though his taste was not the taste of our time, had taste and feeling for language and for literature in a high degree. Christie used this book to teach us a great deal, and he taught us even more when later, in the Seventh, we read with him Sophocles' *Women of Trachis*. Christie could not have interested us so greatly in the language if he had not first interested us in the content. Right at the start of our reading of the *Philoctetes*, he pointed out to us that the young Neoptolemus, ordered to accompany the experienced Odysseus in the dangerous attempt to force or persuade to come to Troy the great archer Philoctetes, whom the Greeks on their way to attack that city had marooned on the desert island of Lemnos ten years earlier, was imagined as being not much older than we were, which caused us to wonder how we might have behaved if ordered by a senior officer to practise a monstrous deception against a person whom we instinctively recognised to be noble and deserving. Christie's reading of Sophocles was to a large degree romantic; he saw heroines like Deianeira and Antigone rather as Tennyson might have done, and he laid more stress on characterisation than it was the fashion to do during the fifties, though perhaps not very much more than we do now. He was always concerned to visualise the action of the play as it was staged, and his feeling for drama and for poetry was constantly alive, so that the most arduous linguistic study seemed infinitely worthwhile.

Since I decided not to take up history, but to go into the Classical Seventh, I read several more books with Christie, who despite all his responsibilities always managed to find time for a little teaching. In those few periods, he did far more for me than any other teacher. David Simpson, Master of the King's Scholars, who taught the Sixth Form at that time, was a careful and conscientious teacher, and I learned much from him. I feel grateful to him for having tried to eradicate faults which I am still conscious of possessing; but he was not gifted with the faculty of encouragement. Christie, being an enthusiast himself, recognised my enthusiasm, and by praising the occasional piece of good work made me ambitious to improve my scholarship.

We read with him parts of the fifth and sixth books of the *Odyssey*; the episode of Nausicaa came across magnificently. We read the *Ion* of Euripides, and Christie made us enjoy as much as he did himself the wonderful passage after the prologue, which presents the boy sweeping the temple steps, scaring away the birds and revealing his pride in being a servant of Apollo to the approaching Queen and her attendants. At Lancing we read the *Birds*, and he made us fully aware of the fun and high spirits of Aristophanes. I was disappointed when the imminence of the school's traditional Latin Play led him to read with us the *Phormio* of Terence; but he soon fully convinced me of the special charm of Terence, the refined elegance of his language, and the appeal of the New Comedy in general. We read with him the fourth book of the *Aeneid*, and I seem to remember that he showed more sympathy for Dido and less for Aeneas than some might have expected. I do not think I ever read a book of Horace with him, but I can vividly remember his presentation of several odes of Horace; Horace was one of the authors he talked about when, during the evacuation, he found time to invite a few members of the Seventh over to his headquarters at the Sussex Pad Inn for informal discussion of the classics. The only Greek prose book I read with him in class was the *Characters* of Theophrastus, in a class which combined amusement with instruction in a particularly high degree.

Christie did not officially teach us composition, by which I mean the translation into Greek or Latin of English prose or verse; but in a few lessons I learned far more from him about it than I did from any other master. Here again his feeling for style and his enthusiasm for literature helped him to teach one much and to make one eager to learn more. Gilbert Murray wrote that this exercise appealed to him because it was the one thing resembling an art which his school education gave him an opportunity to practise. Taste, as well as knowledge and accuracy, is needed for its successful execution, and it can give one a grasp of the principles of language, style and metre as few other modes of training can. The specimens of Christie's own work in this volume, if studied with attention, will show how much skill is needed to do this thing well; but they do not show how much Christie was able to teach by going through one's own attempt, not merely repeating his own polished version, but showing how one might have made better use of such ideas than one, in fact, had.

Christie taught English literature no less memorably than he taught the classics, and in teaching either referred often to the other. Reading Matthew Arnold's *Culture and Anarchy* with him was particularly instructive; Arnold was an author specially congenial to him, and in discussing him he introduced us to many of the personalities and problems of the nineteenth century, in which he felt particularly at home. Among these was Mark Pattison, a central figure through whom one could gain access to many subjects, including German scholarship, of which I then knew nothing. We once read with him Robert Bridges' *Testament of Beauty*, a work even then beginning to go out of fashion but one which Christie used to teach us a good deal; this was the first time that I began to get some notion of Platonism in its ancient and modern forms. Reading *Macbeth* with Christie was exciting, and we read most of the play in class; Christie read magnificently, and helped us to improve our reading.

He introduced us to many authors whom we did not read with him in class, usually making us eager to explore them further. His taste was that of a man of the late nineteenth century; Modernism meant little to him, and he was unaffected by such fashions as that of the demotion of Milton and the exaltation of the Metaphysicals. Nor did he often cite the modern literature of the Continent; English literature and the Greek and Latin classics were his territory. He cared little for the literature of the eighteenth century, and seldom spoke of Swift or Pope. He knew well Wordsworth, Keats and Shelley, but he was intimate with Tennyson and Browning and much appreciated the poetry of Housman. He relished Macaulay, though he often drew attention to his limitations. He had known Scott thoroughly from boyhood, and the Waverley Novels meant much to him. So did Jane

Austen: I do not think he cared so much for the later nineteenth century novelists, though he caused me to read *Middlemarch*. He often spoke of Lytton Strachey, whose attitude to the Victorians was so different from his own, giving him more credit for his good qualities than one might have expected; he never doubted that the Victorians were strong enough to resist Strachey's attacks.

His conversation gave a picture of the old-fashioned English world of education which I found fascinating. We would talk of Rendall, his famous Headmaster at Winchester, and of his senior colleague when he taught at Rugby, Kittermaster, or of T.F. Higham, who had been his tutor at Trinity and of Cyril Bailey of Balliol, who had been kind to him at Oxford. Sometimes he would speak of other Oxford dons, like J.U. Powell, Sir Arthur Pickard-Cambridge or J.D. Denniston. Most of all he spoke of Gilbert Murray, whose lectures and writings meant a good deal to him. Once after I had gone up to Oxford I was running down Gilbert Murray with all the omniscience of youth, and Christie said to me, 'A lot of people got a great kick out of hearing Gilbert Murray say *έάσω κορίζου καὶ σύ κασάνδραν λέγω*'. I was lucky to get an opportunity later to appreciate the force of this. He would also tell us about many other people outside the world of scholarship. He had several stories about Frederick Temple, whose son William was a friend of his. He said that once when Temple was Head Master of Rugby and was taking a parent for a walk in the grounds, the parent was surprised to notice that his companion had disappeared. Looking up, he saw the future Archbishop of Canterbury perched in the branches of a tall tree, into which, using his great height, he had suddenly vaulted. David Pears remarked to me that Christie himself would have been fully capable of such an exploit.

When I went on to Oxford, my tutor at Christ Church was J.G. Barrington-Ward, who even more than Christie belonged to the older world of English classical education. Barrington-Ward's only publications were compositions, and he wrote Latin with much elegance. He did not approve of E.R. Dodds, who had succeeded Gilbert Murray in the Regius Chair of Greek in 1936, or of Eduard Fraenkel, who had become Corpus Professor of Latin a year earlier; but he advised me to attend their lectures, and during the first week of term I realised that I had still a long way to go before I could become a scholar. Fraenkel was the only other teacher I encountered whom I would call a great teacher, and it is instructive to compare him with Christie, even though the two men and the places in which they taught were so entirely different. Fraenkel was by any standard truly learned, both in Greek and Latin, and demanded of us a degree of acquaintance with secondary as well as primary authorities which many of us found too much for them. He was far less sensitive than Christie to the feelings of his pupils. But there was a basic resemblance between the teaching of the two men, for what made them great teachers was their enthusiasm for literature and their eagerness to help others to share the pleasure they derived from it. Fraenkel began by finding us and our old-fashioned kind of classical education hopelessly superficial. But he realised from the first that certain scholars who had their roots in that kind of education, like Edgar Lobel or Sir John Beazley, were great scholars; and he ended by discovering that English undergraduates, ignorant as they might be of secondary authorities, at least knew certain classical texts well and were able to translate them. When Christie returned to Oxford as Principal of Jesus, Fraenkel immediately appreciated his qualities, and worked hard to persuade him to lecture about Terence. Christie was persuaded, but his heart was no longer in it; he felt that classical education at Oxford had been greatly changed since he had been a don at Magdalen, and that he lacked the learning which was now necessary for an Oxford lecturer. But after his retirement he continued for a few years to teach at Westminster; and when during that period he came up to Oxford to speak to an undergraduate society about Horace, he held their attention just as he had held ours thirty years before.

HUGH LLOYD-JONES

SELECTED WRITINGS

Part I · On Education and Teaching

The Queen's Generation: Watching it Grow

'The Queen's Generation' was a series of broadcasts on the BBC in the year of the Coronation, 1953. A number of Her Majesty's contemporaries had spoken about their lives - they included the then world ice-skating champion and the young MP for Bristol South-East, Tony Benn, who had been a pupil of JTC's at Westminster. 'Watching it Grow' was the last talk in the series, the summing up by someone from an older generation.

How various were the subjects of those who contributed to the series entitled The Queen's Generation. Politics of the future; a new view of the Sink; how I composed my poem; life story of a skating champion, and so on. It would be an affectation to pretend that one could trace a single attitude running through them all; nor could I by reading them one after another form a clear impression of a single generation. But it was one I remember very well, the generation at school during the war. In these years, I was head master of an ancient London school; indeed, the first speaker was a pupil of mine. Yes, I have my own picture of those boys, that 'age-group' as we call it now. It was a very small section of it that I knew at close quarters; boys, not girls, and boys from fairly well-to-do homes. But it was a characteristic of that time that this group was much less confined, much less isolated, than it would have been ten years earlier. They rubbed shoulders with the rest of the world, more than their predecessors had, and a good thing too! 'Rubbed shoulders' is the right phrase for close contact in air-raid shelters, in learning first aid, in farming and in the Home Guard during evacuation - not to mention crowded trains and the Food Office! All that, at times, was uncomfortable, though it was education of a very real kind. But I am forgetting: we are not calling it The War Time Generation but The Queen's Generation.

I pondered on that title and what it implies. Here we are, it seems to suggest, nine young persons, all under thirty, and we are contemporaries of the Queen! The Queen - centre of loyalty, symbol of romance, the symbol too of unimaginable responsibility. She has a job, an immensely important and highly-lighted job, but still a job – and we have ours. No disrespect intended: on the contrary, admiration and loyalty, all the more because they have a touch of sympathy and understanding. But doesn't it all suggest something new in our attitude to the monarchy? A healthier, more realistic attitude *I* should say, but with no lack of romance or veneration or sense of history.

Could we easily imagine nine young persons coming forward in 1838, the year following Queen Victoria's accession? A young poet, a young engineer, a young M.P., proclaiming themselves the Queen's Generation? How would that have been received at the early Victorian court? Would the young Queen have liked it, or would a secretary, anticipating several decades, have intimated that 'The Queen was not amused'? And if we jump back to her present Majesty's great namesake, – think of it! 'I am just the age of our gracious Queen,' he or she would be saying in 1559, 'just her age, and what a difficult time we live in, and would you like to hear just what I think about it?' Which of her courtiers, I wonder, would have cared to report those talks to the young Gloriana?

Yes, that phrase The Queen's Generation has a modern ring about it. The sovereign used to stand at the peak of a social pyramid. He or she was at the top, and it sloped down through the grades of aristocracy, each in theory slightly less grand than the one above, but all of them living in a style far beyond the range of the ordinary man. Many of them kept up a state not very different from Buckingham Palace or Windsor Castle. But *now* those intervening stages have gone: no private citizen, however noble, can afford to live like that. Only the Queen keeps her traditional splendour. And the odd thing is that this does not isolate her from us but brings her nearer. To live in a mansion with legions of servants in what was called semi-royal state is no longer practical politics. Earls open their houses to the tourist, and Admirals wash up at the sink! There is not even a pretence that the ideal way to live, if you can afford it, is to live in a palace, like a 'right down, regular, royal queen'. Even the sovereign only does it because her people like to have it so. It symbolizes for them, not the luxury and splendour of a privileged, leisured, ruling class, but an ancient historical tradition. It is the proper setting for a post which, if it brings something in the way of privilege, brings far more in the way of responsibility.

Thoughts like these, I believe, were half consciously in the minds of many of us at the time of the coronation, not least in the minds of the Queen's own contemporaries. They had been through the same mill. We are all the product, Queen or commoner, not only of our homes and our teachers, but of our time. This generation had grown up in the war. As it happens, my own generation too had been at school in war time, 1914–1918. I think our attitude to *that* war was different. For us, it had begun on the high heroic note of Rupert Brooke – too heroic to last. Soon there was the more strident note, of indignation over the whole thing, a war-weariness and cynical criticism of the Staff or the Government. We were uncomfortable, of course, but in England we were safe. This time, in 1940, we were all in it together.

That earlier school generation produced, among those who were left, a different outlook in the early twenties from the young outlook now. We had heard much of how the first war had shaken us all up. I see now how little it had done to shake many of the assumptions of 1910, but those assumptions were no longer valid for 1920. Some of us then felt we had had a fine education to fit us for a world which had vanished. The young man from the leisured home found it was a colder world for him in 1920. What was he to do? Like the man in the Bible 'I cannot dig, to beg I am ashamed'. (But I don't mind doing a little touting.)

The next generation, those I taught when I started schoolmastering in 1922, caught some of this spirit. I remember the clever ones being cynical about England, about the Empire, and about patriotism. Their fathers meantime complained of restrictions and taxation, grimly quoting Lloyd George's promise of 'a land fit for heroes to live in'. They still expected *some* privileges, and they missed them. Their wives bewailed the servant problem. But the next war really did bring us down to earth, all of us, one class with another, the old with the young. We ceased to expect any privileges and wives no longer discussed the servant problem because there were no servants at all, not even enough to constitute a problem! Mother cooks, Anne dusts, and father washes up. There is altogether less 'keeping up of appearances'; less appearances and more time for reality. That is the attitude of the Queen's Generation, as I saw it, and they began learning it in their own homes and schools, under war conditions. In evacuation they had had to make the best they could of dilapidated houses, even glazing and plumbing if they could get a lesson or two; they grew more dependent on themselves. Constantly they found men with far less formal education than their own to be so much better with a rifle or a hoe or a tractor. Boys will always give their admiration to a master of his craft, and some of them discovered for the first time that the craft of the scythe was comparable with the craft of the cricket bat; and far more useful just then.

You can see the sort of young men that such a training would tend to produce, and I would make bold to say that on the whole it has produced them, at any rate among the young people of the kind who get up to a University – a larger proportion of the whole than it was formerly. One can see the effect of their war-time training in many directions – in their work, in their holidays, and in their homes. In their work they think less about appearances and more about the interest of the job; less about pecuniary reward, if only because the Chancellor of the Exchequer subtracts so much of it, and more of the satisfaction they find in the work itself. They take this for granted nowadays. A lady like Mrs. Hichens, who gave one of the talks, combines her housework with an exacting job, without feeling she does anything odd or heroic. The engineer who spoke in this series finds his soul in managing a lonely hydro-electric scheme in the Highlands, without a thought of how it may rank for prestige in the world's eye.

In holidays, too, I notice the same sort of thing. When I was young, going abroad was an enterprise that involved preliminary staff-work with hotels, phrase-books, and even private introductions, and you saved up money for it. Today, when I talk to young people, I am struck by the simplicity and boldness of their travelling arrangements. They have hitch-hiked perhaps from Calais to Marseilles, they work their passage on a steamer to Naples, they live for a fortnight in Italy, with what money they have got, seeing far more of the people than we ever did, and they trust to luck for a lift home. This seems to me admirable; and they may be better ambassadors for their country than some of the professional diplomats. They are typical of the Queen's Generation.

At home they live, as I have said, more simply, and when the time comes to set up their own homes, they expect an equal partnership between husband and wife: both may have jobs, both will do the housework. What a long way we have gone from the accepted pattern of social life as seen in the novels of my youth, when the intending suitor was asked by the young lady's father 'Can you keep my daughter in the secure position to which she has been accustomed?'

The descendants of such young couples today are far less secure. 'Sense of insecurity' – it is a phrase you will find in many modern writers, especially critics: the poetry of today is said to display 'a deep-rooted feeling of insecurity' and that is supposed to be a bad thing. (It certainly makes for rather difficult poetry to one of my age.) But it can be a good thing too. Many young men earlier in this century, who had received a liberal education, were *too* secure. Insecurity has been a spur to them to get out into the world and to show what they could do, regardless of the old hierarchy of respectable, or less respectable, professions.

But you will remind me that I am speaking of a minority. For the greater part of our population there has never before been such great *security*. Security is the watchword of the Welfare State. In so far as that means the banishment of grinding poverty, the mitigation of the haunting anxiety over unemployment – who could call security anything but good? If a man is doing his job well, it is wrong that he should lose his livelihood through no fault of his own. And yet, to feel complete security, to know that your job is safe whatever the standard of the work, whatever the attitude of mind behind it – this may have its dangers, not only in the economic sphere but also in its effects on the spirit of a man in his work and his leisure. We cannot, most of us, choose our work; it is in our freely-chosen leisure that our personality most clearly reveals itself. Is it true that the vastly-increased sense of security in jobs and livelihoods has bred a spirit of too much security, too little enterprise in leisure and spare-time? The Queen's Generation has seen the first flowering of the Welfare State. For the privileged few of that generation it has meant less security and hence more enterprise and more adventure: a good thing. For the unprivileged many, it may at the present time be bringing too little sense of adventure, too much readiness to take our recreation 'laid-on' for us. Every man has the right to some measure of security, some fundamental assurance of safety; but Shakespeare's Hotspur said something true and wise when, being warned that his 'purpose was dangerous', he replied, 'Look you, my lord fool, out of this nettle danger we pluck this flower safety'.

Personality in Education: Three Portraits

This was the first in a series of three papers JTC delivered to Indian educationalists after a lengthy study tour of the Indian Secondary Educational system, sponsored by the Indian Government in 1952–1953.

1. Montague Rendall (Headmaster of Winchester)

I have been meditating on the incalculable importance of *personality* in the world of education.

I have lived in that world myself, first as a boy at school and college for some twelve years, like many of us, and then for over thirty years as a teacher or principal of a college. How easy to say that personality is what matters in a teacher and what a platitude: one of those wide generalizations, you might think, that doesn't carry you far. 'A strong personality': what does that phrase suggest to you applied to a teacher, to a headmaster? A stock figure perhaps, grave, imposing or authoritative; formidable to the offender, Olympian and remote from the whims and impulses of the ordinary mortal. That is the accepted picture, especially in fiction, of the famous headmaster; and lesser men have tried to approximate to it, investing themselves with a more than human solemnity, careful, as it were, never to be caught 'out of cap and gown'. But the picture is not a true one, and it has done more harm than good, because it has limited and hampered the simple spontaneous vitality which most of us – thank Heaven! – keep tucked away behind the official facade.

I want to put before you as vividly as I can three figures whom I knew well at different stages of my life, and to whom I owe more than I can repay. All three have now died, though not so long ago, and I knew them in their prime. I should like to share these thoughts with you because I feel strongly that the future of education in any country does not depend primarily upon organization or text books or bricks and mortar, but upon humanity, the humanity of the teacher – not some special kind of humanity set apart from the miniature world of school, but the abounding surprising energetic humanity that would single a man out whatever his calling – a barrister, a business man, an actor.

The first of my three figures – let us call him M – I see through the eyes of boyhood, for he was the headmaster of the school where I was a boy during the first World War. He was tall, dark, good-looking, and of a whirl-wind energy: thus far he may have resembled the conventional headmaster of fiction or of a fond mother's imagination. But, in truth, 'conventional' was the last word one could apply to him. He had many qualities which are not thought necessary in a headmaster and he lacked certain virtues which headmasters are supposed to need. His study desk was gloriously untidy: he continually mistook the names and identities of boys, even senior boys and prominent athletes. He was by no means a man of method, on one occasion inviting two hundred guests to a garden party and forgetting to order any tea for them. To the conventional eye of the junior English schoolboy, some details of his dress appeared sadly unusual – the tie worn in a brass ring, a black cloak at times thrown over the shoulders. He had been in his day, we were told, a fine athlete, and when he came into class from the Headmaster's house he often preferred running to walking. But over the countryside he was a mighty walker, taking a boy or colleague with him at a brisk pace, breaking now and then into a trot, and vaulting a five-barred gate! We boys laughed at all this, and we imitated his precise and rather rhetorical tones – but strictly behind his back. His sheer vigour and vitality were enough to make him formidable face to face. It was perfectly clear that he liked the company of some boys more than others: no harm surely in having favourites, provided you are careful not to be hard on those who are not favourites. With the chosen few he would take holidays at some beauty-spot in England or on the Continent.

What has all this to do with being a good headmaster, you may say? Was he a good organizer? No. Did he devote his vacations to constructing new time-tables? Emphatically not. He would infuriate his staff by returning from some joyous holiday in the mountains only just in time for the beginning of the term. Why then does he live in my memory and why am I grateful to him? Was he a good teacher? Most certainly he was, for those who were lucky enough to sit under him in the top form for their Classics. Here again it was not patient method or solid instruction that one remembers, but the enthusiasm, the imagination, that could light up some passage of a text by a comic gesture or unexpected inflexion of the voice. There was always something of the actor in him, and how he could make the Latin and Greek Classics live for us – the dialogues of Plato, the comedies or tragedies of ancient Greece, the poetry of Virgil. For two or three weeks of each winter term he would take a double period with every form in the School in turn. How alarmed we felt, we younger boys, as he sailed into our class-room in his silk gown to test us in the work we had done so far. But that was as much as the average boy saw of him as a teacher.

Looking back at him now, I think he never particularly wanted to be a headmaster. With his great natural vigour (he still went striding across the fields when he was over eighty) and his strong old-fashioned sense of duty, he took the responsibilities of a headmaster 'in his stride', and what a stride it was ! But he would have been an equally remarkable personality if he had never been a school-master at all. His ruling passion was for beauty: a statement which makes English boys, and some Englishmen, feel shy and uncomfortable. But of him it was true: all the money he could afford, and he was unmarried, he spent on beautifying the rather gaunt official residence in which he lived, with books and pictures. And it was in sharing these treasures with his boys that we saw him at his best. He would spend an hour in the evening, after school, showing to a small audience lantern slides of famous pictures and sculptures usually from Italy. Attendance here was wholly voluntary, the lectures were racy and informal. I owe to them my first acquaintance with Fine Art and what it can mean to a quite ordinary boy. We took it all for granted, but I realize now what splendid energy and faith it showed to spend an hour in this way, during the first World War when all headmasters were beset with new difficulties and were reading almost every morning familiar names in the list of those who had fallen on the battle field. He himself was no artist, but he was a keen and skilful photographer. He often showed us his pictures, made into slides, of the familiar school buildings or playing fields, taken so as to reveal a beauty in the play of lights and shadows that we had never seen before. What better way to train a boy's eye to notice the everyday beauty of the common life all around him!

Have I said enough to suggest the character and inspiration of the man and the influence he had upon the young? Not because he was first and foremost a great headmaster, but because he had a strong unique personality, far too strong to sink itself in his official position. His abounding vigour and the complete sincerity of his devotion to the things he loved spoke to the vigour and sincerity of youth in us. In his presence we 'had life and we had it abundantly'.

In those days I little thought that I should be a teacher myself and a headmaster for eighteen years. I cannot say that when I was appointed to a headmastership I looked back to him as a figure to follow and to imitate: he was too casual, too unorthodox, too much his unique self to be a model to anyone. But, by my memories of him I am assured of this: that what the young require for their true nourishment and welfare is a man with a strong fearless character, possessing the wisdom of the full grown man but the resilience of youth, a man who follows his ideals and not because they are good for his pupils but because they are the highest he knows and he passionately wants his school to share them. His aim is not to control and organize and regulate his pupils all the time, but in the familiar Christian words 'to govern them and lift them up for ever', and the best way to do that is to be himself lifted up. His watch-word is not 'look at me', but 'do look the way I am looking'.

I am not suggesting that anyone should, or could, model himself on a unique original figure like M. The best headmasters *are* unique: it is the bad ones who are so deplorably alike. To us boys M. was *the* headmaster: we thought then that somehow all headmasters must be something like M. But there, of course, we were wrong. The key quality in M. was his imagination, his enthusiasm, his love of beauty. He was, temperamentally, more concerned with the beauty of Nature, of Art, and of Mankind than with individual boys. He was a kind of Elizabethan figure who would have flourished in the English Renaissance or even in one of the fifteenth-century Italian towns which he knew and loved so well: he was a 'magnificent' man, a bit of a poseur with an affectation which was only the froth on the surface of his deep and vital energy. My next figure was of a more conventional kind.

But M, and he, and my third headmaster as well, were in their several ways *devoted* men: they had no thought of self-advancement or personal prestige; they did not 'stand on their dignity' – they had too much of the natural unconscious dignity for that. These three men were exceptional, I admit, but their example has spoken clearly to a host of pupils and teachers who knew them, and still speaks though they themselves are dead.

2. W.W. Vaughan (Headmaster of Rugby)

'The living personality of the teacher'! Even that aspect of education, if taken in the abstract, could be dull; but to me it is not an abstract subject, it is a frame for pictures. Immediately my memory fills the frame with the features of certain strong, inspiring, well-loved personalities, all teachers by choice and by profession who have meant much to me over the years. I want to share with you my conviction that the teaching and the training of the young is not work suitable only for an ill-paid drudge, but can be a task worthy of the highest qualities and the most devoted energy in the best of men: men who might have chosen some other career with every prospect of success and far greater remuneration, but who in fact chose teaching, and by doing so wielded an influence which continues long after they are dead and gone in the hearts and minds of their pupils.

My second personality, V, was widely different from the first. He was a rugged man, with shaggy grey hair and piercing blue eyes. Plato tells us that Socrates, when talking to a young man, had a trick of suddenly looking up at him like a bull – tauredon. V used to do that as if he were trying to pierce the screen of convention and get right to the heart of the person he was talking to. There was not an atom of pose about him. He took life seriously; it was a battle ground between good and evil and he was a warrior on the side of good. Conventional words, those; and if they suggest to you that he was always talking about religion and morality, with no sense of humour but only a sad sweet smile, than I have certainly misled you. He had a great sense of humour, expressed in gusts and gales of laughter, which boys learned to be slightly afraid of, because the laughter would suddenly end with one of those piercing bull-like glances and some unexpected words which went home to the heart of the hearer.

In all important ways he was a splendid headmaster; I say important because he had lacked the superficial graces with which many headmasters try to recommend themselves and their schools; 'dressing the shop window' as we say. He was, for example, not a fluent speaker; what he said was simple and often repeated with um's and er's. But it came from the heart. As a boy once remarked 'if old V got up and said "it's - ar - um - better to be - ar - good than bad" - you'd think "By Jove, that's very true"'. He was also an untidy man, in this like my first figure M; perhaps his untidiness was part of his scorn for the trivialities of life. If an assistant master or senior boy entered his study for instructions or advice, he would not give you just what the occasion required and no more. There were no neat pigeon-holes in his mind any more than in his study. He would give you the whole of himself, probing behind the question and rejoicing in the chance to know any other human being more intimately; a five minutes interview might thus prolong itself to half an hour.

To V personal relations were the very essence of his duty. He was a good shepherd of his flock: or would it be truer to say that he was a good sheep-dog? Yes, sheep-dog is nearer to the mark; he had the shagginess, the faithfulness, and the sudden barks of laughter which produced in the stranger exhilaration touched with fear. First and foremost he was the guardian of his flock, the boys in his school. He had the qualities that boys admire - directness, determination, and fearlessness. He was fearless in making unpopular decisions; he used to say 'very healthy for Public Opinion to have ah, a shock'. In his younger days he was a courageous and doughty foot-baller. I have been told that once as a young man he was abroad in Europe, and on a visit to a theatre there was a scare of fire on the stage. The curtain came down and the audience stampeded to the doors. V sat perfectly still alone in his stall. Afterwards he said 'I thought it was the only useful thing I could do'. It was not only to his pupils that he was pastor and master. I knew him first when I was a young assistant teacher on his staff, and I learnt from him the very grammar of my trade as a schoolmaster; perhaps he tended to treat us all as if we were senior boys. Indeed, that was his weakness – or would have been if he had yielded to it – the temptation felt by a strong and masterful nature to be overbearing. Like others of that temperament he was irritated by those who tried to flatter or cajole him and he tended to be rough with them. With those who stood up to him he might bark but the bark would end in a gust of laughter. I learnt this lesson early in my days under him and I still remember the way I learnt it. I was anxious to take my class off to the performance of a play, which meant a whole day's absence. With the headmaster I tried the tactful approach saying something about the educational value of the drama. V broke in on my speech: 'ah – young man, don't talk bunkum to me about educational values; you would like a holiday, and so would the boys'. He moved by impulse, but the impulses were right, and we remembered them more than carefully reasoned statements. Once he overheard a boy using foul language: he blazed out at him 'Go and wash your mouth out with Carbolic: go along to the matron and ask for a mouth wash; and tell her why'. Surely the boy remembers that to this day, far longer than he would have remembered a lecture on the evils of swearing.

V knew that he had a hot temper, and he was always ready with a frank and generous apology if he felt he had gone too far. But he knew, also, I think that a fiery temper on the right occasion is a power for good. He showed it, never to resent a personal slight, but to express his indignation at something mean or shameful. It was what the old moralists called 'righteous wrath'. Underneath it was a strong vein of tenderness and wisdom. A colleague and contemporary of mine found himself in his first term unable to keep discipline in his classes. He was unhappy and near to resigning his post: he went to see V with that thought in mind. V at a glance understood his man: this was not a moment for indignation or reproach. He heard the young man out and then said 'I have known very few really good – ah, *really* good schoolmasters who did not begin with difficulties over discipline'. A kind wise word, which changed the life of another human being. V was a humble man; not that he indulged in idle self-depreciation, and he never hesitated to claim for himself the regard due to his position. He had the humility of one whose standards were high but walked conscious of an ideal higher still which he had not yet attained. Still, he was probably more formidable than he knew. He sent for a new boy during the first week of term, and the boy, from the mere sense of loneliness and apprehension, burst into tears before a word was spoken. In a moment V understood the situation and told the boy stories of his own first days at that very school fifty years before. There were some six hundred boys in the school and by the end of the school year, V knew everyone of them by sight, and he would write short revealing comments on them three times a year in the terminal school reports.

I have learned by experience that the potential influence of such friendship on a growing boy is incalculable, and it is education in the truest and deepest sense of the word. Of course, one will not succeed in these relationships as well as one hoped; some boys will have no apparent need of friendship, others will betray one's ideals for them; that is to be expected. But if a headmaster knows well only twenty or thirty pupils during their last year, if he is aware of their ambitions, their home background, their hidden faults and hidden virtues, he will find himself becoming more than a schoolmaster; he will be, to a few boys, perhaps not more than five or six a year, 'a guide, philosopher and friend', to the great enrichment of his own life as well as theirs.

1. R.F. Bailey (Headmaster of Quarry Bank School, Liverpool)

In a teacher personality, alone and unassisted, can produce, if only in a limited circle, that vital spark of wonder and curiosity and desire for knowledge, and resolve to live a certain kind of life, and it is these which make up true education. No doubt, as education spreads, institutions and rules and text-books are inevitable and necessary, but all these without personality are dead.

By far the strongest and most lasting element in my own education, to which I owe very much, was association with stronger and nobler personalities.

The first two figures I have tried to sketch were widely different men, but both were in their generation outstanding. Both, before they died, were recipients of Civil and University Honours. They were recognised figures in the educational world, consulted by Universities and by Committees quite as much after their retirement as when they were in full work. They had surely been marked to rise even from their early days; and the world of education was fortunate when they threw their gifts and energies into teaching. But my third figure, B was not of that calibre. I knew him first not as a schoolmaster at all; he was a relation of mine, and I, as a small boy, liked him because, though there were fifteen years between us, he played with me not as if he were being kind, but as if he enjoyed it. In many respects he was by no means the kind of man that boys make a hero of. He was small and short-sighted, and owing to an accident in babyhood was slightly deformed. In any mixed society he was shy and self-conscious, being most at ease with children and with poor, simple people. He went to one of our great Public Schools with a scholarship: the fees would probably have been beyond his parents' means without that help. Here, one gathered, he was miserable to begin with, mocked and slighted for his physical defects, but the friendships he made there he kept up to the end of his life. At Cambridge he was very happy, doing well but not supremely well in his chosen subject, mathematics; but he never rated his capacity very high and took a post in a preparatory school for small boys. From there to his own surprise he was invited to one of the old and famous schools of England. The headmaster who appointed him had the wit to see beyond the shy and plain exterior and to guess at the great qualities which were developing behind. Even here he was not at first as happy as he hoped, and found some difficulty over discipline. But gradually boys and colleagues came to know the ardent spirit which at first was masked by the bespectacled face and clumsy figure. He was too delicate to serve in the first world war, and became a pillar of strength to the school when many of his colleagues were on the battlefield. When the war ended he was due to become a housemaster; but meantime he had been thinking, on lines which were less familiar thirty years ago in our Public Schools than they are now. 'What right had he' he asked himself 'to enjoy the amenities of a delightful and expensive residential school, when such advantages could be only for a tiny fraction of English boys, say 1%?'. So, much against the advice of some friends and colleagues, he put in his application for the headmastership of a new State School in one of our biggest industrial cities: here if his application were successful he would live in the noise and smoke of a town, with no comfortable traditions behind him, with a new school to organize, a new staff to appoint and new problems to face, and probably some prejudice against him, coming as he did from a public school, a 'snob school' as its opponents delighted to call it. To some men like my two earlier figures such a call would have been a challenge, an opportunity to show their masterful character and their relish for a contest. Not so, B: he knew that he was not the kind of man whom boys admire at sight and colleagues follow with unfaltering loyalty. Nevertheless, he submitted his name, and he was not chosen; he came second on the list. And so, perhaps to his own relief, and the joy of his friends, he returned to the school he loved, ready to serve there for another twenty-five years and with an easier conscience: he had offered his services and he was not wanted: he had hardly expected that he would be. But then came an unexpected turn. The man who had been given the post was found to have forged his testimonials, and he had concealed the fact that he had served a prison sentence.

So after all the post fell to B, and the way things turned out made his position no easier for him at the outset as a headmaster. He had not, on interview, been the choice of the governors, he was unimpressive in appearance and they wondered if they had made a mistake. At first they thought they had; the boys, and still more the parents, let it be seen that *this* was not their idea of a headmaster. The staff were critical and off-hand in their manner. In such a situation there is little doubt what my other personalities would have done. They would have spoken to the boys and then to the staff in clear confident tones and made it very obvious who was the master in that house. There is nothing wrong in such a course; I think I should have tried it myself, but it was not B's way. He was not by nature assertive and had no love for a fight. As far as he personally was concerned, he was wholly unresentful of slights, incapable of wounded vanity, for he had no vanity to wound. Such men are in a strong position; their opponents cannot use one favourite weapon of attack – the barbed word, the slur on the man's self-esteem – because it leaves no mark. If criticism amounted to real disloyalty and was aimed through him at the School, then he spoke out. This he did gently, most reluctantly and quite unsparingly. I never knew anyone who better followed the Christian precept 'to speak the truth in love'. He hated saying what had to be said; he found no relish in telling home truths (how unlike most of us!) and was all the more effective for that. His hearers felt that it was not an expression of personal views, but the voice of the School, at its best, condemning conduct which the offenders themselves knew, in their better moments, was intolerable. The School at length came to recognize in him a mind unclouded by vanity, a heart devoted to the School, a man who lost something on public occasions because he was so simple and so little of a showman, but gained immeasurably by his sincerity and humility.

Within a few years that school was holding its own with some of the best in the country: boys won scholarships at Cambridge and at Oxford, played their part in the sports, debates and other activities of the ancient universities, and all this without any of the advantages of a wealthy home or a privileged background. A strong Old Boy tradition began to spring up; this is a comparatively rare thing among the large day schools in industrial England; and a club was formed in which boys of the school could provide games and recreation and interests for the working boys of the city. In fact that school, with no special resources, no carefully picked boys and no influential backing, was giving to its members most of the advantages and opportunities associated with the expensive, exclusive Public Schools. The airs and graces of the upper class, indeed, the school did not foster, nor did it attempt to, but if it be the aim of a secondary education to lay the foundations of a good citizen, enabling the average boy to find a job and hold his own in the world and for the abler boys opening up a path to the University, than this school was splendidly fulfilling the aims of Secondary Education. At the back of it all was the headmaster, at the back rather than at the front, he remained his own shy self, never in the least caring to impress the outsider. I recall him dropping gently off to sleep on the platform at his own school speech day.

You would not have said that B had any very forceful element in him; but strength there must have been to support him against a cold and unfamiliar background to start with, and against the ever present sense of his own inadequacy. He would be amazed, were he still alive, to know that I was speaking of him, along with M and V. He would have vehemently disowned any comparison. One thing he had in common with V. For both of them everything turned on personal relations. At his school, from the first, he instituted self-government, and gave his trust implicitly to the boy whom he made Captain of the School. This choice was made before the summer holidays for the ensuing school year, and during the holidays he would take this boy away with him for a week or so, usually on a rowing expedition down a river, sleeping in tents. He explained to me that only on some such informal holiday expedition could he really get to know a boy; 'and I take them rowing' he added characteristically 'because it gives us something to do, and it is the only sport at which I can perform without making a fool of myself'.

I hope I have given you something of the man's spirit, the spirit which triumphed so decisively and yet so humbly over the handicaps of the body. He never realized, I believe, what a great thing he had done in creating this school from the beginning. He was never making envious comparisons with other schools more fortunately placed. At length he retired some four years ago: his natural instincts were for country life, but in order to be nearer his friends he lived on in the city, accommodating himself cheerfully in a single room for living and sleeping, and using what money he had saved to support some of his old boys who were in need. But this he never mentioned even to me. That kind of life does not bring wordly fame, but when this man died, all who had met him knew that a life had ended which was higher and better than their lives, and the large church where they held a memorial service was full to overflowing.

There are my three figures: a man of imagination, a man of strength, and a man of love. Each might have chosen a different career from teaching. But I hope there may always be a handful of such men in each generation laying the foundations for the future.

Heads and Hands

An address given to the 27 Club, a dining club of headmasters, at Westminster School.

If I am forgiven this paper, composed rather light-heartedly as a counter-weight to the gloom of the Lent term in London, I will be forgiven anything, including the ambiguity of my title 'Heads and Hands'. Did this perhaps suggest to you theory and practice, the classics versus clay modelling? I rather hope so, because it is not about that at all. The heads are ourselves, you and I, and the hands – they are the instruments by which we make our will known and done – our staff, staffs if you prefer, or should it be staves? An odd word, 'staff', by the way, meaning a body of helpers. Undoubtedly it came to its present usage through the army, but even in a military sense 'staff' barely appears before the nineteenth century, perhaps through its meaning of baton or wand of office. In that sense of course it is as old as English, but not in our sense, and when Prospero threatens to break his staff and bury them some plummets deep in the earth, he does not speak as a Head Master in the ninth week of term. I doubt if even Dr Arnold spoke of his staff; he would have said 'my masters' and in his case there would have been no ambiguity. Nowadays the word denotes groups of various kinds, the school workmen for instance, stokers and so on, who are known in delicate distinction from our colleagues as the 'working staff'. Indeed the applications of the word 'staff' have increased and ramified in the last thirty years, though one usage is now only a memory in its old-fashioned sense: I mean of course domestic staff.

Still, it is the teaching staff I have in mind in their relation to the Head Master. I have listened to a quantity of papers and speeches, wise and unwise, on scholastic subjects, school pensions, school prayers, school punishments etc., but I cannot remember one on this topic. And yet is there any that comes home more closely to our business and bosoms, especially in our early days when we have for the first time committed head-mastery? I do not remember clearly my first sight of the assembled school nor even my first sermon, fortunately: but I recall the very odour of the room in which I held my first masters meeting. How much one's happiness, one's success or failure, is going to depend on those two dozen unknown men sitting in front of one: and no doubt they feel the same. 'You needn't fuss yourself' I was told by an old friend, 'wondering whether or not they are all staring at you: they certainly are'. Of course one may not arrive in utter ignorance of their characters and pecularities; that depends on one's predecessor: one such may give you short and helpful notes

– I speak from experience – such as 'jumpy and idle' or 'good with Science VI, unsafe lower down': another feels it honourable to say only 'due to retire in 1950; charming wife'. One is grateful for these informative comments, but by half term one has forgotten them. You have discovered much for yourself and so have they. What infinite variety among the staff of a single school! And yet – or am I mistaken? – how similar the staff as a whole of Marlchester to the staff of Tunbury! On both, the patient quizzical classic hiding behind a critical manner a passion for the Parthenon and also perhaps for stamp collecting: a man who on speech days tends to cynicism and ennui, but in adversity is very staunch. On both staffs surely the note-writer. His first note received by the young Head Master is deeply disturbing. Beautifully written and dreadfully lucid, it begins 'I fail to understand ...' and goes on to reveal a solecism in the time-table or a piece of injustice to boys not in the Corps until the Head Master begins to feel unworthy of his high office. But the note-writer usually overdoes it: when *any* alteration, major or minor, is followed by a note expressing the writer's failure to understand the Head begins to discount him as one who suffers from what I once called 'high ink pressure'.

One could continue at length with these well-known, and eventually well-loved, types, but as a group they will all be asking one question about the new Head Master – what his policy is. Only the bolder spirits will imitate the journalist and ask him outright: if any do, the truthful answer often is that the Head Master does not know. This does not matter because in his second term he will be told what it is. All he has done in his first term is to keep up with day-to-day problems and running repairs. He has said that the new ablution-rooms in Robinson's house must wait: he has said that Smith's parents must write before Smith is allowed to transfer from the Corps to the Scouts, and so on. But lo and behold, before the second term is well under way, one note begins 'Dear Head Master, I know it is your policy not to encourage any repairs in the boarding houses at present, at the same time I must point out ...' and the eager young Scout master writes 'Dear Head Master, I gather it is to be your policy not to allow any boy to transfer to the Scouts even after gaining Certificate A; while loyally accepting this decision, I must point out ...' A policy has been born though this may not be recognised for some time by the Head Master himself, politique sans qu'il sache.

Of course, he acquires at length a conscious policy: but to begin with it is his unconscious everyday relations with his staff that will be more decisive; and here there is no right way and wrong way. To most of us a regular periodical consultation with masters would seem essential: yet one eminent Head Master never held a masters' meeting in all his twenty-five years of office: perhaps they don't at Eton, I do not know. *One* will move to terms of Christian names with his colleagues as quickly as he can: another will cling to the formality of Mr, at any rate in public. And how are the staff to address their leader? Some still delight in the formal 'Sir'. I do not care myself for Head, still less for Chief, though I have wilted under both ere now. I have been accustomed, as we most of us have, to be addressed as Head Master, though I know that one of my colleagues, a fine man, would modulate into 'Mr. Christie' if the temperature rose above normal. He once entered my study waving a note I had sent him (an innocent note as I thought) crying 'Mr Christie, I was astounded to receive this communication'. All such matters of style and title are imponderable, like questions of when and where to mount cap and gown; when and where to smoke: but they all go to weave the subtle web that attaches the Head to his hands, a web that can, as a by-product, afford such delightful personal friendships: a web that can be liable to such sudden violent tugs and strains. One impression of the independent public schools which I do get is this: that whatever the official relations may be (even if they savour at times of Government and Opposition) personal and private relations are hardly ever as much strained as one might suppose from books about education or novels about schools. An assistant master wrote a book engagingly called 'Thirty Years Hard'. He explained in the preface that he was far better qualified to write on education than most teachers: they were miserably cramped by knowledge of four or five schools at most. He spoke from experience of twenty-three. It was a jaundiced book. I remember one counsel to the staff as a whole: 'Always rally round the member of Common Room who is in the Head Master's black books for the moment'. As to novels and plays a change has crept over the portrait of the Head Master: once he was a man of wrath, dark, tall, humourless and probably unctuous. He corrected Latin proses in the drawing room on the sofa where his wife had lately been talking, very simply, to the Captain of Cricket. But now, following a real trend, and distorting it, as drama does, he is young, loquacious and informal: asking the newest member of the staff if he would care to join the War Memorial Committee (*The Guinea Pig*) settling on the last day of July who is to have a coveted house-mastership in September (*The Browning Version*). The dramatists have got it wrong, but they have got it wrong *from* somewhere. From us of course, and our desire (to give it a kind name) to rule by love rather than by fear. Certainly the days of real hatred and strife between Head and Usher are over. Within these hallowed precincts the great Dr Busby conducted war to the knife by letter, libel and law suit against his recalcitrant under-master Mr Bagshawe, and Mr Bagshawe left his mark even on Busby.

Those days are gone but an assistant here and there may still be awkward. One grows old and sleepy; another ought never to have chosen schoolmastering; what are our duties here? What are our powers? How unfair to a man and his family to discharge him at the age of 45 or 50! But how unfair to the boys to keep him! Ay, there's the rub. It is the hardest decision a Head Master has to make, and for weeks he goes to bed feeling 'uneasy sits the gown that drapes a Head'. And even if he takes the hard hateful and unpopular decision can he be sure of making it effective? As often as not he sits and suffers with an uneasy conscience.

With younger men the problem is less heart-rending: the Heads will deal with their Hands in very different ways. Let us take two Head Masters, Mr X and his successor Mr Y, who are both perturbed by the scanty courtesy, conceited bearing and unbridled tongue of Mr Z, appointed in a rash moment by X and given to commenting freely on his colleagues in school hours. We will follow Mr Z into the study of Head Master X, himself soon to retire.

Z You sent for me, Head Master?

X Yes, I did. I must ask you to be more careful - much more careful - of the way you criticize your colleagues when you are speaking to the VIth form. I gather you even refer to them by their nicknames and you are kind enough to include my sermons, my dogmas as you call them, as topics for the weekly essay.

Z Really, Head Master, I cannot think where you have got this information unless you have been holding an inquisition among the boys. I supposed you wished me to encourage free discussion: I had no idea that you take personal offence at the remarks of immature school boys on what you call your dogmas. Presumably they discuss them among themselves and I cannot imagine you would take what they say seriously. After all, any stigma is good enough to beat a dogma.

X Please don't try your epigrams on me, Z. You know perfectly well what I mean, and I want you to understand that I won't have it. If you are to remain here, you must change your tone – change it completely.

Z I fear I do *not* know perfectly well what you mean, Head Master: but please do not think I cling to my position here for mercenary motives. I could earn three times as much in Fleet Street to-morrow if I cared to. But I believe that I can give my form what no one else can: and in justice to them, I could really not accept anything savouring of dismissal without exercising my right to appeal to the Governors, and indeed – so strongly do I feel this – of appeal to even higher authorities. I hope you will excuse me now, I am already late for my next lesson.

And in due course young Mr Y finds himself in contact with Z, who had been handed on to him with the note 'a live wire; he has ideas of his own'. Mr Y did not send for Z, but Z came in one day to ask if he might read Aldous Huxley's *Ends and Means* for Divinity with his VIth form.

Y A very interesting choice Mr Z. Have you actually ordered the books?

Z I have, Head Master, and they are in the bookshop. I made several efforts to obtain your sanction, but unluckily you always seemed to be out or engaged.

Y Yes, do by all means: an interesting choice as I said, and you will not mind if I come in myself as occasion offers and hear what you have to say. Huxley is far enough, I expect, from what I gather you call my 'dogmas.'

Z Oh, by all means Head Master: it never struck me that you would be sensitive about what the boys, rightly or wrongly, call your 'dogmas'. After all, any stigma is good enough to beat a dogma.

Y (Laughing). Excellent, Mr Z, excellent. I agree with you, and in return for that good epigram you quote from Dean Inge I can only return you a poor one of mine: 'Love me, love my dogma'. I mean, if we are to get on together, I cannot have you using my pronouncements as weekly material for your young puppy-dogs. You have great talents, you know, Mr Z. Did someone tell me you were once a journalist?

Z Indeed no, Head Master. I came here straight from the university at the urgent request of your predecessor. But I could earn three times as much on Fleet Street to-morrow, not that ...

Y Is that so, Mr Z? Well that *is* interesting, though it does not surprise me to hear you say so. But I must not keep you longer. I hope to be along to hear you expound Aldous Huxley on Thursday.

That evening Mr Z had a note from Y saying 'Dear Z, I have been thinking over our talk this morning: I feel sure you are right in saying that your real métier is journalism with its wider freedom and far better prospects. I dare say you have approaches of your own, but I have ventured since we met to write to Lord Kemsley, with whom I have a nodding acquaintance, recommending you to his notice. I am sure this is the right decision which you hinted at in our talk to-day. Yours sincerely'.

Yes, Mr Y can cope with the Zs on his staff. But how he wishes he got on better with old Mr B, so good a teacher, so loyal a colleague and so deeply distressed by every kind of change. Now X was great friends with old B and managed him beautifully.

Certainly there are awkward masters here and there and it is easier to crack jokes about them than to do any justice to the others, the great majority, men living peaceably in their habitations, not leaders maybe, but men without whom no leader could do his work. All these the young Head Master finds *in situ*: they are his data and many of them likely to remain his data for years to come. But gaps occur surprisingly soon. A becomes a head master, old B retires, and Z joins the Daily Telegraph or the B.B.C. A new appointment must be made.

Nothing would be more interesting than to know how head masters interview prospective candidates for a post. Have they stock questions? At what point do they mention the sordid question of salary? Do they make an effort to induce the young man to talk at large? If so, how? If not, can they form any impression of him as a potential teacher? And then next term the neophyte arrives, – the first of one's own appointments. Here surely is a relationship teeming with responsibility, pregnant with possible success or failure and one is tempted to neglect it. I seem to remember every word (and they were not many) which old Vaughan addressed to me my first term at Rugby. 'Ah-h. How are you getting on?' 'Oh, fairly well, I think, so far'. 'Ah-h, not too well I hope.' A simple but shrewd rejoinder. One young man whom I engaged temporarily when asked by his former Head Master how he had got on with me replied 'he hasn't spoken to me so far'. What a damning verdict and alas quite true.

And then how far do Head Masters go round to hear their colleagues teaching? Inevitably it is a practice rather near to espionage: no doubt the class tends to stiffen into unnatural sobriety. But it is not difficult to distinguish the stiffness that follows attention and the stiffness that follows riot. One famous Head, (I expect many people have heard this) used to feel that to invade a classroom without some excuse was ungentlemanly and he entered the class of a young master asking, after a quick glance round, where Mr Hayman was teaching. Now Hayman had been dead seven years.

At any rate there is much to be said for hearing one's young assistants conduct their lessons: less, no doubt, for hearing the older men. They seem to appreciate it less and whatever one's impressions there is not much action to be taken. An acquaintance of mine was appointed to a school in the north of England where he found an ageing and loyal assistant whose modern language teaching had for years been killing all interest in some two dozen boys annually. With rare tact he suggested to him that he might care to go for a week to the famous school whence he, the Head Master, had recently come and there compare notes and listen to the lessons given by that modern language master. The old man agreed with alacrity: on his return the Head Master asked a little guiltily how he had fared. 'Splendid' was the answer 'Splendid. Nothing to learn though. The fellow has got all my dodges'. No, there is not much to be done after a certain age, but for the young men, should we do more than at present in straight instruction about the art of teaching? We pretend we are prevented by modesty: but may there be some laziness in it too? After all, we are gloriously casual about the previous training of our appointments in the art and science of education; I am not advocating the Diploma of Education for everyone: but one thing I learnt from two years examining for Maurice Jacks at Oxford was this. By far the best candidates in my subject 'Practical Education' were those who took it after a few years experience of schoolmastering and a short course taken in their own time. I suppose we should encourage our young men to go for short courses whether in education or in their special subject. It still goes against the grain for an English schoolmaster to devote any part of his 16 weeks holiday to further study at his life's work. 'I am going off this holidays to cure my faults', said a colleague of a former Head Master of Harrow. 'I am taking my iron clubs only'.

And of course we do not appoint men solely for their ability as teachers. If they are to be permanent colleagues and later housemasters we must get to know them, and that quickly, as human beings. For this purpose there are few better methods than a study of the end of term reports. For that reason alone it is worth the Head Master's while to burn that midnight oil three times a year. However much he may or may not learn about the boys, however valuable or trivial his own comments, he learns a vast amount about his staff. I once saw a set of house reports (and this is the nearest approach I make to a tale out of school) – and I admit they were half term reports, a silly institution – in which the housemaster wrote against 70% of his charges 'a sound boy': the boys at the top he called 'a very sound boy' and the newcomers 'A sound boy I think'. How little this told one of the boys! but it told one quite enough about the master.

It is time that these discursions ended and turned again home. When one is young one is critical of one's colleagues, but as one grows older – some Victorian verses come to my mind, beloved and set to music by our forebears, on the subject of old age. They begin:

> I am growing dimmer in my eyes,
> I am growing fainter in my laugh,
> I am growing deeper in my sighs,
> I am growing fonder of my staff.

So it ought to be and so it is. How much more money the Head gets than the Hands: how much more recognition and how much more variety of life! And, often, how much less he deserves it!

The Art of Teaching

Delivered on the Third Programme of the BBC and reprinted in *The Listener* 10 April 1952.

Books pour from the press on the subject of education, and education is 'in the news': nursery schools, technical schools, modern schools; the Burnham scale, state scholarships, local authority grants. There can be few parents, and certainly no educationists, who have not had to grow familiar with such topics, whether they like it or not. And this is surely a good thing if you believe in education at all. But this is not the whole of education. I belong to a discussion group, meeting three or four times a year, which one would call – to use the jargon – 'representative of educational interests'. We discuss education in the sense that we get eminent speakers to talk to us about 'education and local government', or 'the last ten years in education', or school building programmes: and the discussion rarely proceeds far without getting on to finance. But there is one subject that is not often mentioned – teaching.

Professor Gilbert Highet, once an Oxford don, and now a Professor in America, has written a book called *The Art of Teaching* (Methuen, 12s 6d). The professor is a widely-read man, and significantly he can say that for the last twenty years he has been looking for a book, not on 'the curriculum', not on school organisation, not on the 'psychology of the adolescent' or on any particular subject, but on the art and methods of teaching. He failed to find one, and so he has written this book himself.

It is a very good book and extremely readable: though learned, Professor Highet has the light touch. His illustrations from real life are vivacious and relevant. He says some challenging things: he is never what an old kinsman of mine called 'an intrepid defender of undisputed assertions'. Nearly everyone, I believe, who is at all likely to listen to this talk would enjoy the book. Schoolmasters, like doctors, are a class of beings that we have all had experience of: we may have loved them or hated them: we have had to obey them: to many people there is something attractive, in later life, in seeing them as just one more class of fallible human creatures with their own faults and foibles. If you doubt that, think of the way men enjoy recounting, often one suspects 'with advantages', reminiscences of their own teachers: think of the increasing popularity of plays and films of school life. 'Ah', you may say, 'that is arrested development: the full-grown man, the integrated personality' (a favourite word nowadays, 'integrated') 'has put away childish things. He has done with school for better or for worse and to him the man who remembers his school days, the loyal Old Boy, is essentially a type of "infantile regression"'.

But it is precisely to such critical folk that Professor Highet's book may be recommended. In the first place, he shows them that teaching can be, and should be, an art: not just the drumming of a subject or a technique into an unwilling pupil, but the delicate adjustment of one human being to another, the imparting, not of a subject or a dodge, but the sharing of an enthusiasm, the lighting of a spark, the communication of a whole personality. No doubt that is not their picture of education as they remember it: they may have been badly taught, and bitter memories may have infected their whole view of schooling and education, to the great detriment of their own children. In this book they can see what teaching at its best can be; it will give them a standard by which to judge education, and a hope that the schooling for the young of today and tomorrow may be more fruitful than their own. They will be less likely to give their own children a picture of schooldays as a mixture of boredom, escapades and punishments; and it will make them more ready to regard teachers, not as a race apart plying a necessary but hateful trade, but as members of a great profession – 'the worst paid and the most richly rewarded profession in the world', it has been said.

But there is a second reason why this book should appeal not only to teachers but to the man in the street, whether he thinks himself interested in education or not. The truth is that we are all teachers, willy-nilly. To quote our author:

A great deal of teaching is done outside school. Some things – and some of the most important things – are taught by mothers and fathers to their children. This kind of teaching begins as soon as the baby reaches for a knife and his mother takes it away. No, it begins earlier than that. It really begins when the baby gives his first cry and is first answered. In those days, before he can even hear or see properly, he is finding out something about the world and himself: he is communicating and being answered, he is exerting his will, and being victorious or controlled or frustrated; he is being taught to suffer, to fear, to love, to be happy, or to be violent. His mind is being made. Such teaching goes on at a very obscure level, deep down among the foundations. We have all experienced it, and forgotten it. But it is none the less crucially important because it is buried so deep. You know how easy it is for a baby to slice his hand open with a knife or scald his leg with a kettle. The scar is still there, forty years later. Many of the twisted minds and crippled characters in the world were made by careless parents who kept their children away from knives and fires, but put permanent scars on their souls.

All through school, and for years after school, parents continue to teach their children. They do so whether they want to or not. The father who never says more than 'Hello' to his son, and goes out to the nearest pub every evening, is teaching the boy just as emphatically as though he were standing over him with a strap. It is a very tricky business, teaching. He may not be teaching his son to drink and neglect responsibilities. The boy may turn out to be a thinking ascetic devoted to long plans and hard work, like Shaw and Joyce. But, for good or ill, the father is teaching him *something*. Many fathers either do not know this, or do not care. Yet it is impossible to have children without teaching them. Beat them, coddle them, ignore them, force-feed them, shun them or worry about them, love them or hate them, you are still teaching them something, all the time.

And teaching is not confined to parents and professional teachers. In every business and industry, there are learners and teachers. Wherever there are beginners and experts, old and young, there is some kind of learning going on, and some sort of teaching. We are all pupils and we are all teachers. Think

> of your own life as an individual. Much of it is routine. Some of it is amusement. The rest is made up of learning and of teaching: whether you are a doctor enlarging his knowledge of certain types of illness, or a housewife planning her work more effectively, whether you are a trade-union official learning about economics, or a typist learning about life on a minimum wage, whether you are a young husband cheering up his wife, a political speaker influencing an audience, a bus-driver covering a new route, or an author writing a book, you are learning for yourself and teaching others. Most people do not realise how much even of their private life is taken up with amateurish teaching and haphazard learning; and not many understand that most of us, as public beings, either learn or teach incessantly.

This is surely well said, and today especially it needs saying. All through the ages the home used to be a centre of teaching, often the only centre. The parents were the earliest local education authority, the first L.E.A. It is only within this last century, when education has been better organised and on a far wider scale, until today when it is free and compulsory to the age of fifteen – only within the memory of living men, that the home has so largely dropped its conscious responsibilities as a teacher. Throughout history there was a body of – what can one call it? – proverbial wisdom, household skills, nature-lore, fairy tales, religion – that was handed down traditionally round the hearth. 'We have heard with our ears and our fathers have declared unto us ...'. 'And it shall come to pass that when your children shall say unto you, what mean ye by this thing, we shall say unto them ...'. 'This story shall the good man teach his son ...'.

All that has gone. Much that is good has taken its place, but the loss is real. Nevertheless, the important point is that parents are in fact as much teachers as ever they were: what parents (and brothers and sisters) do and say, still has a deep and incalculable effect on the mind and imagination of a child.

Of course, such teaching is largely unconscious, but the principles remain the same for a parent as for a schoolmaster or a schoolmistress. Be honest, be patient, look at the matter through the child's eyes and never be contemptuous. Being honest may involve the frequent admission 'I don't know'. The Victorian parent, anxious from the highest motives to appear irreproachable, could rarely bring himself to say he did not know. He soon lost his reputation for honesty and did not really gain a reputation for omniscience. A child's idea of what is worth knowing is very different from an adult's. I once rebuked a boy for not knowing who wrote *Paradise Lost*. He hung his head, but told a friend later that *I* did not even know how a carburettor worked, which seemed to him more important and far more interesting. The right answer to a question may of course be 'I have no idea, but let us look it up'. The well-educated man is not the one who knows all the answers, but the one who knows where to find them.

And then patience. A child loves repetition. He will read a favourite book over and over again, in this more sensible than his elders: he is ready to repeat the same question endlessly, though not if it is once faithfully answered. Patience with the insistency of the young, and patience too with their inconsistency. While they are growing up, they are quite rightly experimenting with personalities. After all, we encourage this if it suits us: 'Look as if you are enjoying a party even if you aren't'—that is virtually what we recommend to them by precept and example: 'In Church, look devout whatever you may be feeling'. But the young will experiment on their own: a boy will have a period of going tough, and then return to civilization: a girl of fifteen will try to ape nineteen, and so on. These phases are not obstacles to growing up; they are part of the process, and a wise elder, like a wise teacher, will make use of them. A boy will return to school, resolved 'to work like steam this term'; the resolution may not last long, but a teacher will make the most of it, as he will of the next phase - perhaps a romantic enthusiasm for Keats or Marlowe. At all events he will not treat it with disdain as just one more phase. Contempt is surely always wrong, except for meanness. I have known boys and girls kept back for years from civilized behaviour because their first clumsy attempts at party-manners were laughed at by their elders.

These changes of mood are unpredictable, and they do need patience. It is easier to be patient if one can to some degree come down to the child's level and see things through his eyes. This is not condescension; in fact it is the opposite. Condescending people are conscious all the time of the heights which they have left. The good teacher uses all that is still young in himself, to come alongside his pupil. Teachers who are young themselves usually find this easier. 'The market value of a schoolmaster', it has been cynically remarked, 'decreases from his first year onwards'. But this is not true: wider experience need not destroy the youthful heart. Mr de la Mare has dedicated his anthology to 'the young of all ages'. But for most of us it needs an effort to come to the child's natural level. An eminent Professor of Botany once told me that he had been teaching botany to his granddaughter, aged nine. One had to strip off layer after layer of accumulated knowledge, he said, and look at a tree or a plant with a child's fresh eyes, almost as if the thing had a personality of its own. One had to imagine oneself *as* a tree and think how one would behave in spring or winter. And incidentally, he added, one must not forget that a child's eyes were some twelve inches nearer the ground than one's own. There spoke the good teacher.

Honesty, patience, a child's eye: all these are common ground to the wise elder and the wise teacher. But for the teacher they will be woven into a conscious art. Professor Highet writes in inspiring fashion about the routine work of a teacher, his reactions to the individual and to the group; and much that is interesting about great teachers of the past: Socrates, Jesus of Nazareth, and many well-loved teachers of the last century, not least in America. But even with them, it was as much their unconscious attitude to life and learning (in that order) as conscious perfection of their classes or their lectures. Personally, speaking as one who has taught in school or university for thirty years, I can testify that what pupils appear to remember with gratitude are rarely the results of one's long and conscious efforts, necessary as these were. What they remember, and remind you of years later, are things you have wholly forgotten: remarks thrown off in high spirits or the heat of the moment. The reason for this is clear: the teacher's natural unpremeditated sallies, the reflex actions of his mind, you might almost call them – these are the true index of his personality, and it is these that make the deepest and most lasting impression on another personality.

This is observable particularly in dealing with the very young, whose minds are still unformed, but it is true of education at all stages, up to the young man at college learning from his tutor. Professor Highet has some memorable things to say about this stage. Education then, is more a partnership and less a matter of transmitting and receiving. Certainly there are no hard and fast principles for a successful university teacher. Professor Highet sketches for us the methods of a few individuals. They differed widely: charm or severity, ruthless method or romantic enthusiasm – the good teacher uses the quality that is most characteristic of him. But one feature their methods seem to have in common: increasingly the pupil does more and the teacher less. The teacher seems to withdraw himself, sometimes even to the extent of making the pupil despair. 'It is expedient for you that I go away': these words of the Master must have dismayed the first Disciples, but they are good education as well as good theology. Moreover, what matters is not that the learner should reach the right conclusion by the quickest route, but that he should work the question out for himself to a conclusion that may or may not commend itself to the teacher, but will be the disciple's own. Archbishop William Temple used to tell how as a very young man he read an essay, competent and perhaps dogmatic, to his Balliol tutor. After an hour's discussion, the tutor gave him his own views: 'But that is just what I said in my essay', exclaimed Temple. 'Yes, but then you hadn't the right to say it, and now you have'.

There are no set rules for good teaching: that is what makes it an art and not a science. Every teacher has his own personality and will develop his own style, a style which may be subtly modified in dealing with different pupils. The born teacher wields great power and he is not free from the temptations that beset all power. His is a profession which can win admiration and allegiance more easily and more quickly than almost any other, within his own limited circle. But he must never exploit it; he must always be looking on to the stage at which the disciple will have to do without him, and maybe surpass him. Dean Inge says somewhere that education, like authority, must aim at making itself superfluous. The teacher's ultimate command is not 'look at me', but 'look the way I am looking'. And this means that the teacher's horizon must be far beyond the immediate demands of the next lesson or the particular level at which he teaches his subject. There is no learning, no faculty, no hobby, which is wasted in a teacher: they all help to make up his personality, himself: and it is himself that he imparts, himself that goes on influencing his pupils long after his lessons are forgotten and he is gone. The best teaching has the permanence of the best art. The teacher is in truth an artist, and his materials are the hearts and minds of the young – the young of all ages.

The Ancient University

An address delivered to Section L (Education) on 2 September 1954, during the annual meeting of the British Association at Oxford.

When King George III visited the city of Norwich, he remarked to the mayor: 'An ancient City, Mr. Mayor.' 'Indeed, your Majesty,' was the reply, 'but not so ancient as it was.' Nothing can prevent Oxford University from being ancient, chronologically. It still bears, and will always bear, the marks of all institutions that are both ancient and English: the haphazard nature of its growth, its anomalous and illogical organisation, its distrust of too strong a central authority, and its apparent repudiation of the Planning spirit. What planner, in his senses, would try to organise in a single town twenty-two separate Colleges, not to mention a number of more modern appendages, of different size, of different wealth, different traditions and different social status – and then call it a University? I once tried to explain this to a German friend who had descended on me for the afternoon from Heidelberg; he naturally assumed that to each College was allotted a distinct faculty, that, say, Corpus was full of Classics and Magdalen of Mathematicians. I said that this was not so, that at any one College you could find young men studying any one of a dozen different faculties, and he replied 'Is not this very wasteful?' It is. But the loss in economy and in organised tidiness is more than balanced, I have come to believe, by educational gain.

I have seen many Universities in the last few years, in this country, in America, and in India, where I spent seven months on an Educational Commission. I soon realised that Oxford and Cambridge, which still represent for a fairly dominant minority the picture of a normal University, are, in fact, unique exceptions, though it is interesting to observe that in our own newer Universities, a system of Halls of Residence is becoming increasingly common. By the educational gain of such a College-system, I mean precisely the cross-division of faculties which it facilitates. In the same College, nay, on the same staircase, you may find, perhaps, on the ground floor a Rugger-playing Chemist, aiming at a good Third, and opposite him a Theology student, prone to introspection; just above them a shy conventional boy from an ancient boarding school, doing Classics, and across the landing a bright young man from the industrial north, reading English, but chiefly interested in editing a University magazine; above them all, maybe, the College Chaplain. Inherent in that mixture is education, unconscious education, which is the best kind. This was always so, but nowadays it is more important than ever, because nowadays the threat of a narrow specialisation is stronger than it was, and secondly, because the boy from the poorer home with not enough money for books or amenities, needs just this kind of education, almost more than he needs proficiency in his chosen subject, unless he is an especially brilliant person.

Since my own return to Oxford after some twenty years away, I have been struck by the importance of the small informal meetings of College societies – gatherings of two dozen young men in a room intended for the use of one or two, most of them sitting on the floor for lack of chairs, eating chocolate biscuits and discussing, sooner or later (whatever the title of the paper) such subjects as God, Free-Will and Immortality! This may well happen – it certainly should – at any University, but the tradition flourishes more easily in the small residential unit like an Oxford or Cambridge College. It is a tradition which breeds tolerance, interest in other points of view, and the ability to disagree generously – qualities which are sorely needed in a modern democracy, and the ancient Universities are well qualified to provide them. Moreover, the small cross-section division of a University which we know here as a College can confer a corresponding benefit upon the Senior Common Room – on the teachers as well as the taught. An eminent French economist of my acquaintance, who was critical in some directions of the easy-going Oxford spirit, told me that what the Universities of his country most envied was the daily and nightly commerce of the dons' Common Room. Such commerce is only possible when the unit is small. The College system is a part of ancient Oxford, but it still has its effect on seniors as well as juniors and also on the relations between them.

I am thinking, as you may guess, of the tutorial system. There is, I know, more than one view about this tradition. To some, the contact of pupil with tutor, of immaturity with ripe wisdom in the quiet surroundings of a College room, seems to give all that is best in education. To others (and I have heard the view expressed with fervency in Scotland) the tutorial system means spoon-feeding for the pupil and a waste of valuable time for the tutor: 'The young man is old enough to stand on his own feet.' Nevertheless, it is my impression that lecturers at many modern Universities, particularly in Arts subjects with classes of over one hundred, look with envy on a system which can find room for the private hour, when an undergraduate can put private difficulties and a spark can be kindled in the individual mind. I believe that anyone who had himself been an Arts student at Oxford would include the tutorial system among the traditions which are still of value.

In itself, the College system was an integral part of the history of the University as it developed four or five hundred years ago. Some Colleges began by being no more than Halls of Residence for those who came to attend the University; and some of them had a territorial link, Exeter with the south-west, Jesus with Wales, and so on. Something of the same kind was happening in other European Universities: there was the English College at Rome and at Padua. Why was it that the Colleges here, and here only, achieved a status and a wealth which outshone the University? There are, no doubt, several reasons, but one, surely, is to be traced to the English temperament. The Englishman who became eminent in after-life and felt inclined to acknowledge by benefactions his debt to the University where he had been bred, bestowed his bounty not on the larger, more abstract body, the University, but upon the smaller, more intimate community of the College, where he had made his friends, where he had worshipped in the Chapel and sat at meat in the Hall. It was the common life that held for him the deepest memories, and gaining a degree was solemn admission to a full brotherhood. At any rate, whatever the reason, the Colleges became richer and stronger at the expense of the University, and it may be argued that at the end of the last century, their influence was too strong. It was possible for a young man to have his whole education within the walls of his College and to miss the chance of wider contacts which a University is intended to provide. And this was equally true of the dons. If we go back further to the middle of the last century, they were all clerics and all bachelors, a formidable thought for the pupil, and, might one add, the psychologist! A University of that kind was precisely not qualified to meet the needs of a modern world. Oxford has tried to move with the times, to shed what was narrow and cramping but to keep alive traditions, some of them very ancient, which still have their contribution to make.

And certainly the times have been moving. Oxford has changed; she is, as I said at the outset, less ancient than she was. She has changed, in spite of her traditional background, in more directions than I could hope to discuss in a short time. But I will take two, both of them obvious and unmistakable, one academic and the other social. Academically, there has been in the last forty years a wide and swift expansion of Natural Science. Let those who remember Oxford long ago take a walk round the Parks. Laboratories and Institutes have sprung up on every side, some of them for the study of Sciences whose names were hardly known when I was a boy. It would be absurd to label this great expansion as either good or bad. It was inevitable, and Oxford would not have been true to the cause of learning and the needs of her children if she had not made such provision. But it is worth reflecting for a moment on the attendant changes which have been introduced by this rapid development. One change that might have been expected, a diminishing number of Arts students, has not been conspicuous at Oxford. Although the Science student is needed by industry and by the Government, although he can look forward to a secure post even without a First Class degree, although Science is subsidised by the State – in spite of all this, the students of History, Modern Languages, even of Classics, remain surprisingly steady. This, I imagine, is far less true of the modern Universities, and Oxford on the Arts side is perhaps flourishing at the expense of her younger brothers and sisters. At any rate in Oxford there is still the right mixture of Arts and Sciences to provide a background for that wider informal education, which is conducted by discussion and by living together in a College.

However, it is certainly true that the development of Science has been a centralizing force, a force that pulls against the preponderating influence of the College. The young Scientist no longer works mainly within his College. In the old days, Colleges often had their own laboratories, but clearly they could not meet the new demands of individual Sciences, and now the student spends a great part of his working day in a University laboratory, consorting with fellow students in his own subject. There is little danger now that the College could exert too strong an influence, as it may have done in previous generations. Economically and educationally, the University is coming into its own again, with the rapid development of Science. All the more important, therefore, that the closer and more intimate life of the College should continue to exert its effect on Science student and Arts student alike.

I said just now that the University had come into its own economically as against the Colleges. Oxford, like other Universities, receives large subsidies from public funds. There were at first many voices raised against such an innovation: the independence of Oxford was threatened and 'those who paid the piper would soon be calling the tune'. (And in these days of State control, it is easy to forget just how great was the freedom of University and College from outside control. The Head of one wealthy College entirely refused to admit the members of a nineteenth-century commission within his walls.) *Prima facie*, the receipt of State money has not brought State control, and Oxford is still largely free to spend as it likes, not only its own wealth but the Treasury's subvention. I say *prima facie* because, from a wider aspect, it is possible to see the effect of public demands on University education in ways of which most of us are surprisingly unconscious. We accept these demands as normal and justified, and fail to realise that in fact they are substituting a different educational ideal from that which our fathers and grandfathers took for granted.

This ideal was admittedly limited in its range of application;

for centuries it was an ideal only for the privileged few. But for them it set up a fine and liberal standard. We may call it vaguely the ideal of Christian Humanism: it combined, with varying emphasis at different times, the Christian view of every child as potentially a child of God; the desire for knowledge and beauty for their own sake, a view taken ultimately from Athens and reinterpreted at the Renaissance; and a practical sense of justice and of the art of ruling, which came from ancient Rome. It was an ideal down the centuries which shone and faded and shone again. The point for our consideration here is that it was an ideal dictated by the character of the individual: his calling would be decided by his gifts and his natural endowments, and his schooling must enable him to make the most of them. To this ideal we still pay lip-service, but, under the phrase 'education for the community,' are we in fact admitting tacitly quite a different ideal, viz. that the schools and Universities exist to supply the community with men trained as the community requires and in just the proportions needed from time to time?

Perhaps this *is* what the modern world is bound to demand of its educational system; certainly we educationists acquiesce in such demands. We are told, let us say, 'There is still room for biochemists. You should train more biochemists. Why is not Oxford making its full contribution to bio-chemistry?' The interesting thing is that so many of us humbly accept the criticism and feel that we really must do better in our production of biochemists and induce more students to take it as their main course. There may be nothing wrong in this; but at least we ought to observe that such an assumption is quietly changing the old educational ideal of the man educated to make the most of himself along his own best line. At its worst this 'education for the community' may lead to directed education (as is bound to be the case with soldiers in war-time) where the State dictates the whole syllabus with an eye on its own immediate needs. We are still far from that position in England, but we have diverged sufficiently from the old ideal to make many classic statements of educational aims sound strangely irrelevant to-day.

You would not, incidentally, find the blessed word *Research* mentioned in old-fashioned essays on the functions of a University, and I may interpose a word here on the immense development of Research in all Universities, and especially for the postgraduate student. The number of postgraduate students at every College has, I imagine, increased by five-fold since I was an undergraduate. This development is due of course primarily to the ramification of Science, and industry's increasing demand for it, and in that there is nothing to be deplored. Research is the life-blood of Science: and an ancient University, like any other, must take the demand into account. Research has an immediate effect on the practical uses of Science, though every student of the history of Science knows that many far-reaching discoveries have not been made by men who set out to solve a particular problem or to confer a particular benefit, but by those who pursued their inquiries in a spirit of pure curiosity, true to the principle that a University can never afford to lose sight of 'knowledge for its own sake' as one of its ideals. But the spirit of Research has spread to other subjects, and it is possible to ask whether Oxford has not gone too far in its efforts to keep up with the times in encouraging second-rate Research in Arts subjects. Such Research is not always educative: is it really enlarging the boundaries of knowledge? The researchers claim that you cannot build a house without bricks: I wonder sometimes whether the bricks which they laboriously gather are destined, not for a house, but a brick-heap! There is of course always room for the *first-rate* researcher: but when the average young man comes to me asking for a fourth year at Oxford to research into an author whom he had scarcely heard of till his tutor mentioned his name, I am reminded of the wise-crack: 'to copy from one book is cheating; to copy from two is research'. In this respect, an ancient University ought not to follow the fashion too readily.

Such would be the view of what we may call the University idealists – like Dr Hutchins of Chicago: and their warning is salutary. But in their championship of pure and 'useless' knowledge, they go too far. They would claim, and there are some in this country to follow them, that an ancient University like Oxford has become too technical and too vocational. The two epithets are frequently used together in educational literature as if they were almost interchangeable; of course they are not. Technical education involves the learning of a specific technique or craft, and all scientific education must be technical to a more or less degree. The question is whether the acquisition of a technique is an end in itself or a stage in acquiring new knowledge, to which the technique is only a means. If it is the first, the proper place for it is a Technical Institute. Scientific training for the average student *may* be no more than acquiring a technique. This is a standing danger at a University: and the remedy lies not so much in modifying the training but in ensuring that the teacher himself is not just a technologist, but one who is able to see means and ends in proper proportion and perspective.

The risk that a University should become too technological, with a stultifying effect on the minds of the pupils, is one that applies mainly to the Scientific faculty. When a University is accused of being 'too vocational,' all faculties are involved. There is undoubtedly a danger here of which a University must take note, and one can see what the critics have in their minds. But here too some of them overstate their case. They speak as though only in materialist modern times has a University become vocational. But from the earliest times Oxford prepared young men for the Law, the Church and for Medicine. And still a University is bound to be vocational in this one respect if in no other: it must train some of the students to recruit its own ranks as University teachers. No doubt in the eighteenth and nineteenth centuries when a University was confined to a small privileged class, there was little in the education which could be called vocational, unless it is a vocation to lead a life of leisured culture on an inherited income. Would the idealists like us to return to that standard? No: but nevertheless the standard implied in the abused word 'culture' must not wholly disappear. To the ordinary man, the reader of the cheaper daily newspaper, for example, there is no *danger* in a University becoming vocational: as far as he thinks about a University at all, he regards it as a superior institution for getting better-paid jobs for its members - a kind of superior high school. I once heard a parent speak of a grammar school as a 'place where you get the School Certificate from.' Similarly the University would be 'a place where you get a degree from'. In many Eastern countries it is, alas, regarded in just this light. The result is that everyone wanting a Government job - which means a large percentage of the educated class - presses into a University. The numbers swell and swell: the classes become more and more unmanageable, the education more stereotyped and less satisfying. The product is not an educated man, not even a man able to get a Government job, because, as one may imagine, there are not nearly enough jobs to go round. The more effective part of a student's education is the extra-curricular part, education in student-politics – the tactics of strikes, the best way to challenge authority. (I am thinking of what I saw during seven months in the East.) This sort of education added to a high rate of unemployment is a difficult mixture for any country to digest. And one cause of it is the view of a University as solely vocational. It is by no means confined to Science students: it extends equally, or even more, to the faculties such as Law or Economics. When I returned from India to Oxford, I asked myself why our undergraduates, quite as full of spirit and youthful ideals, were not as preoccupied with politics – University or national. No doubt the English temperament and the absence of grinding poverty are partly responsible. But one reason surely is that education at our Universities is not solely vocational, not just a means to an end, but sufficiently interesting in itself to satisfy the active questing mind of the young, and they have less need to look for excitement in other quarters. The ideal of a strictly 'non-vocational' University cannot to-day by itself be sufficient for Oxford, even as an ideal (and one may doubt if it ever was so), but it must remain one element in the ideal: knowledge for its own sake, culture, education for leisure, and civilised intercourse – these are previous parts of our heritage and perhaps an ancient University has a special responsibility to preserve them.

But it can only do so, if the young people themselves arrive at a University with a background of sufficient general education to understand that knowledge *can* be pursued for its own sake, and is not mere material for examinations. I myself have taught classical students, well-crammed for their scholarships, who seemed to think that if they did not get a First, then Virgil lived in vain. A boy may have advanced far along the road of his own speciality, and yet have little idea of its relation to other branches of knowledge or to civilisation, and have no wish to make the necessary co-ordination in his own mind. At the newest of our Universities, Lord Lindsay, the founder of Keele, was keenly alive to such a danger, and laid great stress on two things: 1. The preliminary year of general education, and 2. The residential quality of the University: for he knew from Oxford how much of education depends not on the lecture room but on the common life. Is there implicit here some measure of criticism of an ancient University? The shared life we have always had: but are we too ready to allow young men of limited background and narrowly specialised education to continue along the same groove, and thus to endanger their best and earliest opportunity to 'see life steadily, and see it whole'?

In the old days at Oxford and Cambridge, though there was much idleness, much aimlessness, and much self-indulgence, the young men who did any work at all, at least approached it with some half-conscious sense of humanistic values and the unity of knowledge: they brought it with them, not usually from their schools, but from their homes, with history all about them, in buildings or pictures, homes with books on the shelves and good talk at the table; homes that observed the seasons in the fields and at the church. I should never be in favour of a return to such days, even if such a return were possible which it is not. The older Universities then produced, like the Public Schools which largely fed them, eminent and able men; but, again like the Public Schools, they took the credit of producing rulers, who would in fact have ruled by virtue of class, apart from their education. There was a host of Victorian writers, artists and reformers who owed nothing whatever to a University and had a more abiding influence than the statesmen. In those days the smaller, less famous Colleges were sometimes half empty: the University was far from working at 100 per cent. efficiency. To-day, the picture has completely changed.

And this brings me to the second great adjustment which an ancient University has had to make – and is making – to keep up with modern conditions. It is primarily a social and economic change, though it has its effects on academic education. Within my own lifetime, the two ancient Universities were regarded as the properly succeeding stage to the Public Schools. Not all Public School boys entered the University, but those that did, set the dominating tone. The fees of Public School and University alike were far beyond the range of any but 2 or 3 per cent. of the population. There were of course brilliant boys who paved a road for themselves with scholarships: they were still the exception. On the whole, it would have been said, the older Universities and the Public Schools drew on the same privileged well-to-do class, and would sink or swim together. That would have been the forecast in, say, 1910. How mistaken it has proved! The Public Schools are still dependent on the private means of parents, now in prosperity and now in depression, with no prospect of state-aid. Educationally, I am convinced, they have made a steady advance: but economically can they hope to continue as they are, when parents are already paying out capital to meet the fees? But Oxford and Cambridge have never in their whole history been as prosperous as they are to-day, if prosperity is measured by the number of applications for entry. At the College I know best over five hundred applications were received in a single year. No doubt some of these applicants asked for admission elsewhere too. But in any one year we could have had a hundred and fifty candidates sitting for admission for some forty-five places as commoners: for the figure I have given excludes scholarship candidates who take a different, more competitive examination. My only object in mentioning these rough figures is to show that all Colleges at the ancient Universities reject annually a number of young men who appear well-qualified for entry, simply because there is no room for them. At each of the five women's Colleges in Oxford three or four hundred girls every year are actually examined at their schools; about a fifth of that number interviewed, and the successful candidates drawn after scrutiny from among those who gain an interview. As is well known, the great majority of these young men and women come up to the University on public money: and no doubt they must live carefully and many work in the vacation. (On that vexed question may I say in parenthesis about vacation work that, in my experience, the best pupils *can* combine vacation work with academic study, though others are ready to give vacation work as an excuse for academic deficiency, provided you do not inquire too closely what they did in their vacation while they were *not* working!) They must as I say live without extravagance, and there are of course temptations to be extravagant: but I recall what an old member of Jesus College said to me who had come up fifty years ago on an exiguous emolument: 'These lads do not know what it means to be really poor.' If that is true, all the better: there is a poverty which stimulates, but there is also a poverty which can isolate. At any rate here the undergraduates are (State Scholars or locally assisted, most of them), in far greater numbers than ever before in Oxford. Their presence represents the greatest adjustment to modern conditions which an ancient University has had to make. Compared to the Oxford of forty years ago, there is some loss: but there is far more gain. I have known Oxford intimately at three different periods: as an undergraduate in the early 1920s, as a young don in the early 30s, and as the head of a College in the 50s. Of the three, the Oxford of the 1950s seems to me the healthiest and the best accommodated to the needs of the time.

The development of this social adjustment has been, like so many processes at Oxford, largely unconscious. At no one stage did the University say 'let us now be more democratic.' But the change would never have come about if the voice of the traditional ruling class had been the true voice of the University. If heads of Colleges before the first war had carefully discriminated man from man, according to accent and manner and social agility, then Oxford might well have been left high and dry, with what is vulgarly termed 'snob-value,' but without the true educational value that has impressed itself even on the Treasury and the Ministry of Education. As it is, she is assisted up to the hilt by the State, to keep her registers full and her laboratories up to date. We owe a debt that may easily be forgotten to those far-seeing men at the beginning of this century who determined to throw the gates of Oxford wider and wider open to all who could profit by an Oxford education. As a consequence, the Oxford of to-day is more representative of the whole community and more homogeneous in itself. The clear-cut social distinctions between Colleges, so common once and so apt to breed unconscious arrogance and hidden resentment, are breaking down: on the exclusively social level of the dance and the dining club they still exist. But these are in fact less important than the College discussion group, the Oxford Union, the river and the playing-fields: here the social levels and the different 'income-groups' mix freely, with the great benefit on both sides of the dividing line. Perhaps Oxford has no right to take the credit for this trend: she is only reflecting a tendency seen throughout the country: perhaps, ultimately, any University reflects the social ideals of its age. But at least she is not hanging back: she is not championing the lost cause of the inherited income and the life of ease. Naturally the preponderance of the State Schools (in the widest sense) presents the University with a new problem.

For most of these young people, Oxford is not the top-dressing – the very pleasant top-dressing – on a plant nurtured in a leisured home, an expensive preparatory school and an ancient, beautiful and rather Spartan Public School. They must acquire in their own way, from three years at Oxford, what earlier generations had absorbed in twenty. And very well most of them set about it. Some of them work too hard, or at least take their work and their examinations in too grave a spirit. I can fully understand the reason for that, and I appreciate their conscientious ambitions. But they are not getting the most from their University. Last year for the first time, in addressing Freshmen, I warned them (with, I hope, suitable qualifications) not to work too hard. When I thought of the extreme improbability of my old President at Trinity addressing such a warning to me in 1919, I felt that Oxford was indeed adjusting itself to new conditions! Most of these young men, I hope, are learning, and will learn, to combine, during their three or four years, the foreground with the background of their Oxford life: their immediate task with the age-old traditions of an ancient seat of youth and of learning. Oxford herself, in adapting her ways to new demands, has in many cases broken new ground: in coping with the spread of Science, with an increasingly complex organisation, with the requirements of a University Grants Committee. But in providing a suitable education for what was called long ago 'the poor scholar', she is only going back to the ideals professed by many of those who founded her Colleges. By ceasing to be class-conscious and exclusive, she has been true to her tradition.

What my audience was expecting from this paper I cannot tell: I trust they did not pitch their hopes high. I am well aware that much has been omitted, that no very startling conclusions have been reached, and no bold prophecies thrown out. The disjointed observations I have made are at least based on personal experience, and are, I expect, open to question. But it has ever been the Oxford system not to look for truth in the pupil's essay, but in the discussion which follows it. Oxford 'is not so ancient as she was,' but she is Oxford still, and I am proud to speak as her representative.

SELECTED WRITINGS

Part II · On the Classics

INCLUDING A SELECTION OF LATIN AND GREEK COMPOSITIONS

Prologus

JTC wrote both the Prologue and the translation when their Majesties, King George VI and Queen Elizabeth, attended the second performance of the Westminster School Latin play, Terence's *Adelphi*, on 20 December 1937.

Ipsum quid ante Regem alumni regii
decentve agentve? sic tuum, illustrissime,
excepit olim illustrem proavum prologus:
ex quo die unum saeculum abiit amplius.
prisci theatri rudia ad haec subsellia
venere clari militia, clari toga;
venere et aliqui regio orti sanguine.
ad non adhuc Rex ipse, veteris fabulae
spectator, huc descendit in nostros Lares.
salvete vos qui adestis optatissimi;
vos omnis hic consessus fausto cum omine
salvere ter quaterque primum hodie iubet:
iterum scholares, more queis patrio datur
regem ut salutent omnium primi suum
diadema avitum in Aede sumpturum Petri
quanta recenter vobis adclamavimus
pietate, tanta nunc quoque 'Vivat Rex' precor
'Vivat Regina Elissa', quos servet Deus.

Rex optime et tu, Domina clementissima,
propitii, quaeso, aspicite nostra haec ludicra.
ridere, si quid ridiculum, dignemini;
si claudicat quid, detis indulgentiam.
hoc certum habeatis, hunc scholaribus diem
fore praeter omnes lapide dignum candido,
quod qui repetimus gloriosam originem
a prisca Elissa, nobis hodie denuo
Elissa praesens annuit ludentibus.

Prologue

'What deeds, what words shall fitly be addressed
By royal Scholars to the Royal Guest?'
Thus, standing here, the Prologue spake long since
To your great ancestor, illustrious Prince.
A hundred years ago he spake, and more;
And hither lights of learning, chiefs of war,
Hither e'en princes of the blood have come
To our rude theatre in its ancient home.
But ne'er since then have England's King and Queen
Honoured our hearth and shone upon our scene.
Hail then, all-hail, long-looked-for Royal Pair,
Warm be your welcome and the omens fair:
So cries this whole assembly at the Play
And offers you their first 'all-hail' today;
For them the first: for us the second, Sire,
Us scholars who by right in duteous choir
With earliest homage made the Abbey ring
With Vivat! Vivat! to our Sovereign King.
Now with like duty and as dear delight
'God save the King and Queen' we pray tonight.

Sire, and most gentle Lady, this our play
We beg you with indulgent eye survey.
A smile, we ask, if aught for smiles be here,
Or if we falter, frowns not too severe.
In our own memories, so much is sure,
This day beyond all others shall endure.
Children of good Queen Bess, we set the scene
Once more to greet Elizabeth, our Queen.

The Study of Classical Civilization without Classical Languages?

The substance of an address given at Cambridge to a Conference for teachers of the Classics and published in *Greece and Rome*, Second Series, Vol. XIII, Number 2, in October 1966. There were many colleagues, and indeed publishers, who pleaded with JTC to write a study of the Classics as part of modern education. He completed various synopses of putative books on the theme, but this is the only full paper on the subject that remains extant.

I know that it is a commonplace to begin with apologies, but the Head Master of Eton did so earlier, and hence let me say that you are doomed to disappointment if, at the end of your splendid and varied programme, you are expecting a sonorous peroration on 'The Spirit of Antiquity' or 'The Greeks and what they mean to us'. You know the kind of thing I mean: 'Greek simplicity recalls to us the central interests of the human heart. Greek truthfulness is a challenge to see the world as it is and to shun the falsities of rhetoric or sentiment. Greek beauty is a memorial of an aspect of the Universe to which ages of thought are often blind.' Noble words, and as you hear them, some of you are no doubt murmuring 'Dr Livingstone, I presume', and like Stanley you would be right. Originally I was billed to talk about Verse Composition but this was changed to something about the Greek Anthology, and finally I find myself responsible for the conclud-ing lecture. I fear it will be for me not to heighten the tone but to lower it. I have myself attended conferences of this kind and drawn much profit from them. You have listened to masters of their craft, speaking on subjects which they know, some of them, more about than anyone in England. They have inspired you to lift up your eyes and look, to gain a glimpse of the heights, and a picture of some of the highways and byways; but I am still at heart a schoolmaster, a teacher, and I cannot forget that you too are teachers, and will, after a well-earned holiday, return to your desks, much enriched by the Cambridge conference. But you will not always find that the pearls which have been displayed before you here can be exhibited again just as they are, with the same dazzling effect upon your classes at the beginning of a Christmas term.

I have much in mind of course the Sixth Form teacher. I spent the happiest and, I think, the best years of my life teaching a good Sixth Form, and there is no calling more delightful or more richly rewarded. But I remember Cyril Alington's pregnant paradox: 'Any fool can teach a Sixth Form'. (He is said to have added 'and some do'.) At any rate most of the boys there want to learn and most of them *can* appreciate something of the values of Classical Antiquity – the relevance of Roman History, the romance of Greek Archaeology, and this indeed without knowing Latin or Greek. And they can appreciate, would you say, the realism of Thucydides and the nobility of the *Aeneid*, even perhaps in translation? Even in translation: that is one of the questions I want to raise. Is there some value, some element in Classical Antiquity, which comes solely and indispensably from the languages themselves? That is a question not only for Sixth Form masters, but for teachers at all stages of Latin and Greek. While those two languages enjoyed the enormous and, I fear, exaggerated prestige which they had for centuries, right on to my own days at school fifty years ago, one could treat the early stages as mere preparation, as dull and as dry as you like, for that fuller knowledge which could unlock the gate to Virgil and Sophocles, and (more important for some dominies of the older generation), open the way to Greek and Latin Composition. Incidentally, what tremendous claims were made for that typically English exercise; delightful and profitable if you happen to have a turn for it, but not, I am sure, 'generally necessary to salvation'. In this very town of Cambridge many years ago there was a Preparatory Schools Conference and one headmaster was reported as saying, 'the education that we Preparatory Schools aim at providing is nothing less than an all-round preparation for life on which a boy can build and specialize as he likes afterwards'. A blameless ideal surely, but mark the next sentence: 'for this all-round education there is no subject in the world so well suited as Greek Composition'! There were many highly intelligent boys who were simply not suited to such training. When William Bateson left Rugby in 1879, destined to First Classes in Science at Cambridge and subsequent fame as a geneticist, the

Headmaster wrote on his last school-report that he could not imagine that anything was to be gained by sending so aimless a boy to the University. Composition no longer holds its old commanding place, and even Virgil and Sophocles, though I was put into them at the age of ten, far too young, are nowadays the perquisites of Sixth Forms; even there, are there not some boys and girls incapable of understanding these writers as a whole with sympathy and imagination, though no doubt in the General Paper they may reproduce the enthusiasm of Livingstone or Mackail?

In that connexion, I well remember marking Classical scripts at a celebrated Public School when the boys were asked to write a few lines 'on any three of the following'. One was Sappho. The first paper I looked at gave some facts and added, 'she has a bird-throated clarity'. This struck me as rather charming and I marked it accordingly. The second boy was something of a scholar and quoted one or two lines in Greek, adding that she was the most famous of all women poets and had a bird-throated clarity. The third merely said that Sappho wrote Sapphics: 'she is famous because she liked women more than men, and also for her bird-throated clarity'. We were warned last night of the damage of cramming second-hand views, and I warmly agree.

I would ask you now by an effort of imagination to divest yourselves of your own long familiarity with the great Classical writers, to go back to your own Sixth Form days and even beyond that to O-level as it would now be called, long before you could read and appreciate classical literature as such. That is the time when a lasting antipathy to Latin can so easily begin. That is the stage at which pupils may decide that whatever else they may choose for further study, it will not be Classics.

When I went to Repton more than thirty years ago, I found an Upper Sixth Form of four boys; the stream that might have fed the Classics had dried up and the waters, diverted after School Certificate, flowed 'brimming and bright and large' into History and Modern Languages. For two years I taught, just at that point, the slowest stream, together with a Greek set of beginners. A few hours with the Latinists showed me that the shutter had come down long ago, at the very mention of the word Latin. In that respect, as Sophocles himself says, 'God had taken away even the wits that nature had endowed them with'. Wandering in the jungle of moods and tenses, of conditional sentences and oratio obliqua, they had lost heart. These dry matters of course had ultimately to be understood and learnt, but first that shutter must be rolled up. They must see some relevance in Latin to their own thoughts and their own surroundings and, if possible, even at that early stage, the peculiar strength and virtue in the language itself. I sometimes gave them by way of preparation half an hour to study some chosen Latin epitaphs in the school chapel and the village church, both near at hand. In epitaphs there is no oratio obliqua, and in epitaphs conditional clauses are mostly out of place. A massive principal verb, several adjectives in the genitive, perhaps an ablative of quality, and a couple of relative clauses are all you need. Then together, or in small groups, we would compose a Latin epitaph for ourselves – on George V say, or Rudyard Kipling, both topical just then, or Florence Nightingale, or as I recall (in anticipation of favours to come, in 1935), on Mussolini.

This sort of thing was only a sweetener, a tin-opener as one might call it, and in itself of little use for the School Certificate, but at least it was nearer to the boys' contemporary world than 'The General who persuaded the legions not to return into winter quarters: it would, he said, be all over with the army'. But, further, I verily believe that the boys thus acquired half-consciously a glimpse of the strength and economy of the Latin tongue, the quality which a French critic calls 'l'art romain de frapper une pensée en medaille'. The best I know in this kind has often been quoted: the words appended to the long Roll of Honour after the First War on the walls of Berlin University: the memorial to all those young men who had died before the defeat of their country, which was erected by those who had known defeat but were resolved to live on and to conquer. INVICTIS VICTI VICTURI: just those three words, and one remembers that *victuri* can come from *vivo* as well as *vinco*.

If any boy, before he abandoned Latin for good, could appreciate that, he would retain something worth remembering; and if he did continue his Classics, he would meet with this peculiar virtue of the Roman tongue on every page of his authors; but he must read them in Latin. This force of plainness and simplicity is not, of course, peculiar to Latin, though a Classic, I should hope, will be quicker to detect it in any language. If he learns to do this in youth even in English, he will have achieved much more than an appreciation of certain strong bare lines. The average English boy – and even more perhaps the girl – is a natural romantic, and very right too. Marlowe and Keats and Tennyson are the food for his burgeoning imagination. But if he can further make for himself the discovery that his heart can equally be pierced by lines that have no mighty words and no startling colour but are the right words in the right place in the right context, he has opened the way to a whole new range of effects which will chasten and delight him for the rest of his days. I have seen it happen. No doubt, all literatures can attain this effect but especially the Classics. Virgil's greatest effects are his simplest. Moreover, the Classical tongues can draw upon another power which Modern Languages cannot match – their inflexions. With inflexions the whole immense range and delicate power of word-order rises into view. I hardly dare give you examples of something so obvious. Who am I to have the presumption to instruct you in this strain when you know it only too well already, I a retired schoolmaster and you, young, keen, and efficient? Consider that very sentence! Latin can take these 31 words, cut them to 13 and thrust them together in such a way that we can feel the force of contrast. 'Egone vos, haec nimis bene nota, magister emeritus, iuvenes acres diligentes, adrogans edocebo? Who am I, to you, this familiar stuff, retired schoolmaster, keen efficient young men, have the cheek to instruct?' One cannot do it in English, you see; the nearest thing is the style of Mr Alfred Jingle; he, as we know, though not a Classical scholar, was a forceful speaker.

Obvious enough you say; nevertheless, I remember doing the *Odes* of Horace at school pretty thoroughly, and not once was our attention drawn to this quality of the Latin tongue which Horace illustrates better than any other author; and one need not be a gifted scholar to appreciate it. My own father spent five years at Winchester without reaching the Sixth Form, and read History at Oxford. He would have mocked at the very idea of his being a scholar but he had been made to learn his Horace and would in the old Erasmian pronunciation quote

dis te minorem quod geris imperas.

I should never have dared to lecture him on the nicety of word-order; but is it not that which makes the line so specially memorable? There are six ways of arranging the three short words, and Horace, by thrusting to the front the word *dis* followed by *te* gives the final emphasis. Only Latin can do that. Translators can try as hard as they like but they are prevented by the very structure of our language from producing any equivalent of Horace. (Here are some standard translations of the line: *Lytton* – Thou ruls't by being to the gods subjected. *Conington* – Revering Heaven, you rule below. *Marsh* – Ruler of man, but minister of heaven.)

I would say to Latin teachers, never forget at any stage, from lowest to highest, the virtue of the Latin tongue; so often seen at its best and strongest not in its elaborate rhetoric but in the simpler authors, traditionally supposed, God save the mark!, too elementary for Sixth Forms. Never forget its special powers through the ordering of words; and of course, its sound. Every sentence translated in class ought to be sounded aloud at least twice, once by the pupil and then by the teacher (and here I would add through learning by heart, but I am afraid that nowadays this is crying for the moon). Reading by the eye is a comparatively modern faculty; for classical students it is a danger to their comprehension of the text and an insult to the authors themselves.

The Greeks even more than the Romans were supremely alive to the sound and character of words. Words were winged creatures bursting through the cage of the teeth, flying from one speaker to another, speeded by joy, burdened with omen, to be repulsed, or captured and appropriated, the moment they left the other speaker's lips. I seem to have made my transition to Greek and if any of you take classes in elementary Greek, you may be thinking '"winged words" indeed, "exquisite delicacy of language"! What poles asunder from what we have to teach – the use of the optative and the verbs in -μι.' Indeed elementary tuition in Greek is for the teacher a difficult matter compared to Latin. At least, so it seemed to me with my Greek Set of 14-year olds. What barren acres of grammar, both accidence and syntax! Those early stages are bound to be largely preparation for the shape of things to come. I do not doubt that without a knowledge of the language one can gain from the *Realien* – buildings, sculpture, pottery, and above all, visits to the country – something truly valuable and genuinely Greek. What room then does that leave for the laborious learning of this lovely language? Will no translation do as well? It is certainly better than nothing. The vitality, the quick wit, and the directness of the Greek spirit declare themselves in any product of the Greek genius, and will survive many approximations and transmogrifications. I remember old Professor Myres describing in a lecture at Oxford, how an archaeologist would dig through layer after layer of relics from various civilizations and then suddenly one would encounter with instant recognition an unmistakable trace of 'that human champagne, the Hellene'. Well, that human champagne can stand a deal of decanting and rebottling and knocking about, but in literature, a translation is no substitute for the real thing.

It is my cue to speak this morning, not about the heights of scholarship or the mature appreciation of the Classics, but more about what we can give as classical teachers to our still struggling pupils that may stir their imagination by simple effects that are within their grasp. The Greek language is infinitely richer and more flexible than Latin. L. and S. Greek contains about ten times as many words as L. and S. Latin.[1] That richness one can explore later, but Greek has its own matchless simplicity, quieter and less rhetorical than Latin, and not hard to understand by those who are beginning a second or third year of Greek. Sooner or later, of course, comes Homer. A man who has not read Homer, said Walter Bagehot, is like one who has not seen the sea. Only it is fair to remind oneself how formidable the language is to a schoolboy, whose vocabulary is based on Xenophon and whose grammar (what he has of it) is Attic; but Homer eventually, for fairly fast and extensive, not intensive, reading. (I was positively put off my first taste of Homer by spending a fortnight on the first ten lines of Iliad XV, with long discourses on Dialects, the Digamma, and the Thematic Aorist.) For intensive reading, there is much to be said for the Greek Anthology which I mention because it is not used enough. It is unique in its length of span, 650 B.C. to 700 A.D. at least; and in its variety, ranging from solemn public epitaphs to a world of playful fancy and casual daily life – the sort of thing represented to us visually by Tanagra statuettes. In it one can find so many of the true notes of the Greek genius in a small compass, and the shapeliness of a single whole. The couplets are simple, sometimes to the point of non-

[1] Liddell and Scott's Greek Lexicon; Lewis and Short's Latin Dictionary.

chalance, so unlike the continual snap and sparkle of Latin epigrams. The Greek too can be witty, but in a kindlier way, and always there is the heart-rending bareness of the epitaphs. I have only time for a few examples, but I hope you will agree that though their full implications go deep, their language is easy to understand, and that they cannot yield their secret except in the original tongue.

One could illustrate from the Greek Anthology many aspects of the Greek language in a little space: its richness, its flexibility, its humour. Take, for example, vi. 10 in Mackail's *Selection*, with those rare, graceful, compound-epithets in the first couplet, *ὑψαύχην* suggesting not only the shape but the stiff-necked solemn character of the disappointingly empty wine-jar (cf. the last line). And a boy would be quick to seize the point of i. 44 if after construing it he were given the happy rendering:

> I send you some eau de Cologne, dear;
> 'Tis to it that the favour is shown,
> For the odour you have of your own, dear,
> Can add odour to eau de Cologne.

But even more does the Anthology exemplify the bare simplicity of Greek, the refusal to embroider, the power to state the plain fact without being commonplace, e.g. vii. 20. Even Mackail's translation is far behind the Greek:

> Gazing upon my husband as my last thread was spun, I praised the gods of death, and I praised the gods of marriage, those that I left my husband alive, and these that he was even such an one; may he remain, a father for the children who are his and mine.

Line 3 is obviously moving in its strong brevity: *τοὺς δ' ὅτι τοῖον*, but one might well miss the implications of that simple word *ημετέροις* - children that are mine as well as his. The author lived at the end of the sixth century A.D. but he still knew the secret. Or again vii. 17 by a writer as completely unknown as many of the artists who carved the gravestones now in the museum at Athens. The tomb speaks: I am as yet the tomb of no one and so may I remain for a long time

> *εἰ δ' ἄρα καὶ δεῖ,*
> *δεξαίμην ἐν ἐμοὶ τοὺς προτέρους προτέρους*

If death does come, as it must, then all I ask is to receive the eldest first. Could anything be more starkly simple or more serenely appropriate?

And finally, the celebrated lines of Simonides on the dead at Thermopylae (iii.4). When I read this first in class as a schoolboy, I remember feeling and, I think, saying that I did not see 'anything very marvellous' about it, in spite of the master's reverent enthusiasm. Perhaps he might have drawn our attention to the mere sound of the words – the long wailing diphthongs – and still more to the implications of ξεῖνε; the passing stranger must carry the message home. No Spartan was left to do that; they were all dead. He might have stressed the strict translation of πειθόμενοι, not just 'obedient' as it is often rendered, but the present participle 'still obeying'. They were ordered to stay, and staying they still were, in death as in life.

I must make an end of these rambling and too personal reflections. The thought that I would leave with you is this. As Classical teachers we believe profoundly in the study of classical antiquity for reasons which are no less true because they have been stated so often. Greece and Rome between them, and in varying proportions, nourish the roots of our rich western way of life – in Philosophy, in Religion, in Literature. The visible marks of their civilization – the Arts of Greece, the Roads of Rome, the Architecture of both alike – still furnish us with standards unmatched through the centuries. All that is part of our heritage and it behoves the teacher to hand it on with all the knowledge he can command. It needs training in the pupil to appreciate it, but there they still stand, the things themselves, – statues, vases, aqueducts, temples – eloquent of the genius which produced them. A cast, a picture, a reproduction is *not* the same. But the greatest of these legacies, the most ample, the most accessible, and the least defaced, is their literature. Translations can serve as commentaries and sometimes as things of beauty in their own right, though of a highly subjective kind (think of Murray's Euripides). But ultimately, all translations are substitutes. The actual languages of antiquity give a more faithful and more detailed map of the classical world, for most of us, than its concrete relics; and some knowledge of those tongues under the right teacher brings its own rich and lasting reward, not only to the promising scholar who may himself become a schoolmaster or a don, but also, in its measure (and this was the faith of our forebears) to the men who passed from a classical education into the wider world. Under the right teacher, I said; in the old days our profession has sinned in this respect. Only last week I was reading in the new Life of Lord Halifax, a naturally civilized soul if ever there was, how glad he would have been if he had been allowed at his preparatory school and at Eton to enjoy the Classics. As it was, he found the teaching so dry and dusty, that the whole literature of antiquity was a sealed book to him. All depends on the teacher. Deep down, 'felt in the blood and felt along the heart', as Wordsworth says, he must have this loving interest in the language, to the height of his capacity. He must not show off, however much it may win the temporary admiration of his young hearers who will be tempted to reverence him and not his subject; they will not see the stars for the fireworks. Yet he must keep his lesson bright and variable, not at the expense of drudgery but with a break here and there to sweeten it.

For all this one does not need profound learning. Of course, let every teacher be as learned as he can; even more important, let him be learning. With beginners, let him vary his approach. With a Sixth Form, let him embark on new texts, if only for an hour a week, not clinging to the old safe round. (At Winchester I remember a friend of mine gained an unexpected remove from the lower division of the Sixth Form to the higher because, so we understood, he had been four terms in the lower, and if he remained, the master would be inhibited from taking the *Antigone* again, with which our young friend was already familiar, though not nearly so familiar as the teacher.)

Is the idea of a classical education for general culture rather at a discount today? In the Universities classical study becomes every year more professional, more specialized, and more fragmented. Such professionals are our standard-bearers and pioneers, and if they combine their deep learning (like a Page or a Lloyd-Jones) with a sympathy and an imagination that can appeal to the plainer man, then they are best of all. But, as I said, I am a schoolmaster at heart and I am sometimes alarmed by the narrow vehemence of some young don pouring his whole soul into a new solution of an obscure problem in a fragmentary work by a forgotten author.

I venerate all true learning, especially in my own subject, and far better to be dry and learned than dry and unlearned, like some old schoolmasters of the past. But there is a species of truly learned men whose gifts do not primarily fit them to hand on the torch of the Humanities to a struggling and doubtful younger generation who nowadays need some coaxing. If such a one had ever come to me as a headmaster (which is highly unlikely) applying to teach a Sixth Form, I think I should have remembered the Platonic treatment of the poets in the *Republic*; with great respect I should crown him with white wool and send him to another city. Compared to these learned professional scholars, whether of the dry sort or of the life-giving variety, we schoolmasters are admittedly amateurs, even dilettantes if you like; no need to be ashamed of that if we press the meaning of those words – those who love what they do, those who delight in their calling. Best of all, be lively and right, but better be lively and at moments wrong, than be for hours right and boring.

Finally, we classical teachers have mostly come up the hard way; it has taken us much toil to acquire our due share of classical languages. Let us not regard this precious personal heritage as simply the basis of our teaching which may, through no fault of ours, be limited to classes small in number and mediocre in quality. Let us use it for our own delight. Let us dedicate *some* portion of our weeks of vacation to exploring for ourselves the boundless garden of the Muses into which we have earned the right of entry. Forget your form and your syllabus now and then. Read where your fancy takes you: the *Metamorphoses* of Ovid, the best book of stories in the world; the letters of Erasmus; the dialogues of Lucian; Homer, and again Homer. Thus will your teaching all unconsciously grow better and more inspiring, because you who teach will be fuller men, speaking out of abundance. Your class will cease to look at you and will look the way you are looking, and they may, the best of them, carry away something that will last a lifetime and colour all their thought. Think first of the Humanities and then of yourselves as interpreters. That is the right order of precedence. Horace's famous line is still in my head and I would say to you, and indeed to myself – how can I put it? –

Musa minorem te gere; carior
sic Musa fiet tuque gregi tuo.

Put first the Muse and then yourself; e'en so
To your young flock shall both the dearer grow.

But there; even Latin which is bad sounds worse in translation; *a fortiori*, Latin that is good. That is just my point.

On Translating Homer

From the Times Literary Supplement, 14 March 1968, reviewing Richmond Lattimore's *The Odyssey of Homer*

If every age has its own concept of Odysseus - not for nothing was that Protean wanderer called *πολύτροπος*, a 'man of many turns' - it also tends to create its own *Odyssey*. Allegorized by Chapman, formalized by Pope, redone as a pre-Raphaelite dream by Butcher and Lang and a medieval Kelmscott confection by William Morris, brought down to earth by Samuel Butler, stuffed with technicalities and tight-lipped understatements by T.E. Lawrence, turned into Omar Khayyám quatrains by J.W. Mackail and a flat if jolly novel by Dr E.V. Rieu, successively augmented with Augustan conceits, purged of its oral formulas, shackled in rhyme, and fragmented into *vers libre*, the *Odyssey* nevertheless survives, archetypal and indomitable, weathering each fresh generation of experimentalists with granite aplomb, a never-failing source of inspiration and delight to scholar, sailor, mystic, feminist, and ordinary readers from every level and walk of life. The first English paperback translation, that by Dr Rieu, sold well over a million copies, and the demand shows no signs of slackening.

Whether poets or scholars have made a more successful job of the *Odyssey* is still a fairly moot point. Cowper's version is hardly calculated to set the Aegean on fire; but then many of what Cicero called the *grammatici interpretes poetarum* have hardly done better. Perhaps the man who most felicitously combines both roles today is Richmond Lattimore, Paul Shorey Professor of Greek at Bryn Mawr, a fine poet in his own right, and, by general consent, the most distinguished living verse-translator of the classics into English. Professor Lattimore is a founder-member of that dynamic modernizing movement which numbers among its practitioners such names as David Grene, William Arrowsmith, Robert Fitzgerald, and, in England, the present Poet Laureate.[1] He has produced immensely influential versions of Hesiod, the *Iliad*, the *Oresteia*, Pindar, and the Greek lyric poets. The appearance of Professor Lattimore's *Odyssey* is, therefore, something of an occasion.

How near does this new version get to Homer's original Greek, in style, verbal usage, rhythm, and formal design? And what (scarcely less interesting) does it tell us about current fashions or tastes in literary appreciation? What sort of world does this new *Odyssey* reflect, what readers does it presuppose? Let us take an example at random, and through it trace some of the poem's vicissitudes in translation down the ages: the passage from Book V describing Hermes's flight to the island of Calypso. First, the version by George Chapman:

> He stoopt *Piéria*, and thence
> Glid through the aire; and *Neptune's* Confluence
> Kist as he flew, and checkt the waves as light
> As any Sea-mew, in her fishing flight,
> Her thicke wings soucing in the savorie seas.
> Like her, he pass'd a world of wildernesse;
> But when the far-off Ile he toucht, he went
> Up from the blue sea, to the Continent,
> And reacht the ample Caverne of the Queene:
> Whom he within found, without, seldome seene.

This, for Chapman, is pretty compact (despite the awkwardness of the last line) and not excessively embroidered. He only runs half a line longer than his original; and though 'kist *Neptune's* Confluence' may be thought a flowery and gratuitously Latinate rendering of 'reached sea-level', and 'a world of wildernesse' certainly adds romantic overtones to 'the multitudinous waves', in general he sticks closely enough to his brief. One line at least, 'her thicke wings soucing in the savorie seas', is both literal and striking in its own right. Indeed, Chapman's main sins are those of omission. Where in this version is Homer's 'unhar-

[1] C. Day Lewis; John Masefield had died in 1967.

vested sea'? Why tacitly ignore Calypso's beautiful tresses, however formulaic they may be? And what (most important of all) has become of the Homeric hexameter?

The truth is, of course, that Chapman, like nearly all translators, was inescapably a child of his age, and his age is not ours. It did not occur to him for one moment that Homer's metre is an intrinsic element in Homeric poetry, and should not on any account be jettisoned; his business, as he saw it, was to dress this rude Greek in decent English broadcloth. Besides, there was the horrid, and all too recent, example of Gabriel Harvey and Richard Stanyhurst to show what perils might befall the translator who dabbled in outlandish foreign prosody; and no Elizabethan Milman Parry had arisen to point out that Homeric epithets, though alien to English usage, were integral to what was, after all, essentially oral poetry - or that English rhymes utterly destroyed the natural over-running flow of Homer's dactylic lines. In any case, the gentlemen and scholars for whom this version was designed knew the original as a matter of course, after long drudging years in the schoolroom, with liberal visitations of birch or tawse to reinforce the lesson.

Here, in embryo, we can see all the main assumptions which were held by English classical translators until a very short time ago. Their central and unquestioned tenet was that the convenience of their audience came first, and honest adherence to the original, in the widest sense, a very poor second. It could, indeed, be argued that this consideration still applies up to a point today. The changes that have taken place, between Chapman's time and our own, in the methodology of classical translation have been produced by the demands of a new reading public rather than by any radical reappraisal of working axioms. Pope's Homer was produced for educated *cognoscenti*, and merely reflected the poetic fashions of the day: it is not till near the end of the nineteenth century that any significant progress becomes apparent, and then the motives for it are, beyond doubt, social rather than literary.

Compulsory universal education and adult evening classes, together with the establishment of public libraries, produced a wholly new class of reader - eager to explore their classical heritage, but unprovided with any formal grounding in Greek or Latin. When Dr Johnson asked the boy who rowed him what he would give to learn about the Argonauts, the boy replied: 'Sir, I would give what I have'. It is a moving aspiration; but not for well over 100 years was it destined to be fulfilled, and then in a singularly unsatisfactory way. Yet whatever we may think of the pedestrian and 'literal' prose in which Bohn's Classical Translations were written, for that boy's humble descendants they represented manna from heaven indeed.

Anyone leafing through them, and other similar late-Victorian translations, will at once be struck by several considerations. In the first place, poetry, as such, has gone by the board: the denotational meaning, the sense, the message, is all. 'Tell us what they said', cried Carlyle; 'none of your silly poetry.' In the second, there is a conscious, albeit clumsy, movement towards archaizing, which expressed itself in a (to us) abominable convention described by R.L. Stevenson as 'tushery', and known more generally as 'Wardour Street English'. This phenomenon has never had quite the attention it deserves. It was, indeed, as fake as that 1930s architecture which Mr Osbert Lancaster so memorably labelled Stockbrokers' Tudor; but it did reflect one immensely important shift forward in the public attitude to *temps perdu*. People now began, however haltingly, to develop a sense of period, of context and perspective. The past, they saw, was different.

This discovery had immediate repercussion. When the Pre-Raphaelites painted a medieval scene they made an honest attempt to reproduce it in medieval terms; the result may not have been wholly successful, but the intention was there. Similar considerations apply to that newly popular phenomenon, the historical novel. The artists of the Quattrocento, who blithely put Jewish zealots and Roman centurions into their own contemporary fashions (or, indeed, the Elizabethan acting companies which dealt in equally cavalier fashion with Shakespeare's historical plays) would have been baffled by such antiquarian niceties of interpretation. The change was revolutionary, and of untold significance.

This realignment of the past may have been due, *inter alia*, to the newly arisen science of anthropology, which very early on acquired the invaluable trick of examining disparate cultures from a strictly relative viewpoint (unhelpful, incidentally, to the unthinking self-confidence hitherto apparent in Church missionaries). Be that as it may, translators also became aware that some kind of 'distancing' was required of them. Their audience had changed beyond recognition; those who still chose to write for their peers could now only depend on a minority public; sooner or later the demands of the newly literate (to whom the classics, in their original tongue, remained a closed book) were bound to prevail. These demands included a strict adherence to the sense of the original (on which no individual check could now be made), and at least some lip-service to the remoteness, the alien context, of the author whom they were studying.

The change affected all translations, not merely those with a consciously educational aim. Many factors were involved in determining just how this sense of period should be conveyed. Ruskin and William Morris and the 'Merrie England' cult probably played a large part in it. Morris's *Odyssey*, with its long rocking-horse couplets and synthetic archaisms, shows the pseudo medievalizing trend at its very worst – as here in Odysseus's account of his dealings with the Cyclops:

> So I spake, and he took it and drank, and became exceeding fain
> Of that sweet drink that I gave him, and besought me of drink again
> 'Come give me the drink and be blythe, and straightway tell me thy name,
> That a guest-gift I may give thee to gladden thy heart with the same ...'.

To those who argued that this kind of stuff was artificial as well as abominable, a form of speech which no one had ever employed in any period, its practitioners could reply, with a certain specious plausibility, that the same was true of Homer's own epic dialect. The real point – that it called up misleading associations – does not seem to have occurred to anybody. The vagaries of English classical teaching also helped here: if sixth-formers were set to turn passages of Malory into Herodotean Greek, why not English Herodotus into a pastiche of Malory, with equally spurious overtones borrowed from Doughty's *Arabia Deserta*? (This particular habit dies hard, as Mr Enoch Powell's version all too eloquently demonstrates.)

Reactions against the archaizing trend came, predictably enough, from exponents of the New Rationalism, who purged Homer so effectively of his primitive quirks and formulaic repetitions that most of the poetry vanished at the same time. For them the story came first, and the 'silly poetry' nowhere. The first *Odyssey* to appear under this aegis - the first Drab *Odyssey*, C.S. Lewis might have called it - was the remarkable version by Samuel Butler, from which those by T.E. Lawrence and Dr Rieu are directly descended. In one sense, of course, Butler represents a reversion to Pope's position, since his characters are as unmistakably late-Victorian as Pope's are Augustan. This tends to produce the same kind of disarming incongruity in both cases:

> The prudent chief with calm attention heard;
> Then mildly thus: 'Excuse, if youth hath err'd;
> Superior as thou art, forgive the offence.
> Nor I thy equal, or in years, or sense.'

That passage from Pope's *Iliad* earned a kind of dubious immortality from its resurrection in *The Stuffed Owl*; but Butler's rendering of the way Odysseus was greeted by his wife on returning, at long last, to Ithaca is, surely, an equally strong candidate for inclusion:

> 'My dear', answered Penelope, 'I have no wish to set myself up, nor to depreciate you; but I am not struck by your appearance, for I very well remember what kind of a man you were when you set sail from Ithaca....'

It might be Paula Tanqueray speaking; the entire epic context has been boldly discarded.

Somewhere between these two extremes a compromise had to be struck; and struck it was, with remarkable skill, by a pair of highly talented Scotsmen, Andrew Lang and S.H. Butcher, the latter an energetic Professor of Greek at Edinburgh University. They retained Butler's flexible prose, but sparingly heightened it with enough archaisms to suggest the epic flavour; they reproduced the meaning of Homer's Greek with uncommon fidelity, formulas and all; and they set an overall tone which, while discreetly romantic, never slipped into the kind of fustian rant which all too often mars the pages of such works as *Ivanhoe* or *The Last Days of Pompeii*. Here is their version of the passage quoted above in Chapman's translation:

> Above Pieria he passed and leapt from the upper air into the deep. Then he sped along the wave like the cormorant, that chaseth the fishes through the perilous gulfs of the unharvested sea, and wetteth his thick plumage in the brine. Such like did Hermes ride upon the press of the waves. But when he had now reached that far-off isle, he went forth from the sea of violet-blue to get himself up into the land, till he came to a great cave, wherein dwelt the nymph of the braided tresses: and he found her within.

This makes pleasant if mildly saccharine reading; it still remains the most acceptable version - oddly enough - for children. But no one could possibly guess from it that the *Odyssey* was a great *poem*, and a poem, moreover, created in the oral tradition. Now in the half-century since Butcher and Lang published their translation, our knowledge of Homer in general, and of oral techniques in particular, has increased out of all recognition. We now see the precise value and function of those stylized formulaic epithets; we can talk knowingly (if not always accurately) of Achaeans and Luwians and the Linear B tablets; we take it for granted that Homer without the hexameter is scarcely Homer at all, that the medium, as they say, is the message. On the other hand, the number of those who can actually read the *Odyssey* in the original is probably lower, absolutely speaking, than it was 100 years ago.

Such a state of affairs cannot but force the translator to a radical reappraisal of the task confronting him - though still, be it noted, very much in terms of the new audience for which he has to cater. Clearly, in an age which has read and digested the important work done by such scholars as Parry, Lord, Bowra, Page and Kirk (most of it now easily available in paperback editions) the idea of Homer as an adventure-novelist for tired businessmen simply will not do. The poetry has to be restored, with all its traditional formulas and epic associations: and to restore the poetry means, first and foremost, restoring the hexameter, or something as near it as the natural patterns and rhythms of the English language will allow.

This, of course, constitutes a formidable barrier. The strict English stress-hexameter (having no metrical counterpoint to stiffen it) is about as dead a verse-form as the mind of man could devise; most translators considering it for the *Odyssey* must have remembered the disastrous version by H.B. Cotterill, and hastily cast around for something less risky. No sane man wants to spend vast time and trouble sinking himself in a kind of prosodic graveyard. The solution now generally accepted is the long, elastic six-beat line used by Mr Day Lewis for his rendering of Virgil, and since then by Professor Lattimore himself to deal with Hesiod and the *Iliad*. (Contrary to general opinion, others had been experimenting with such a line long before the Poet Laureate published his *Georgics*. It was employed, very successfully, for two passages of Homer included in the *Oxford Book of Greek Verse in Translation*, one by Mr Michael Balkwill, the other by Professor E.R. Dodds.)

It must be said at once, without qualification, that in this *Odyssey* Professor Lattimore has achieved his *chef-d'oeuvre* as a translator. Studied in retrospect, much of his previous work takes on the appearance, technically speaking, of prolegomena to this dazzling and well-nigh flawless performance. *Crescit eundo*. Above all, he now, as never before, displays a virtuoso mastery over the deceptively simple-looking verse-form he has chosen to employ. Nothing, as we know, is harder to write than good *vers libre*; it calls for a control of pace, texture and rhythm at least as subtle as that displayed by a first-class concert pianist. In the hands of any lesser exponent, the six-beat line's wide-ranging flexibility will always prove its greatest danger. The discipline must be imposed from within. Too rigid a control leads to stiffness of movement and rhythmic constraint; but the perils of over-relaxation are even more insidious.

Because the line is so accommodating, there is a constant temptation to exploit it to the limit, and to throw any kind of casual verbal rubble into it as a 'fill'. In prosody as elsewhere, Parkinson's Law applies. The result, very often, is barely distinguishable from prose – one of the most telling arguments adduced against the medium by its hostile critics. It also (as they are not slow to point out) seems to generate its own special brand of inappropriately demotic jauntiness, a fault of which Mr Day Lewis's *Aeneid* provides several unforgettable examples. For instance, 'Quo fugis, Aenea? thalamos ne desere pactos' emerges as: 'Where are you off to, Aeneas? Don't welsh on your marriage contract.' The ghost of Stanyhurst, it would seem, still haunts the English hexameter, or hexameter-equivalent.

But no one could accuse Professor Lattimore of failing to profit by his own mistakes, let alone those of his fellow-practitioners. In both his *Iliad* and his Hesiod the tone, tempo, and variations of rhythm are still, to some extent, in the experimental stage. This may well have been due, partially at least, to the intractable nature of the material he was translating. Much of the *Iliad* is as stiffly heraldic as those complex designs portrayed on Achilles' shield, and the formality of texture too often breeds a parallel constraint in Professor Lattimore's empathic imitation. Hesiod, on the other hand, reads at times like an uneasy cross between Genesis and Old Moore's Almanac. To find an acceptable yet faithful equivalent for this in modern English would tax anyone's ingenuity; and if Professor Lattimore's version occasionally suggests some mid-West agricultural journalist with a passion for Sunday hot-gospelling, that is not, perhaps, altogether the translator's fault.

But in the *Odyssey* he has found the ideal poem both for himself and for his audience; and he has come to it at the very height of his powers. All the qualities which distinguish the *Odyssey* from the *Iliad* – greater variety of scene and incident; the shift of interest to more private, even domestic issues, with a corresponding emphasis on individual characterization; the new element of magic and romance; the strikingly modern approach to, and interest in, women – combine to make this great poem about as perfect a subject for Professor Lattimore's remarkable interpretative talent as anything in the whole extant corpus of classical literature. But to say so much is not to minimize the way he has risen to the very considerable challenge which such a task presents. Here is a master in perfect control of his medium. The apparent ease with which he surmounts every problem, the perfect balance struck and maintained between vivid, fast-moving narrative and epic formality, the rhythmic subtleties, the freshness and vigour of language displayed from first page to last – all these make his *Odyssey* a landmark in the history of modern translation.

But – as in the parallel case of the pianist – the air of effortlessness is deceptive. It would be hard to assess (and perhaps only a fellow-translator could even surmise) just how much hard-won technical knowledge, poetic sensibility, and patient searching for the *mot juste* have enabled Professor Lattimore to sustain his Homeric evocation at epic length and on so majestically confident a scale. All translation, we know, is a matter of compromise and artifice: half-loaves are better than no bread. The reader is willingly deceived: but the least false step can shatter his sense of illusion. Professor Lattimore has proved himself the most skilful magician of them all; his verbal sleight-of-hand never falters as he steers a triumphant course between the twin perils of false archaism and misleading modernity.

He has, in fact, come about as near as any man could to conveying, in English, the utterly alien movement and structure of Homer's poetry, with its bardic conventions and sharp, fast-moving, predominantly visual use of paratactical sentence-formation. Yet he has managed this without the least grotesqueness, without any irrelevant literary associations; his language suggests neither period pastiche nor jarring colloquialism. It flows as crystal-clear and swift-moving as a mountain stream; yet even as we read we know that this stream has its sources in no English hills.

Consider, once again, the example with which we began. It is fascinating to observe how neatly Professor Lattimore avoids the mistakes committed by his predecessors:

> He stood on Pieria and launched himself from the bright air
> across the sea and sped the wave tops, like a shearwater
> who along the deadly deep ways of the barren salt sea
> goes hunting fish and sprays quick beating wings in the salt brine.
> In such a likeness, Hermes rode over much tossing water.
> But after he had made his way to the far-lying island,
> he stepped then out of the dark blue sea, and walked on over
> the dry land, till he came to the great cave, where the lovely-haired
> nymph was at home, and he found that she was inside.

The temptation to prolong the quotation is irresistible, and illustrates the range and subtlety of this translation's achievement:

> There was
> a great fire blazing on the hearth, and the smell of cedar
> split in billets, and sweetwood burning, spread all over
> the island. She was singing inside the cave with a sweet voice
> as she went up and down the loom and wove with a golden shuttle.

This is the pastoral mood; but Professor Lattimore can catch Homer's fierceness and pathos and harsh irony with equal skill –

the archetypal nightmare of the Cyclops's cave, Odysseus's last meeting with his dog Argos (a passage which, despite its familiarity, can still reduce the reader to tears as here translated), Circe's dark enchantments, that last climactic rain of arrows down the great hall. It is a splendid and monumental achievement. To bring the dead to life, as Mr Robert Graves has said, may be no great magic; but it would be a crime to underestimate the miraculous and self-effacing artistry with which Professor Lattimore has reanimated Homer for this generation, and perhaps for other generations to come. All Greekless lovers of literature owe him an incalculable debt of gratitude; if the blind man from rocky Chios lives on as a force and an inspiration in western culture, it is such dedicated interpreters whom we must thank for it.

On Horace

An address to the Horatian Society given at the House of Lords on 16 July 1959

I have been reading the addresses of earlier speakers to this Society and I have noted with admiration and some sinking of the heart the gentle wit and mellow wisdom of their words. Of course they have varied in their approach to our common theme, but, on the whole, the roads seem to lead to one side of Horace, one aspect of him happily attuned to the festive mood of this distinguished audience – Horace the companionable, the quotable, the *bon vivant*; Horace the amateur as opposed to the professional; Horace the gentleman, indeed the English gentleman. A figure rises before one, in toga and sandals of course, but otherwise rather like a cross between Thackeray and Charles Lamb. This, no doubt, is one aspect of the poet, and Thackeray, himself the most Horatian of authors, helped to turn it into something of a legend. Horace does share with Thackeray the wistful charm, the happy phrase, the kindly commonsense, which we all love. But of course, if that were all, Thackeray would not have lasted a hundred years, nor Horace two thousand.

Is it possible, without sounding too harsh a discord in this atmosphere of Horatian post-prandial ease – good food, good wine, while tobacco may do duty for the *unguenta*, and the best of good company (only our Neaeras are lacking) – is it possible to remind ourselves that Horace was a genius, a great originator and a unique craftsman in the art of words? This is not just a question for academics: in any case, I shall not detain you long, asking you for a few minutes to sit in patience – *cubita remanere presso*. When Jeanie Deans, in *The Heart of Midlothian*, was safely married to her Reuben Butler at the end of that great story, and he used to wax somewhat prosy about Politics and the Kirk, Jeanie heard him out, remembering, Scott says, 'that the man was mortal, and had been a schoolmaster'.

With this address in mind I have been reading *The Odes* again as a single work. How unique it is, and how original! Virgil and Ovid had their clumsy predecessors and their endlessly clever progeny; but there was nothing like *The Odes*. There were Latin lyrics before Horace, but he owes nothing to them; Catullus' favourite metre he ignores; and he has had no successors. One may easily forget the originality of Horace until one reconsiders him against the background of Latin literature. *The Odes* are unique, and a whole; each of us has his favourites, his special gems. But the gems are threaded on a string with great subtlety of variation in theme and in metre. That first Ode in the first book, *To Maecenas*, is in the simplest of all his metres, and he never uses it again until the very end of the third book. The opening Ode is a humble prelude to his first lyric publication; the last Ode is majestic and proud, as who should say 'what do you think of me now, reader of my Odes?' The first has the simplicity of modesty, the last the simplicity of grandeur, in the same metre. This was no chance, but surely an example of Horace's quiet ironical perfection as a craftsman.

(One may of course be interested in metre for a variety of reasons; not many of us for the reason which appealed to Mr William Crowe, Public Orator at Oxford in the last century: he was composing a history of poetry and writes to his friend, Samuel Rogers, as follows:

'If the part on versification could be out before the middle of April it would find a present sale in Oxford, for this reason:

there are above four score young poets who start every year for the English prize, and as I am one of the five judges to decide it they would (many of them) buy a copy to know my doctrine on the subject. The compositions are delivered in about the beginning of May.')

Certainly a re-reading of *The Odes* with a roving eye for the changing metres gives one a new pleasure in *numerosus Horatius* – Horace with the tunes. At school we cared little for such things and we missed much by not caring. About 100 years ago an aspiring young Wykehamist, aged 12, was asked *viva voce* to scan the line 'Dulce et decorum est pro patria mori' Now one thing the boy knew for certain – that a Latin Verse was either a hexameter or a pentameter and he replied –

dūlcĕ ĕt dēcōrūm ēst prŏ pătrīă mŏrī

Noting that the examiners were less than satisfied he tried with confidence the only possible alternative –

dūlcē ēt dēcōrūm ēst prō pātrĭă mōrī

Without suggesting that any mature lover of Horace believes that he wrote in Elegiacs – 'longs and shorts' as Etonians used boldly to call them – I know many true Horatians who care little what the metre is; and of course it is not the metre's name that matters, Asclepiad, etc., but the melody.

After that first Ode in the simple short Asclepiad we have a series of nine, all in different measures, some never used again. It is a metre-parade: the colts canter round the ring showing off their paces, but only a few are chosen. One would have liked to hear more of one or two among them:–

'Lydia, dic, per omnes
te deos oro, Sybarin cur properes amando . . .'

But Horace knew what he was about, and for the rest of his lyrics he almost confines himself to Alcaic, Sapphic and the various Asclepiads. There are one or two unique metres later on, notably the bold and entirely successful poem about poor Neobule who is kept closely under hatches with a scolding uncle in monotonous confinement. The metre breathes monotony, and Horace carefully comes to an end just before we feel we have had too much of it.

'Miserarum est neque amori dare ludum neque dulci
mala vino lavere, aut exanimari metuentes
patruae verbera linguae ...'

This metre has had few, if any, imitations until the immortal 'Book V' of *The Odes* by Ronald Knox and his friends, where the poor uncle is persecuted by his energetic niece.

'Her equipment is amphibious: she can swim a mile or more;
Her appearance in the saddle I both envy and adore;
She's the super-Atalanta of the young;
She declines to ply her needle, and she never reads a book,
But she withers me completely with a single scorching look,
And she cows me with the lashing of her tongue.'

And the Latin is even better than the English.

But it is in the First Book, as one would expect, that one finds most of the experiments in metre and in subject: Sapphics used for a weighty theme, Alcaics for a light one; the opposite of the poet's final practice. And if Book I is experimental, Book II is personal. The great majority are Alcaic or Sapphic, poems of advice or greeting to his growing company of friends: to poor Dellius, immortalized by the single crushing epithet *moriture Delli*. (If I received a letter one morning beginning '*Moriture Christie* ...' I should not soon forget it.) To Xanthias, in love with his housemaid; to a pair of old boon-companions, Septimus and Pompeius; and then suddenly a scorching little Ode to Barine, the notorious *fille de joie*, Barine. I have seen in the margin of a school text a very passable portrait of Barine in the fashions of 1924. How his indignation breaks out in the first line! *Ulla si iuris* – 'is there *any* oath you are not prepared to break?', and its incomparable ending:

'Let young wives take care when husbands are coming home from the office; one waft from the *femme fatale* and they have lost their bearings.'

tua ne retardet aura maritos.

And then the gentle counsellor continues: to Grosphus; riches are not happiness. To Postumus; time marches on.

If Book II is personal, Book III is more of Horace the politician, the poet laureate. Those first six great Odes are really one poem in six cantos, all in the same Alcaic metre at its most majestic. They are the heart and centre of *The Odes* and show every aspect of Horace, the person, the politician and the poet. The Regulus Ode is, I suppose, the best known single poem that has come down to us from antiquity, at any rate for Englishmen. I expect you recall Francis Doyle's poem about the Private of the Buffs who refused to kowtow to the Lords of China.

> 'Ay, tear his body limb from limb,
> Bring cord and axe and flame,
> He only knows that not through him
> Shall England come to shame.'

The contrast between west and east that Doyle develops in three verses, Horace's Latin can give us in a few words: *sub rege Medo Marsus et Apulus*: the Seaforth Highlanders serving the great Mogul. Every resource of rhetoric and word-order is used to bring home the shame. And then as he reaches his climax, the words become as simple as they can be. *Fertur pudicae*, etc.; that skilful *fertur* – so runs the tale; 'this story shall the goodman teach his son'. You all remember it; and then in conclusion what a surprise! How glibly could the classical schoolboy have finished off this patriotic Ode, e.g.

> (diiudicata lita relinqueret)
> sic ibat in dirum serenus
>   supplicium indomitusque mortem!

and what do we get,

> tendens Venafranos in agros
>   aut Lacedaemonium Tarentum.

Here is Horace, not the friendly personality, not the politician, but the great poet in his own right.

And then, when this great music has died away, in Ode VII, we have the Asterie Ode – delicate, ironic, intriguing, a novel in a nutshell.

> 'Weep not Asterie; spring breezes will bring your Gyges home. He will not listen to the foreign charmers; and you, meantime – young Enipeus is around, so keep your window shut at nightfall.'

This Ode employs the fifth Asclepiad which Horace uses with perhaps more mastery than any other. It is his favourite metre for the sudden picture, the dramatic lyric, the *chose vue*. The famous Pyrrha Ode, for instance, which the late Sir Ronald Storrs (*multis ille bonis flebilis occidit*) had reproduced in 144 renderings. It is the metre for the fountain of Bandusia, and for the gallant ship making for port in a storm, with tackle torn and yard-arms groaning.

Indeed each of these Asclepiads came to have its own character and its own theme. Hardly one of them is a poem of friendly advice. That is left to Sapphics and Alcaics. The Third, (short line and long line alternating)

> Donec gratus eram tibi
> nec quisquam potior brachia candidae ...

is for emotion, and especially love. The Fourth - (three of a kind with a shorter line to end, like the breaking of a wave) - is low-toned: the refusal of the poet to attempt a higher theme; the lover's moan, stretched outside his mistress' door; the lament for Quintilius.

> ergo Quinctilium perpetuus sopor
> urget! cui Pudor et Iustitiae soror
> incorrupta Fides, nudaque Veritas
> quando ullum inveniet parem?

It has something of the mood and melody of Tennyson's *In Memoriam*.

I will not linger here, but I must pay a passing tribute to *vixi puellis nuper idoneus* ('*vixi puellis semper uninteresting*,' as a bachelor don of my acquaintance once said). This metre had by now come to be the regular measure for the weighty poem, and this is in fact a charming parody. *Vixi* he begins, a solemn valedictory word; and it ends with mock-serious entreaty to the Goddess of Love with her temples in Cyprus and in Memphis. Memphis 'which lacks Sithonian snow' - no wonder, in the sands of Egypt! The whole joke comes at the end and Horace sharpens the point with every word:

> regina, sublimi flagello
> tange Chloën semel arrogantem.

Arrogantem is kept for the end, 'Give Chloe just a flick, the little hussy'. And the Third Book ends with the proud, soberly proud, *exegi monumentum aere perennius.*

There remains Book IV, of which it was the fashion in my youth to speak with disapproval. So T.E. Page, but don't believe him. It has some splendid poetry and is highly relevant to my theme. Just as a composer in the last movement of his symphony will sometimes leave cards, as it were, *pour prendre congé* on the melodies he has already used, so Horace, in this last and much later book, looks back on his seven principal metres and gives us specimens of each. The Alcaic has come to stay, for the swelling imperial theme: elaborate and a trifle stiff, but fine and memorable. A change has come over the light-footed Sapphic. Instead of the tripping movement –

> Integer vitae scelerisque purus
> non eget Mauris iaculis neque arcu

we get a different break with a far more sonorous effect. This change was due in part, I am sure, to the official *Carmen Saeculare* which Horace was commanded by Augustus to compose. Those Sapphics were sung aloud by choirs of youths and maidens in antiphon, and Horace had come to see the superior effect, for music, of a more varied rhythm:

> pulcher! o laudande! canam, recepto
> Caesare felix.
> tuque dum procedis, io Triumphe,
> non semel dicemus, io Triumphe.

One Ode in this book, the fifth, is in the tranquil low-toned metre which has hitherto been used for sadness or refusal. Here the theme is the great Augustan peace brooding over city and countryside. The tone is confident and imperturbable; but the tempo is Andante. (Somehow it always puts me in mind of the mood of those lines which Shakespeare (if it was Shakespeare) puts into the mouth of Cranmer at the christening of the babe who was to become Queen Bess –

> 'Upon this land a thousand, thousand blessings
> Which time shall bring to ripeness; good grows with her.
> In her days every man shall eat in safety
> Under his own vine what he plants, and sing
> The merry songs of peace to all his neighbours.')

Very near the end of the book we meet once more with an old flame; who but Lyce, last heard of when Horace, so he would have us think, lay all one frosty night across her threshold pleading with the cruel fair to bestow her favours upon him? That poem was in the quiet, sad measure of the fourth Asclepiad, and we might have expected, with the reappearance of Lyce, to meet the measure once again. But no. It is all an old story now. Horace can recollect his emotion in tranquility, look at the picture of his younger self ('Look back and regretfully wonder, What we were like in our work and our play') and so we have the poem, one of his best, in his favourite Pyrrha and Bandusia metre. Horace is quite impossible to translate with satisfaction to anyone but the translator himself. (Translations, you may remember, were like wives, the Frenchman said, either *belles* or *fidèles*, but rarely both.) Still, I have often thought that Calverley's first stanza was as good as it could be:

> 'Lyce, the Gods have listened to my prayer;
> The Gods have listened Lyce; thou art grey;
> Yet still wouldst thou seem fair,
> Still unshamed drink and play'
>
> Audivere, Lyce, di mea vota, di
> audivere, Lyce: fis anus, et tamen
>   vis formosa videri
>   ludisque et bibis impudens.

But he misses inevitably the hissing sounds of *fis anus*, etc. It is, of course, a poem of revenge; in this way like *Parcius iunctas*, with that bitter picture of the courtesan now grown old, standing in the draughty alleyway, raddled with old age and desire, on a moonless night while the wind blows cold from Thrace. But there is little real bitterness in *Audivere, Lyce*, and Horace looks back with a touch of sentiment, rather as Thackeray looked back at the ardours and endurances of his own young days in *Vanity Fair*. And here is Thackeray popping his head up in a talk on Horace, despite what I said of him to start with. But it is not the sentiment that makes Horace immortal, nor the charming personality, nor the patriotism, nor the calm good sense. These live because they lie embalmed in poetry of just proportions and perfect form.

In conclusion, let me quote, as a grateful child of Trinity, Oxford, some words from one of her greatest sons –

'Let us consider, too, how differently young and old are affected by the words of some classic author, such as Homer or Horace. Passages, which to a boy are but rhetorical common-places, neither better nor worse than a hundred others which any clever writer might supply, which he gets by heart and thinks very fine, and imitates, as he thinks, successfully, in his own flowing versification, at length come home to him, when long years have passed, and he has had experience of life, and pierce him, as if he had never known them, with their sad earnestness and vivid exactness. Then he comes to understand how it is that lines, the birth of some chance morning or evening at an Ionian festival, or among the Sabine hills, have lasted generation after generation, for thousands of years, with a power over the mind, and a charm, which the current literature of his own day, with all its obvious advantages, is utterly unable to rival.'

Thus far John Henry Newman.

How comes it that this company dines year after year to think together of Horace as humorist, philosopher, comforter and friend? All these he truly is, but so were others. Horace still lives because behind it all he is a master of his craft.

Bentley's *Horace*

The 'Host's Paper' delivered to 'The Society', a dining club at Oxford, in the late 1950s

I expect that most of us here find themselves happy members of various small groups that meet at intervals more or less frequent with aims more or less academic - groups, graduating in my case from Classics once a fortnight with tea and crumpets, through a plain Monday lunch garnished with the gas and gossip of the week, up to the stark self-indulgence of a terminal dinner alternately at Oxford and Cambridge where the only aim professed is to eat and to drink. Among these, The Society holds a modest place for its traditional aims - in no sense academical, but falling just short of appetite unalloyed, because the host is supposed to supply a digestive for the body and a spur to the mind by talking continuously about something or other, while the rest can indulge in rumination or repose.

For the guests, I hope, this should be no great hardship, but it sets a little problem for the host. The Society used, I believe, to abound in University politicians - liberal but tenacious, and growing less liberal, as ageing Liberals do. That day has long gone by. In recent years, the School of English Lang. and Lit. has been strongly represented among us by Scholars who might not be amused by the literary amateur talking about his pet poets. At present perhaps we are more varied in interest and the host-speaker had better stick to his last.

My last, so far as I have one, is Classics: an arid field, you would say, for the non-specialist? Maybe, but there still *can* be found areas in which the bleak rigour of the ancient tongues is lightened by sparks of controversial abuse, by the rumbustious character of the disputants, and by the atmosphere of battles long ago, fought, *à outrance*, over points so minute and so irrelevant to present problems and the Franks Commission, as to be positively heart-warming.

So let me speak for a few digestive minutes about Richard Bentley. I would not insult a cultivated audience by retailing, even in abridgement, his claim to immortality: supreme scholar in the Republic of Letters, not only in his own century, but in the whole annals of classical scholarship, by whose side, says Housman (and Housman was not given to eulogy), Scaliger himself 'seems but a marvellous boy'; Master of Trinity from 1700–1742, he was at war for over 20 years of this period, first with the Fellows whom he regarded as illiterate priests, then with the College Visitor, the Bishop of Ely, and at length with the Lord Chancellor and the law of the land. He defeated them all. Formally ejected from his Mastership and deprived of all his degrees, he never budged from the Master's Lodge. It was against this background that he produced many of the works which were the admiration, or at least the wonder, of the learned world. But rather than talk in generalities of this unique phenomenon, I will turn to one work Bentley's *Horace* which displays in all their abundance his qualities of learning, pugnacity and scorn; the superb Latin style which flowed from his pen more readily and more racily than English; his emendations, here and there palmary, more often wholly unacceptable, but in both kinds supported by battalions of quotations gathered from authors of every period, from Homer to the early Middle Ages – authors whom he often emends, *en courant*, as he quotes them.

Let us look first at the Preface. This celebrated book, to be for ever afterwards regarded as a kind of Pole Star by editors, was, we learn, undertaken as a distraction from more mundane anxieties. It was the fruit of his 'horae subsecivae' 'aestivis tantum mensibus', in fact his long vacation leisure. He calls it unpremeditated, 'αὐτοσχέδια:' the sheets were sent off wet to the printer. No doubt we must not take all this too seriously: Bentley, like Lord Macaulay according to Matthew Arnold, 'had his own heightened and telling way of putting things'. It is true that the years he spent on his *Horace* were the years of the bitterest battles with his colleagues when he was deprived of the Mastership by the Visitor and refused to move. He meant the *Horace* to appear in 1707, but it was not published until 1711. For some of those years he could not work at it even in the summer and much of the work was done in the last six months. Even so, this represents an astonishing power of concentration – to produce in such circumstances a work which most scholars would be well content to regard as the 'magnum opus' of a life time. It was an inverted pride which made Bentley speak with this mock modesty: pride of a more direct sort soon appears in the Preface. Textual critics are a rare and chosen race, he tells us: they must possess learning, shrewdness, power of divination ('μαντική'), and I Bentley possess them all. Where have we heard this brave language before? Why, of course, in A.E. Housman's estimate of himself. There are times when Bentley reminds one of Housman: in his ferocity and in his ample learning, learning of the kind that could never be gathered from lexicons or indexes. But fundamentally the men are different. Bentley enjoyed a fight in life as in letters: Housman, Professor Garrod has told us, 'bit his lip' at life and scholarship. Bentley shook his fist. He does not spare his fellow scholars, saying of those who are too timid to trust the light of reason, that they find in the variety of manuscript readings 'something to flatter their morbid itch for making perverse emendations'. For himself his motto is 'Per te sapere aude', 'have the courage of your convictions' founded upon a learning wide and deep. Mr. Denniston in his *Greek Particles* has bidden us 'bathe in examples': Bentley collects his examples for less peaceful purposes, 'that so, chafe or struggle as they may, my enemies should by the sheer weight of my reasons and the host of my examples be overwhelmed'. Those who are more recalcitrant he will 'drag over to our side by the scruff of the neck', 'obtorto collo'; a favourite metaphor of Bentley's, this. In dealing with other opponents he will 'dissimulate his resources that the dunces may find themselves taken in the toils unaware, a source of jest and merriment to men of a finer discernment', 'risum nasutioribus daturi'.

Turning now to Bentley's own notes, one or two things strike one immediately: first that they are readable, instructive and often highly entertaining quite apart from the correctness of his conclusions. A summary (or even an abridgment) of Bentley would have little value; the amplitude of his commentary is its virtue. Secondly, that Bentley's instant recognition of a good reading found in only one or two among the vast number of manuscripts, hitherto overlooked, was at the period of primary importance for the text of Horace, and does almost as much credit to Bentley as his 'merae coniecturae'. Thirdly, it was a time when accepted texts of Horace still printed readings that were wildly impossible and Bentley swept them into oblivion once for all.

At Odes 1.3.18, 'qui siccis oculis monstra natantia ... vidit', we come to Bentley's renowned and wholly unconvincing change of 'siccis oculis' to 'rectis oculis', without a shadow of manuscript authority. 'No sign of courage', says Bentley, 'to look on monsters of the deep with dry eyes, without weeping; no: "rectis oculis", without flinching.' Unfortunately for Bentley tears *were* frequently taken as a sign of terror in the ancient world: but even so, we should regret the loss of Bentley's note. First, parallels to 'siccis oculis', meaning 'without tears': (Bentley leaves nothing to chance). He goes on, 'No merit even in a woman to refrain from tears in the presence of terror; we weep from pity, love, regret, shame, slight danger, or recollection of the past; but faced with overpowering danger, there is no place for tears even in a baby girl. Then we stiffen and grow pale; [hosts of parallels]. Therefore read 'rectis oculis'; this is so certain as to outweigh the authority of two hundred copyists.' Parallels to 'rectis oculis' follow from Seneca, Suetonius, Tacitus, Elder Pliny, more Seneca, Cicero, Statius, Juvenal, Boethius; the Greek for 'rectis oculis' is 'ὀρθοῖς ὄμμασιν' and on we go with parallels from Sophocles, Theocritus, Arrian, Xenophon, Hierax quoted by Stobaeus, Aristides, and pass to a parallel from Oppian who is emended by the way: this leads to another emendation, in Hesychius the lexicographer. It is an astonishing performance and a good instance of Bentley's avowed intention of overwhelming his opponents by sheer weight of examples: unhappily here, as often, in the process he overwhelms himself and his own better judgment.

Passing over much that is wrong-headed and some things that are cogent – and all readable – we come to Odes 1.23.5. The manuscripts with almost complete unanimity give 'nam seu mobilibus *veris* inhorruit *adventus* foliis' 'or whether through the light-hung leaves hath run the ripple of spring's approach', (Wickham). I was taught to regard this as one of Horace's most exquisite pieces of word-painting, and for years I believed it: it sorted well with romantic memories of Swinburne's 'Lisp of leaves and ripple of rain'. But I can believe it no longer: that the *arrival* of spring, not spring itself, should be said to ripple in the leaves, without any reference to spring breezes – this, as Bentley is always saying, 'concoquere non possum': I cannot swallow it. Bentley, as we all know, following a hint from Muretus, reads 'seu mobilibus *vepris* inhorruit *ad ventum* foliis': 'or whether the light-leaved thornbush trembles in the wind'. This accords better with the other details in Horace's simile; the frightened fawn, seeking its mother, and the lizards parting the brambles. The frightened fawn was more likely to tremble at a quiver in the undergrowth than at the approach of spring. But Bentley bases his view on less delicate considerations: (1) the arrival of spring cannot quiver in the leaves because there *are* no leaves till the spring has arrived. (2) Fawns do not seek out their mothers in early spring because they are not yet born; nor (3) do green lizards part the brambles in early spring, because they are still hibernating. Bentley's rough common sense is not always suited to lyric poetry, as we shall see; but I believe that he is right here. His bold 'vepris' is well picked up in the next line by 'rubum', [bramble-bush]; and as for beauty, is not the picture of the bramble-leaf quivering in the summer wind more beautiful, and certainly more classical, than the vague notion of spring's trembling arrival? Many editors follow Bentley, though Page speaks of this emendation as 'a correction, the mechanical ingenuity of which is as marvellous as it is misplaced'. Page, like many rugged housemasters, was at heart a romantic.

Jebb, in his admirable short life of Bentley, regrets that the great scholar confined himself to textual notes on Horace and did not write expository notes on the subject-matter; if he had, it would have been a *μέγα βιβλίον* with a vengeance. But in truth, while ostensibly emending the text, Bentley touches on all departments of antiquity – linguistic, grammatical and philological of course, but also on social customs, mythology, epigraphy, history and geography. Take his note on Odes 4.4.17. The manuscripts give 'videre Raeti bella sub Alpibus Drusum gerentem Vindelici'. The old commentators here talk happily of Raeti Vindelici as a single tribe. Nothing will 'extort agreement' to this view out of Bentley, nor will he accept the easy solution of 'et Vindelici'. The Rhaetians did not see *Drusus* waging war: they saw *Tiberius*. Read 'Raetis ... Alpibus'. This he amply supports by purely historical evidence from V. Paterculus and Tacitus' *Germania*, with geographical inferences from Claudian: no expository commentator could go further.

I should say that Bentley was more essential for a student of the Satires and Epistles than for a student of the Odes: satire, in the widest sense, was more suited to his taste than lyric; but on the whole he is less lively. There are however exceptions. I am thinking, as you may guess, of Epistles 1.7.29 – the fable of the fox in the corn bin. The fox, 'volpecula', crept into the corn bin ['cumeram'] when he was thin and ate so much that he was too fat to get out. Bentley, with no shred of support from manuscripts, on the ground that foxes do not eat corn, reads *nitedula*, shrew-mouse. I do not believe in this change for a moment: we are in the land of fable, where animals talk and laugh and behave in all kinds of unlikely ways, especially foxes. Bentley's suggestion, though applauded by the great Lachmann, has met with little approval. But who would willingly forgo Bentley's note? It is not a note, hardly even an essay, though it runs to some 1,500 words. It is the speech of an advocate. 'Prick up your ears, gentle reader; give me your attention while we probe this passage to the very quick' (the usual text is quoted). 'If these are the words not of some dozing scribe but of our own Horace, then I fear he may turn into a Bavius or a Maevius before our eyes. Huntsmen, countrymen, naturalists, I cry your mercy: 'vestram fidem, venatores, rustici, physici ...'. The fox eating corn! Who ever heard the like? Why, no hunger in the world would drive a fox to eat grain: his broad flat teeth cannot bite it, nor his stomach digest it. Can we believe that our Horace was such a dolt, such a feather-pate, as not to know *that*? Or that none of the friends he read his verses to, knew it and would put him right? Dacier indeed read 'Cameram frumenti' for 'cumeram': so, quoth he, Horace's reputation is saved. 'Cameram frumenti'! 'Camera' means an arch, a domed building. Whoever heard of an arch of corn? He quotes Columella; he might equally have appealed to Frontinus but it would avail him nothing. They speak of the Camera of a granary ('horreum'), not a 'camera' of corn. The fox, says Dacier, got in not to eat corn but to catch the chickens and the pigeons. Bah! What a flippant and dishonest note! 'Vah! facetum et callidum commentum'. Nay, my good sir, turn where you may, this is a blot that will cling to Horace, and not all the water in the wide sea can wash it away. What do I hear you say? A fox crept in through that tiny crevice! And do not pretend that 'volpecula' means a fox cub: in Cicero *de Officiis* 1.13.2 it means a full-grown fox. And even if it were a cub, would it not grow bigger in the course of nature, whether it ate much or little, and so could not get out in any case?' (And so on for another three hundred words or so, and he ends) 'Could anyone bring himself to believe *this* – that a fox could eat corn, and in order to eat corn could creep through a crack only large enough for a mouse, could creep through such a crack into a bin, itself within four walls of a house, and that there, in the midst of the enemy camp, inside the house inside the bin, though twice a captive, ('bis captiva licet' – echo of Virgil) should calmly enjoy himself till he grew fat, and then should be so feckless, so forgetful of his ancient arts that he knew not where to turn.' No; 'volpecula' will never do: and Bentley suggests one by one the qualities of the animal required to suit the conditions and incidentally the quantity required to fill the hexameter. At last, with the flourish of the conjurer he produces it: 'nitedula', a shrew-mouse – with examples, though hardly as many, one feels, as he would have liked, to establish its meaning and its metrical quantity. Q.E.D.

On the *Ars Poetica* Bentley is, if not at his best, certainly at his fullest and most vigorous. Were one trying to establish the critical value of his *Horace* and not merely recommending it as a book to study for scholarly enjoyment, one would scarcely need to go beyond these 450 lines. The *Ars Poetica* is a difficult work: the more often I read it, the odder and the harder it seems to me to be.

His most celebrated note is one which has gained and has deserved the least acceptance. It is at 441: 'et male tornatos incudi reddere versus': 'he bids you take verses that have been badly *turned* and put them back on the *anvil*'. In a speech for the prosecution running to nearly 3,000 words Bentley condemns 'male tornatos' and reads 'male ter natos'. Like many forensic arguments Bentley's will not bear scrutiny. There is no necessary inconsistency between 'tornus' and 'incus', the lathe and the anvil. There is no mixture of metaphors and, if there were, Horace *does* mix his metaphors. 'Male ter natos' cannot bear the meaning of 'ter male natos'. But Bentley had a special affection for this emendation. He had published it some sixteen years before in a note on Callimachus and scholars had already judged it. Here Bentley cannot be acquitted of some petulance and vanity, so keen for approval, so sensitive to criticism. 'Graevius', he tells us, 'Graevius, that most discerning critic by temperament and by training, had written me a precious letter on 2nd December 1702 saying that this was no conjecture but a certain restoration. It is a wise provision of nature', he continues, 'that in the world of literature there should be a cheap and plentiful supply of moles to furnish amusement to scholars with better eyesight, and by contrast to heighten their own renown: 'in his Gronovius nomen profitetur suum' – Gronovius, who was pleased to caw like the crow he is [cornicari voluit] against this emendation of mine and for the last ten years has pursued me with insults'. (Then follows the body of the discourse, with much about woodwork and smith's work and sculpture in the ancient world, and the correct terms in Greek as well as in Latin.) It is good reading and the note ends – indeed it is almost the end of the complete commentary, page 802 – with Bentley at his most defiant, Bentley at bay: 'As for the book which he, Gronovius, and another have put out against me, it is wasted labour. I do not yet reckon their strokes so weighty as to think it worth while to give them another thrashing. Indeed their hides are so hardened to the whip, beyond any slave in comedy, that I fancy they only draw fresh spirit from their beatings and will one day emerge fiercer than ever. This note I have drawn out to a greater length than is my wont, for I felt bound to protect this emendation which was the earnest and the first-fruits of my studies in Horace. Furthermore, I would have all to know who are ready to risk themselves against me that, in Pindar's phrase, "my quiver yet hath store of shafts", wherewith, if need be, I can defend what I have said aright: what may be proved amiss, since any man may err, especially when he has frequent distractions, this I shall be the first to abandon, and leave whoso will to refute and carp at it, without retaliation'.

I find something touching in this resolve of Bentley's, if proved wrong, to be humble under correction. Mr. Darcy in *Pride and Prejudice* tells Elizabeth that all his life he has been unselfish in principle but not in practice. So with Bentley's humility: he remained arbitrary and masterful to the end, dislodging traditional readings from the texts as if they had been so many Fellows of Trinity, until with his edition of Milton, that freak of literature, his passion for emendation becomes fantastic and pathetic. But in his Horace he is still far from that point.

Anyone with a moderate knowledge of Latin, a sense of humour and affection for Horace can take this volume away with him on vacation and be sure of a unique experience – the experience of enjoying Bentley's *Horace*.

Let me add in conclusion that originally I had thought of

taking for my subject this evening Bentley's *Milton* – the greatest example on record of misguided pedantry: it would be easy – and rather dull – to make Richard Bentley out as 'a driveller and a show'. But just as his famous *Horace*, for all its merits and entertainment value, is *more* outrageous than is commonly supposed, so the notorious *Milton* for all its demerits (its donnish rebukes and incredible emendations) is *less* outrageous than tradition paints it. The comments are often fair, though the 'improvements' are nearly all indefensible. After all, Milton *was* blind; and his proof reading must have been less thorough than most. Bentley's edition is a pleasant book to 'leaf over'; but the *Horace* is a prodigious, incomparable book. What other commentary could be named so full of vitality and character, and withal so readable? Most of us once knew Munro's *Lucretius*, Jebb's *Sophocles*, but they breathe a soberer and more academic air.

Oxford Compositions

JTC enjoyed the discipline and excelled particularly in the art of turning English verse into Latin or Greek equivalents. These examples are taken from *More Oxford Compositions*, edited by T.F. Higham, Oxford, at the Clarendon Press, 1964.

It was a tall young oysterman lived by the river-side,
His shop was just upon the bank, his boat was on the tide;
The daughter of a fisherman, that was so straight and slim,
Lived over on the other bank, right opposite to him.

It was the pensive oysterman that saw a lovely maid,
Upon a moonlight evening, a-sitting in the shade!
He saw her wave her handkerchief, as much as if to say,
'I'm wide awake, young oysterman, and all the folks away.'

Then up arose the oysterman, and to himself said he,
'I guess I'll leave the skiff at home, for fear that folks should see;
I read it in the story-book, that, for to kiss his dear,
Leander swam the Hellespont – and I will swim this here.'

And he has leaped into the waves, and crossed the shining stream,
And he has clambered up the bank, all in the moonlight gleam;
Oh, there were kisses sweet as dew, and words as soft as rain, –
But they have heard her father's step, and in he leaps again!

Out spoke the ancient fisherman: 'Oh, what was that, my daughter?'
''Twas nothing but a pebble, sir, I threw into the water.'
'And what is that, pray tell me, love, that paddles off so fast?'
'It's nothing but a porpoise, sir, that's been a-swimming past.'

Out spoke the ancient fisherman: 'Now bring me my harpoon!
I'll get into my fishing-boat, and fix the fellow soon.'
Down fell that pretty innocent, as falls a snow-white lamb!
Her hair drooped round her pallid cheeks, like seaweed on a
clam.

Alas for those two loving ones! she waked not from her swound,
And he was taken with the cramp, and in the waves was drowned!
But Fate has metamorphosed them, in pity of their woe,
And now they keep an oyster-shop for mermaids down below.

OLIVER WENDELL HOLMES

Ostrea ab amne legit Corydon, collecta per oram
  venditat; in promptu cumba ligata natat.,
margine in adverso procera filia forma
  piscatore larem cum patre Phyllis habet.
hanc iuvenis secum meditans lucente Diana
  conspicit; umbroso tegmine operta sedet.
ecce, puella agitat mappam, nec fallit amantem
  quid velit: 'hic vigilo sola relicta domi.'
surgit et 'hic maneat' tacitus sic cogitat ille
  'cumba; viam prodet cumba soluta meam.
tu freta trans Helles, fama est, Leandre, petebas
  Sestidos amplexus; sic ego, Phylli, tuos.'
in freta desiliit: nitidas iam traicit undas,
  iam manibus cupidis altera ripa datur.
roscida blanditiis dum miscent oscula, patris
  planta sonat; Corydon mersus in amne fugit.
'ecquid, nata,' senex 'crepuit?' rogat; illa roganti
  'nil nisi quem ieci, mi pater, ipsa, lapis'.
'quid tamen e visu quod remigat ocius istud?'
  'nil nisi delphinum pe freta nare vides.'
'qua mihi, qua iaculum? iaculum modo missile vibrem
  e rate; sic, pestis, conficieris' ait.
concidit ad terram castissima Phyllis, ut insons
  ante aram nivei corporis agna cadit;
ora fluunt laxi circum pallentia crines,
  in placido fluitans fertur ut alga mari.
heu, miseros! non illa animam collapsa recepit;
  hunc rapuit medio frigoris amne rigor.
mutati faciem fatis miserantibus ambo
  sub mare nunc vendunt ostrea Nereisin.

JTC

From *Atys*

'Lydians, lords of Hermus river,
Sifters of the golden loam,
See you yet the lances quiver
And the hunt returning home?'

'King, the star that shuts the even
Calls the sheep from Tmolus down;
Home return the doves from heaven,
And the prince to Sardis town.'

From the hunting heavy laden
Up the Mysian road they ride;
And the star that mates the maiden
Leads his son to Croesus' side.

'Lydians, under stream and fountain
Finders of the golden vein,
Riding from Olympic mountain,
Lydians, see you Atys plain?'

'King, I see the Phrygian stranger
And the guards in hunter's trim,
Saviours of thy son from danger;
Them I see. I see not him.'

'Lydians, as the troop advances,
– It is eve and I am old –
Tell me why they trail their lances,
Washers of the sands of gold.

'I am old and day is ending
And the wildering night comes on;
Up the Mysian entry wending,
Lydians, Lydians, what is yon?'

Hounds behind their master whining,
Huntsmen pacing dumb beside,
On his breast the boar-spear shining,
Home they bear his father's pride.

A.E. HOUSMAN

'Lydorvm proceres, vestri qui quaeritis Hermi
  cribis aurifero quod later amne lutum,
anne redit silvis venatrix turba relictis?
  iam procul aspicitis tela micare virum?'
'Rex, monitu stellae quae sera crepuscula claudit,
  cogitur a Tmoli grex ad ovile iugo;
huc procul e caelo repetunt sua tecta columbae,
  rege satus Sardes huc puer ipse suas.'
nunc sublimis equo, Mysis ubi trames ab agris
  scanditur, exuviis fertur onusta cohors;
sidus idem, iuvenem gaudet quod iungere nuptae,
  hoc simul ad Croesi limina ducit Atyn.
'vos, mihi vena quibus rimantibus emicat auri
  fluminis aut flava condita fontis aqua,
respondete patri, num liquerit ardua Olympi
  filius huc reduci conspiciendus equo.'
'Rex, comites adeunt silvestri more recincti,
  et novus e Phrygiis finibus hospes adit:
quos dederas, raperent ne forte pericula natum,
  praesidio, est omnes cernere; natus abest.'
'turma subit, proceres: hoc quaeso dicite regi;
  (nam senis obscuro vespere visus hebet)
vos, quibus e lota faex aurea manat arena,
  dicite cur isti spicula prona trahant;
iam vergente die caecam nox promovet umbram
  et gravis annosum me premit umbra senem.
dicite – namque aditus iam Mysius excipit agmen –
  quid velit, O Lydi, quid velit istud onus.'
incedit taciturna cohors; arguta querentes
  ignarum catuli pone sequuntur erum.
ecce, super iuvenis pectus nitet hasta perempti;
  sic redit, heu, patris spesque decusque domum.

JTC

Muse and Poet

MUSE Will Love again awake,
That lies asleep so long?
POET O hush! ye tongues that shake
The drowsy night with song.
MUSE It is a lady fair
Whom once he deigned to praise,
That at the door doth dare
Her sad complaint to raise.
POET She must be fair of face,
As bold of heart she seems,
If she would match her grace
With the delight of dreams.
MUSE Her beauty would surprise
Gazers on Autumn eves,
Who watched the broad moon rise
Upon the scattered sheaves.
POET O sweet must be the voice
He shall descend to hear,
Who doth in Heaven rejoice
His most enchanted ear.
MUSE The smile, that rests to play
Upon her lip, foretells
What musical array
Tricks her sweet syllables.
POET And yet her smiles have danced
In vain, if her discourse
Win not the soul entranced
In divine intercourse.
MUSE She will encounter all
This trial without shame,
Her eyes men Beauty call,
And Wisdom is her name.
POET Throw back the portals then,
Ye guards, your watch that keep,
Love will awake again
That lay so long asleep.

ROBERT BRIDGES

M. Iam sopitus Amor diu
longae vincla velit solvere inertiae?
P. vox, quae carmine languidae
noctis sollicitas otia, quin taces?
M. en, adsto querimoniam
portis ausa tuis edere lugubrem,
virgo non sine gratia,
non indigna tuae laude prius lyrae.
P. quanto tu magis es procax,
tanto candidior fac niteat tuus
vultus, ne mihi sordeas
his prae deliciis, somnia quas ferunt.
M. mirarine procul iuvat
aestivo speciem vespere Cynthiae
messes dispositas super
surgentis? videar vel speciosior.
P. at me non nisi dulcius
quam mortale sonans elicies polo,
qui sublimis apud deos
caelesti penitus carmine gaudeam.
M. praedicas ab amabili
risu labra super qui vagus enitet,
quantus consona vestiat
dulci verba lepos ore fluentia.
P. at tu riseris irritum
si sermone minus captus ero tuo,
qui deleniar audiens
quali colloquio di soleant frui.
M. en hic omne quod exigis
praesto, nec pudor est, nomine quam vocant
mortales Sapientiam,
nec deest vera Venus luminibus meis.
P. ergo pandite ianuam,
custodes quibus est praesidium domus:
sic sopitus Amor diu
nunc demum excutiens surget inertiam.

JTC

To the Translator's Muse

Dear Muse, ere age benumb my hand and heart,
Accept a grateful tribute to thy art.
Mine is but mimic verse; yet he that woos,
Even in Latin, still may court the Muse.
Some only strive to win her, some succeed;
But both alike, methinks, enjoy their meed.
In many a guise dost thou thy servant tend –
Joy, comfort, sage, seducer, teacher, friend.
In childhood thou the learner's step didst guide,
And still in age thou walkest at my side.
Nor have I sought thee solely to impart
To boys some relish for thy ancient art.
Today's head master is beset with cares –
Shortage of funds, no servants, School repairs.
By tasks so dull and so diverse appalled,
Never in vain upon my Muse I called.
Wroth not with youthful naughtiness alone
Ashamed more oft at lapses of my own,
To thee I turn; my heart revives again.
Thy strict demand brings comfort in its train.
Gentle thy touch upon my trembling ear
With counsel for the inmost mind to hear:
'No Bank, no public building craves thy care;
Hand on the sacred torch 'tis thine to bear.
Profit for thee and thine my art will show;
Where duty and desire direct thee, go.'
Alas, ill-prompting pandar! to my cost
Too well I hearken, waver and am lost.
'Gainst thee, enchantress, duty calls in vain;
That Siren song rings ever in my brain.
Yet practice bad, I grant, for Virtue's ways
May teach at least a turn for Latin phrase.
Who better than a mistress gay and young
To train the tiro in some foreign tongue?
What plaint is this? Nay, be not wroth dear Muse
Welcome in any mask that thou shalt choose –
My joy, my guide, my comfort in distress,
Inspirer sweet in hours of idleness.
Howe'er thou com'st, however rude my skill,
Thou art my strength and stay, my trusty comrade still.

JTC

An ex-headmaster reflects on the practice of Latin Verse Composition

Haec prius a grato capias, mea Musa, ministro
  quam mea torpescat mens rigeatque manus.
nil nisi docta parum veterumque imitamina finxi;
  his tamen est aliquid te coluisse modis.
gaudia contingunt eadem, nisi fallor, utrisque –
  quique placent Musae quique placere volunt.
a! quot agis dudum partes mihi, diva – voluptas,
  solamen, monitor, lena, magistra, comes.
te duce laetabar teneris tironis ab annis,
  nec minus oblector te comitante senex.
non modo te colui melius si forte docerem
  discipulos prisci carminis arte frui;
Orbiliis hodie sunt multa negotia curae –
  fiscus inops, famuli, nec bene sarta domus.
numquam defuerunt, memini, solacia Musae
  cum vexat varii triste laboris onus.
saepe acuere meam pueri, grex improbus, iram;
  saepius angebar spretor et ipse mei.
te meditor; studio recipit mens otia ab ipso
  et relevat curas quod, dea, poscis opus.
poscis opus monitorque simul mihi molliter aurem
  vellis, et haec ima mente notanda refers:
'non aedilis,' ais, 'non argentarius audis.
  est tibi doctrinae fax data; trade facem.
quin, prodest pueris, prodest tibi fingere versus;
  i, pete iucundam qua decet ire viam.'
audivi; nimis, heu!, copi te audire monentem;
  lena parum stabili fis malesuada mihi.
pellicior; iusti mihi fers oblivia pensi;
  quicquid ago, Siren non fugienda sonas.
vix ita, confiteor, virtus discenda; sed usu
  promptior ad versus lingua Latina venit.
nemo virum melius ridente docebit amica,
  verba cupit linguae qui didicisse novae.
quid loquor? irasci noli, mea Musa, querenti.
  grata mihi, facie qualibet usa, subis.
delectasque docesque, eadem solare dolorem;
  est ubi desidiae gaudia dulce canis.
sis quaecunque voles, ego sim licet inscius artis,
  tu tamen adiutrix, tu mihi fida comes.

JTC

from *Hassan*

CALIPH WHY did you abandon me, Ishak, and flee into the night? I do not know if I shall forgive you.

ISHAK I was weary of you, Haroun-al-Raschid.

CALIPH And if I weary of you?

ISHAK You will one day or another, and you will have me slain.

CALIPH And what of this day that dawns?

ISHAK Dawn is the hour when most men die.

CALIPH Your death is granted you, Ishak; you have but to kneel.

[*A red glow on the horizon*

MASRUR It is the Caliph's dawn.

JAFAR Thy dawn, O Master!

ISHAK Thy dawn, O Master of the World, thy dawn;
The hour the lilies open on the lawn,
The hour the grey wings pass beyond the mountains,
The hour of silence, when we hear the fountains,
The hour that dreams are brighter and winds colder,
The hour that young love wakes on a white shoulder,
O Master of the world, the Persian Dawn.
That hour, O Master, shall be bright for thee:
Thy merchants chase the morning down the sea,
The braves who fight thy war unsheathe the sabre,
The slaves who work thy mines are lashed to labour,
For thee the waggons of the world are drawn—
The ebony of night, the red of dawn!

CALIPH Sheathe your sword, Masrur! Would you kill my friend?

J.E. FLECKER

K. Τί δὴ θέλων σὺ προύλιπές μ᾽ οὕτω μόνον
φυγὼν ἐς ὄρφνην; μὴ οὐχὶ συγγνωστὸν τόδ᾽ ᾖ.
I. λυπεῖς γάρ, ὦναξ, ἐκ μακρᾶς συνουσίας.
K. τί δ᾽ ἦν σὺ δὴ κἄμοιγε λυπηρὸς γένῃ;
I. κεῖν᾽ ἦμαρ ἥξει, κἀμ᾽ ἀποκτενεῖς τότε.
K. καὶ τοὐπιὸν τόδ᾽ οὐχὶ σὺν καιρῷ πάρα;
I. ἀλλ᾽ ὀρθρίους τοί φασι τοὺς πλείστους θανεῖν.
K. θανεῖν ἄρ᾽ αἰτεῖς, κἀξ ἔμουγ᾽ οὐδεὶς φθόνος.
κάμψον τὰ γούνατ᾽ αὐτίχ᾽ ὡς θανούμενος.
Χο. καὶ μὴν ἕως φλογωπὸς αἴθεται πόλῳ
ὡς ξύμμετρος παροῦσα σοῖς κελεύσμασι.
M. σὸν δῆτ᾽ ἄρ᾽, ὦναξ, καὶ τόδ᾽ ὄρθριον σέλας.
I. σή δή ᾽στιν ἕως, δέσποτα πάντων,
ὅτ᾽ ἀνεπτύχθη κρίνον ἐν κήποις,
πτερύγεσσι δ᾽ ὄρη δνοφεραῖς φρούδη
νὺξ ὑπερέπτα·
κἀπὸ σιωπῆς τῆλε δι᾽ ὤτων
πίτυλος πηγῶν ἠρέμα βάλλει·
νῦν γὰρ ὀνείρατα μᾶλλον ἐναργῆ,
νῦν δ᾽ ὀξυτέρα Βορέου ῥίπη,
λευκῷ δὲ κλιθεὶς ἀγκῶνι κόρης
ἔγρετ᾽ ἐραστής.
σοὶ πάνθ᾽ ὅσ᾽ ἕως ἐφορᾷ, βασιλεῦ
Περσῶν πάνταρχ᾽, ὑπακούει.
φαιδρὸν ἀνίσχει σοὶ τόδε φέγγος,
πηγὰς ὅθ᾽ ἕους καθ᾽ ἅλ᾽ ἰχνεύων
ὁλκάδα ναύτης σὴν χάριν αἴρει.
σοὶ νῦν γυμνοῦσι μαχαιροφόροι
φάσγαν᾽ ἐπ᾽ ἐχθρούς, ἐν δὲ μετάλλοις
τὸ σὸν ἐκμοχθοῦσ᾽ ὑπὸ μαστίγων
πλήγματι δοῦλοι.
σοὶ νυκτὸς ὄχοι μελανοπτέρυγος
κυκλοῦσιν ὁδόν· σή, δέσποθ᾽, ἕως
φλογερῶν ἐπιβᾶσα τεθρίππων.
K. ἔα·
μέθες μάχαιραν· μῶν ἐμὸν σφάξεις φίλον;

JTC

from *The Path to Rome*

THE DUCHESS. ? ? ? ? ?

CHARLES. ——!

THE DUCHESS. ! ! ! ! !

CLARA [*sobs*]. ♪♪♪♪♪♪♪♪♪♪

THE DUCHESS [*to Major Charles*]. ☛

CHARLES. ∿∿∿∿∿∿∿∿∿∿∿∿∿∿∿∿∿∿∿∿ (*exit*).

THE DUCHESS [*to Clara, sharply*]. %%%%%% ? % ? $!

CLARA.

THE DUCHESS [*in great anger*]. ? ♯ * ‖ § ‡ ¶ † ⚔ !

CLARA. ▬ ▬ ▬ ▬

HILAIRE BELLOC

Ἀρήτη Ὀδυσσεύς Ναυσικάα Χορός

Αρ. ἔα· τί τοῦτο; μῶν ἐφωράθης, τέκνον,
ξὺν τῷδ᾽ ἰοῦσα διὰ φιλημάτων ξένῳ;
Οδ. διαρραγείης ὡς ἐν οὐ καιρῷ πάρει.
Αρ. ἀλλ᾽ οὔ γέ τοι χαίρουσα, μὴ δόκει τόδε,
ὦ θρέμμ᾽ ἀναιδές, ὧδ᾽ ἀπαλλάξεις ποτέ.
Να. αἰαῖ.
τητωμένην γὰρ ἀνδρὸς αἰάζειν με δεῖ,
λιγυρὸν χέουσαν ὥστ᾽ ἀηδόνος γόον.
Αρ. ὅπως φθερεῖ σὺ τῆσδ᾽ ἀπὸ στέγης τάχα.
Οδ. ἀπορῶ· τίν᾽ ὀργῇ τῇσδε προύχωμαι λόγον;
Χο. βέβηκεν ἁνὴρ τρομερὸν ἐκκλέψας πόδα.
Αρ. ἦ γὰρ σύ γ᾽ ἔτλης, ἥνπερ ἐκ δόμων τινὶ
ἀρχαιοπλούτων κοιράνῳ καταξιῶ
ἕδνων γαμεῖσθαι σὺν πολυχρύσῳ χλιδῇ,
μνηστῆρα δὴ τοιοῦτον ὧδ᾽ ἐπελπίσαι
ὃς οὔτι χαλκοῦν, οὐχ ὅπως χρυσόν, φέρει;
Χο. ἀλλ᾽ οὐδὲν ὡς ἔοικεν ἀντερεῖ κόρη,
φόβῳ δ᾽ ἀφώνῳ γλῶσσαν ἐγκλῄσασ᾽ ἔχει.
Αρ. καὶ δῆτ᾽ ἐτόλμας τῷδε τῷ ξένῳ λάθρᾳ
λόγους συνάπτειν πατρὸς ἀντειρηκότος;
ἐπίστασ᾽ οὖν, εἰ κεῖν᾽ ἀπομνύναι θέλεις
μὴ κρᾶτα τοῦδ᾽ εἰσαῦθις ὄψεσθαί ποτε
μηδ᾽ ἄγγελον πέμψειν τιν᾽—εἰ δὲ μή, τέκνον,
ἄσπονδον ἤδη τοὐπ᾽ ἔμ᾽ ὀφλήσεις χόλον.
Να. αἰαῖ αἰαῖ·
ἔκανες, ὦ μᾶτερ, τοιαύτᾳ μ᾽ ἀρᾷ·
βλέφαρά μοι κνέφας σκότιον ἀμπέχει,
μελαίνᾳ τε συγκέκραμαι δύᾳ.

JTC

SELECTED WRITINGS

Part III · On English Literature

AND SELECTED JEUX D'ESPRIT

Shakespeare's *Macbeth*

JTC was following a Dragon School tradition in basing the theme of a sermon on a school play performed at the end of the summer term, in this instance in 1954.

It is dangerous to use Shakespeare as a theme for a sermon. Shakespeare would not have liked it and he will have his revenge on you by not, after all, giving you the moral that you hope to draw. I suppose the obvious moral warning for you in *Macbeth* is if in later life you are entertaining a great man for the night and you stand to gain by his death, do not murder him, however much your wife may try to persuade you, not even if you become king thereby! You will only rouse grave suspicions, and if you are at all sensitive, you will never have another quiet night. This is very true; but there needs no great genius, no great poetry to tell us that.

When I was your age, school preachers, after telling a rousing story, sometimes from the Bible, used to pause and then say 'What does this mean to us?' and then one knew there would be about fifteen minutes more to run. Unfortunately you know this story and I have already told you the most obvious moral from it, but I am expected to speak to you for more than two-and-a-half minutes!

'Would you rather know or not know the plot of a play or a story before reading it?' A good question that: in my experience most people under twelve say they would much rather not know the plot. What point in reading the story if you know already how it ends? (When I was a master at Rugby, we had a play-reading circle on Sunday evenings. I asked a boy who had not come before if he would care to read *Romeo and Juliet* with us. Very politely he refused, explaining that he had read the play already!) People over twelve (perhaps younger if they are young Dragons) sometimes say they would rather know the plot because, as one boy explained in a Winchester Scholarship paper, 'you can spot the clues better'. He was right; and when you are quite old – eighteen perhaps – you say 'I should prefer to know the story first, because then you can see how the author works out the plot'. I think that is very true.

Duncan is just saying these words

> He was a gentleman on whom I built
> An absolute trust . . .

Enter Macbeth, and Duncan goes on

> O worthiest cousin
> The sin of my ingratitude even now
> Was heavy on me.

How does that sound in our ears when we know that a few hours later Duncan will lie dead, murdered by the man he trusted? On which side lay the ingratitude then?

We know that the Castle of Glamis is to be the scene of a dark and bloody deed, but remember Duncan's words as he comes up to the gate:

> This Castle hath a pleasant seat; the air
> Nimbly and sweetly recommends itself
> Unto our gentle senses.

And finally, just before Duncan enters his room for his last night on earth, he sends to Lady Macbeth a message 'To the most kind hostess'. That means one thing to Duncan, another thing to us, and we feel frightened. And what of Lady Macbeth herself just after the murder, 'A little water clears us of this deed'. If we know our play we at once remember – 'All the perfumes of Arabia will not sweeten this little hand'. Or again:

> MACBETH Fail not our feast.
> BANQUO My lord, I will not.

Banquo dead keeps the engagement for Banquo living.

In such master strokes as these, there is no moral lesson: we never want to say 'this only shows that you ought or ought not to do so and so'. And yet, when we ponder on them they do give rise – even if we are quite young – to deep thoughts. We think about the outward appearance of things and their inward truth; we think of Duncan's opinion of Macbeth and Macbeth's true character: we say how dreadful that Duncan understood the real Macbeth so little and was his unsuspecting victim. But we know that such things happen in real life. Or again, we think how strange and terrible that Lady Macbeth in her high self-confidence should know her real self so little, and so soon after her moment of triumph shall be herself a victim. Whose victim? The victim of fate, some would say; or according to others, the victim of some mocking devil, who makes us say these confident things when all the time we are rotten at heart. This is not particularly a Christian idea. Indeed, if we think that the supreme power is a mocking, unkind spirit that enjoys deceiving men, that is a definitely un-Christian idea. But it is a deep thought and one you can ponder on for a long time. How do I know, I that am so happy, am so sure of myself, that my own weakness may not bowl me over and ruin my ambitions? Or, more subtly, that I may gain all my ambitions and then find that they are dust and ashes? Every now and then we ought to think about such matters, and the Sunday after *Macbeth* is a better time than most. We shall not regret it, and we shall come to admire Shakespeare more and more. That is my first point this morning.

All this aspect of the play is due to Shakespeare. The original story from which he took the plot has nothing of it. There Macbeth is just a strong man who was angry, with some justification, at Malcolm being declared the heir to the throne. And he killed Duncan in fury because he thought *he* had a better right to be king. Lady Macbeth is hardly mentioned at all. The original Macbeth was a bold, unscrupulous fellow, without much imagination and at first quite a good king. Shakespeare has added to him a deep sense of right and wrong and a strong imagination. Imagination means seeing with the eye of the mind things that other people cannot see with their ordinary eyes – like the dagger hanging in the air or the ghost of Banquo. Imagination is neither good nor bad in itself; it is a great power. Its goodness or badness depends on whether it shows us the light or the dark; and Macbeth's imagination was dark. If I was producing a film of this play, I should try to give some quality of darkness to all the scenes in the first two acts where Macbeth appears. Whatever the conditions outside were, it was dark in Macbeth's heart. It reminds one of that terrible short sentence in the Gospels, when Judas Iscariot left the Last Supper: 'And he went out and it was night'; night, because the sun had set, but deeper night in the heart of Judas. Once your imagination controls you, you are at its mercy. And if it is a dark imagination, it is stronger than all good principles and high resolutions. It is the pictures that you and I are forming in our hearts every day, unknown to anyone else, that are slowly and surely shaping our character and our fate. 'Keep diligently thy heart' says the Bible 'for out of it are the issues of life'. There is a second thing to think about.

And a third thing is this. When Macbeth has got what he wanted, what he plotted for, lied for and killed for, what does he make of it? The achievement of his ambitions makes him supremely unhappy – and unhappy at once. He does not get five minutes of happiness out of it.

> There is nothing serious in mortality:
> All is but toys.

That is said the moment after the murder is discovered. He is not just frightened of an avenger, like a man in a thriller, but bored and weary of life: irritable and tired, even of the things he used to love and admire. Even his wife means nothing to him in the end;

> The Queen, my Lord, is dead.
>
> She should have died hereafter
> There would have been a time for such a word.

I suppose he means: 'Really, she might have chosen a more suitable time. Why not wait to die until this whole, silly meaningless Play of Life is over and done with? The woman really ought not to have died just now: she missed her cue'. Can you imagine a more bitter and callous way of responding to the news of your wife's death? Then follows the greatest expression in English literature of the view that life is not worth while

> It is a tale
> Told by an idiot, full of sound and fury
> Signifying nothing.

After despair, bad temper: the innocent messenger he strikes, calls him 'liar and slave' and threatens to hang him up alive until he starves to death. Only one quality is left to Macbeth, brute courage like an animal at bay. 'They have tied me to a stake, I cannot fly.' He has cut himself off forever from the support that others can find in the thought of God overruling all – others like Banquo: 'In the great hand of God I stand and thence I fight'; or like Old Siward hearing of his son's death with all his wounds in front 'Why, then, God's soldier be he'. Such people as Banquo and Siward are still living in a world where life has some purpose, a world guided by God's providence in spite of loss and sin. Siward can be proud even in the loss of his son. Banquo felt the temptation, surely, to be a Macbeth, but resisted it. Noakes made this clear to us. After all, the Witches prophesied great things for him too. According to tradition, his descendants were Kings of Scotland right down through King Robert II to our own Stuarts. (Perhaps Banquo is the remote ancestor of our present Queen!) But Banquo finally followed the light and not the darkness: he was the Peter, not the Judas. He and the other chief characters serve as a contrast and a foil to Macbeth. The gracious, saintly Duncan, the fierce, down-right Macduff, even the perky, innocent little Macduff – they still have a world about them to enjoy or to fight for, undarkened by the secret thoughts of their own hearts. Compare Macduff's reaction to the news of *his* wife's death with Macbeth's response when they tell him the Queen is dead. These men lack Macbeth's terrifying power of imagination. They are smaller men than he, but they are much better men and much happier.

Are you always the better and happier for lacking imagination? Surely not. Lady Macbeth is as bad as anyone could be, but she had very little imagination and no sympathy with it in other people. 'We must kill this old man and then you will be King and I shall be Queen. Why don't you go and *do* it instead of mouthing all this poetry? ("Infirm of purpose, give me the daggers") 'I would have done the thing myself if the old King had not had a curious look of my father as he slept.' Macbeth, surely, would have given us some memorable lines if he had seen a resemblance to *his* father in the sleeping Duncan. Lady Macbeth seems to note it as a mere curiosity. Macbeth had a fierce struggle with his conscience, and his conscience was never wholly defeated. It survived to take all the zest and joy out of his life after he had done the deed, but he dies bravely in the daylight. His wife crushed down her conscience: no doubts, no qualms, no remorse. But wait! We are forgetting the greatest single scene in the whole of Shakespeare, when she walks in her sleep. Her conscience was killed, but it went rotten inside her and set up a poisonous infection, which would not let her rest and at length killed her. In the end, the suffering of Lady Macbeth is just as great as her husband's, and her death less noble.

Well, what is the moral of this tremendous play? It has no moral, I think. Shakespeare as always looks at life with sympathy and imagination, seeming to say 'Here are two characters in a bloodthirsty old story - one full of ambition with a Christian conscience and a poet's imagination; the other, equally ambitious, with no conscience and very little imagination. Between them they achieved exactly what they plotted for, and I will show you what happened to them afterwards. Think about this story, following in my footsteps, and you will understand more about man and life, and about the Being that men call God.'

Scott's *Old Mortality*

Because of his well-known love of the work of Sir Walter Scott, JTC was commissioned to write a series of new introductions to Scott's novels republished by Collins in the 1950s.

In *Old Mortality* we find Scott at the height of his powers. During the year 1816 when it was published, he was still confident and happy and his health had not yet given way under the burden of an over-busy life. In this book, he knew his period as intimately as he knew the Scotland of his own day: he knew his characters and had talked with some of their descendants: and he knew the country. The background is always important in the Scottish novels, and this is especially true of *Old Mortality*. Scott felt for Lanarkshire a particular affection, and it was there that his imagination wandered even when, as a dying man, he was visiting Naples many years later.

The idea of the story came to him from a conversation with Joseph Train, the antiquary, who, breakfasting one day with Scott, noticed on the wall a romantic portrait of Claverhouse, presented hitherto by most Scottish historians as a ruffian and a villain. Scott defended his character, and Train suggested that he might well be made the hero of a Scottish romance: and what if the story were told as if from the lips of 'Old Mortality'? This was the nickname given to Robert Paterson (not Peter Paterson as Lockhart has it) a maker of tombstones who spent many years of a wandering life renewing the inscriptions on the graves of the Covenanters. Scott had seen him in a kirkyard more than twenty years before – just the kind of character to set his imagination working. And so the seed of the story was sown, though 'Old Mortality' only appears in the introduction, nor is Claverhouse the central or even the most memorable figure.

It was an immediate success. Lord Holland, asked for his opinion, replied 'Opinion! We did not one of us go to bed last night: nothing slept but my gout'. For many readers to this day it remains the favourite in the whole series; as Andrew Lang used to remark, whatever else you put first, *Old Mortality* comes second. It shows few of Scott's weaknesses. Admittedly the lovers, as always, are stagey. Scott could never compass the language of passion between gentleman and lady, either in his books nor, one suspects, in his own life. But Miss Bellenden's letter pleading for a last-minute rescue of her lover and smuggled out of the castle by night has a lighter tone than many such epistles, the whole point being huddled up into a Postscript! Morton in love is a man of straw, but Morton in action is better than most of the heroes, not, at any rate, 'a sneaking piece of imbecility', which was the phrase that Scott, so disarmingly, applied to Edward Waverley.

To some readers the introduction might seem a weakness. Why are all these imaginary sources – the Landlord, Jedediah Cleishbotham, etc. – piled up before we get to the story? To lovers of Scott this familiar piece of mystification is endearing – a childlike trait which he never quite outgrew; and at this time the 'mystifying' mood seems to have been strongly upon him. He changed his publisher; the novel was not ascribed on the title page to 'The Author of Waverley', and a long anonymous review which the book received in *The Quarterly* was in part by Scott himself.

But when this has been said, there is left Scott at his strongest. We have the solid grasp and the bold presentment of large public events, equally vivid in the councils of the great and as they are reflected in the taverns and cottages of the humble. This power of seeing the big and the little together is a quality which distinguishes Scott among the novelists. As Bagehot said, if Scott had described the panic aroused by the Young Pretender's race to Derby, we should have had a picture of the Bank of England paying out money in sixpences and the loves of the cashier. Moreover, in *Old Mortality* we have pre-eminently the fair-mindedness of Scott. The religious wars of Scotland were long over but their spirit was still bitterly alive. As soon as the book was published, Dr Thomas McCrie, the biographer of John Knox, launched an attack on Scott's lack of sympathy towards the national faith of Scotland, himself displaying some of the intemperate zeal which he criticized Scott for finding in the Covenanters.[1] If one regards these men as a Church regards its accredited Saints, one can understand the indignation of Dr McCrie. But if they are to be counted as fallible men, narrow in outlook though admirable in their devotion to a cause, one can only praise Scott's realism and sympathy. He shows us their fondness for theological dispute in the hour of trial and their love of tyranny in success; but we are left in no doubt of their burning faith or of the readiness, in the best of them, to suffer for the cause. Among these ministers of religion, none of them naturally congenial to Scott's tolerant heart, there is wide variety: the canny Poundtext, the windy Kettledrummle, Mucklewrath the ecstatic visionary, and the true martyr Macbriar. No one fresh from reading the trial and death of Macbriar could maintain that Scott lacked all sympathy for the Covenanters.

Scott saw these things as an historian, but the history here does not obtrude itself. We do not begin *Old Mortality* with a long introductory slab of history, such as has often blunted younger appetites in the other novels. The beginning is swift and eventful: the comic catastrophe of Goose Gibbie leads quickly to the matchless scene at the inn, where the two sides that are to conflict throughout the book are found in sharp collision, watched by Niel Blane, the landlord, careful to offend neither side; and there we are given our first sight of Balfour of Burley, fresh from the murder of the Archbishop, proposing his mysterious and

[1]See an essay *Walter Scott and Thomas McCrie* by R.S. Rait in *Sir Walter Scott To-day* (Constable: 1932).

ominous toast. Thereafter one vivid picture succeeds another: battle scenes and night-pieces (there is much darkness in *Old Mortality*) and the siege of the Castle, until we reach a climax in the moorland hut, where Morton waits for the clock to reach the hour of midnight and bring him to his death. It was bold of Scott to introduce a lapse of some years before we reach the closing scenes. This conclusion makes for a more finished historical survey and it might well have spoilt the story, but this it certainly does not do. In the earlier chapters there is something of Homer in the battle-scenes and the defiant challenges in mid-field: in the narrative of Morton's return one remembers the Odyssey. The master moves unrecognized among his old servants; the delightful Jenny Dennison is quick to discover him but says no word. Ailie Wilson the old housekeeper, the 'grave dame' of the Homeric household, treats him as a stranger, until the dog (a true Scott touch) leaps up at him like Argus at his master Odysseus, and Ailie's eyes are opened: 'God guide us, it is my ain bairn'. And that is not the end: there is still the tremendous interview with Balfour of Burley in his fastness, where Morton only saves himself by a heroic leap across the ravine, reminding one of the leap of Albert Lee in *Woodstock*.

Here is fine story-telling to delight 'the young of all ages', and Scott's style rises to the demands of every high point in the story – the death of Bothwell, the rescue of Morton from the hut, the last foray between Balfour and his pursuers. In the Scottish dialogue, the author's craft never fails him, whether it be the cultivated Scots of Lady Margaret at the Castle or the broad dialect of Cuddie and his mother. Even in English, Scott rises to real eloquence when Claverhouse speaks, as in his noble words on death and honour. In this novel, beyond all others, Scott shows his command of that particular brand of Scottish eloquence, particularly, in the Scotland of the seventeenth century, the denunciation and the sermon, steeped in the phrasing and the imagery of the Hebrew prophets. It is, no doubt, a sort of pastiche and at times gently satirical, but when he wishes, the author can breathe spirit into the dry bones. In Macbriar's sermon on the evening of the battle we have a discourse which needs to be read aloud if it is to be fully appreciated.

The hero, Henry Morton, is not a character to rouse our affection though, as has been remarked, he is less insipid than many other of Scott's *jeunes premiers*. A man of honour, he suffers from divided loyalties. Like Walter Scott himself, he felt the attraction of all that was old and traditional and truly national, but his reason approved the cause of order and good government. It is the same kind of conflict, though in different circumstances, that we find in *Rob Roy* or *Redgauntlet*. In *Old Mortality* the division runs along a religious line. Scott was a loyal Presbyterian, but he loved the beauty and the seemliness of the English liturgy. (When Morton stands bound before his enemies in the hut, they overhear the prayers he is murmuring to himself in his extremity: they are drawn from the Book of Common Prayer, and this whets their indignation to fury.) Scott allows the story to end happily though not conventionally. It is not Evandale, the romantic aristocrat, who gains the lady's hand, but Morton. A schoolboy wrote to Scott in later years 'Oh, Sir Walter, how could you take the lady from the gallant cavalier and give her to the prick-eared Covenanter?' Morton is the central figure not Claverhouse, as Scott may at first have intended. In truth the figure of Claverhouse was one which always haunted Scott's imagination. Who that has ever read Wandering Willie's Tale in *Redgauntlet* can forget the vision of Claverhouse at the ghostly revel among the fierce and dissolute spirits of his boon companions: 'And there was Claverhouse, as beautiful as when he lived, with his long dark curled locks streaming down over his laced buff-coat . . . He sat apart from them all and looked at them with a melancholy haughty countenance, while the rest hallooed and sung and laughed that the room rang'? It is a picture of high romance, based no doubt on the picture that hangs today on the staircase at Abbotsford; perhaps Scott felt unable to bring Claverhouse wholly down to earth. In drawing the character of Balfour of Burley, Scott had no such compunction. He is magnificently done, brave, masterful, bigoted, with a fanaticism that easily turned to religious mania and visions of the Evil One; he has in him all the best and the worst of Puritanism.

Old Mortality is a grim book, grimmer than many of its fellows, and the light relief is mostly in the same key. But how good it is! Other authors might have given us something like Balfour or Lady Margaret or even Claverhouse, but Mause Headrigg and her son Cuddie are peculiarly Scott's own. Only a man of his wide humanity could, in real life, have known such people well enough to hear them talking unabashed. The division in poor Mause's heart between mother-love and her devotion to The Covenant comes out with a dozen deft and delightful touches; and through all her speeches there sounds the native eloquence of 'the people of a Book – and that Book the Bible'. Mause must have been a sore trial to live with and a terrible bore. But it is the privilege of a novelist, like Jane Austen with Miss Bates, to portray an obvious bore who in the story is never boring. We laugh at Mause, but we end by loving her. And as for poor simple Cuddie – after all, it is he who rescues the hero in the nick of time. Jenny Dennison, light-hearted, flirtatious and loyal, is one of a long line of free-spoken young waiting-women in the novels and comedies of English literature. There is none better. I have even heard a good Scotsman say – oh heresy! – that he would rather have had her to wife than Jeannie Deans.

Virginia Woolf's *Between the Acts*

This letter to his sister-in-law, the composer Elizabeth Maconchy, was dashed off one evening on paper torn from a school exercise book, at a time when JTC was living in a lonely farmhouse beyond the Bromyard Downs, where Westminster was in evacuation to Herefordshire during the war.

May 10 1941

Hill House Farm
Bromyard: Herefordshire

My dear Betty

Here I am, alone, like you; & I feel inclined to break a lance with you in reference of V. Woolf's last book 'Between the Acts'. So this letter will have no practical importance whatever, & you can put it aside till you next have to stand in a butter queue. But I thought the few Reviews I saw of it didn't do justice to it either. I know you're fond of V.W., &, mind you, I'm not putting this anywhere near The Waves or To The Lighthouse: but to someone who likes her mind, it seems very relevant, besides being good fun in itself. I mean, anyone lecturing on her couldn't afford to ignore it, as I believe they could The Years. What I find in it first – and this of course is a matter of taste – is what my dear Jane [Christie not Austen!] calls '*Great Fun*'. That's a side of V.W. which her earnest interpreters seem to me to forget: there wasn't much of it in The Waves. But she has, hasn't she, a real and exquisite wit: the sort of wit that can come out in Parody & in grave descriptions of absurdities. As to Parody, I thought the whole of the Elizabethan Scene was superb in B. the A: Eliza Clark as Q.E., on the soap box with the ruff which won't stick on: & her horrific Webster-like stuff, half funny half mad. It carries on from the best bits of Orlando – in fact Orlando is what it's most akin to throughout; and then the Congreve stuff, the old harridan match-making, with her maid, called of course Deborah. You may not like this sort of thing: but I do think V.W. did. Look at the Common Reader: isn't the very first essay on Elizabethan Drama? laughing at it & loving it, for its wonder & dressing up & its gusto & its childishness. (She liked dressing-up herself: wasn't she in the famous Sultan of Zanzibar hoax on the Man of War about 1910?) And think of Orlando again, in fact read it again. It improves with keeping. The Reviews remember, treated it with absurd gravity: of course the deep-down ideas are serious, but the whole thing at one level is a firework display of intellectual high-spirits, making fun of all the pillars of Society, including Time & Space. Now there's quite a bit of *that* in B. the A., of the V.W. of The C. Reader & Orlando. I don't think it's an entirely superficial streak, either: this wild & fanciful humour. It reminded me often of Hamlet himself: taking a conventional phrase and repeating it gravely till it sounds funny. Near madness, as it was in Hamlet. She did, I gather, kill herself because she was afraid of madness. Look at the gramophone, on p. 218 foll. & p. 220–21 you get one of the underlying pictures of The Waves 'jazzed' as it were. And *then*, the comic parson; good, I thought, but a little less fastidious than her usual standard. But of course this wild fanciful literary working strain is only one in the book: & not the most important. (But it definitely made me laugh, &, so to say, clap my hands.) The whole structure of the book is extraordinarily characteristic, if one can use that word of a writer whose books are so individual and peculiar each to itself.

All understanding of her of course (the preceptor begins!) must start from 'Mr Bennett & Mrs Brown' the pamphlet which no doubt you know. Novelists want to give you LIFE at its most living: how? Dingy suburbs in the Potteries, says Bennett, with every stain & wrinkle & loose tile & dirty bus-ticket put in. No, says V.W., for me purely in the twistings & flickerings of the mind: the wild rush of images, the chance words, the random tunes, that go tearing through a mind as a preliminary to any action or any remark. And on *this* level, there isn't the same hard distinction between Reality (bricks & mortar in the Potteries) & Fiction or Imaginings. On *this* level, Hamlet is as real as Mr Psmith: nay, realler because deeper & more self-consistent. (Plato wd. agree there.) So Books & Pictures & wild fantasies have all got to take their place alongside Tea & Dinner & "Two lumps?" etc. You remember Lily in To the Lighthouse how her Tree (symbol of the difficulty of her Art) kept popping up at dinner: & oh – best of all – Mr Ramsay switching away at the shrubs, trying to get just that one stage further in his philosophy which would make him a *great* philosopher: get him down to P & Q, not simply O. O was lurking in the azaleas, & P *just* hidden there, & then it fled. That's rather irrelevant: only just illustrating what I mean by the mental & the material being kept in the same plane. Now this plane, & this whole method, involves one in saying such the deuce of a lot about the 'events' of six hours or so, that one can quite easily fill a book with it – with an exquisitely minute picture – of life shimmering and pulsating between 3 or 4 minds. Is this really life? No it isn't; because it's virtually *static*. Already in Mrs. Dalloway the striking of a clock is invested with great significance. And in a moment one's up against the problem that fascinated V.W. for all the 2nd half of her life: TIME. *What is* something, somebody? Not what it or he or she is to-day: but long long before that – what 'he' was when his great-grandmother was in the womb herself. The strains of male & female in him; of father & mother, of remote traditions. Hence, of course, 'Orlando'. Her dearest friend – V. Sackville West: who, what, was she? She was a part of all that she had been, centuries before her birth. In fact, that's the answer *there* to this Time Problem: The Reality of something is found in the whole sweep of time that has produced it, not in the here & now, only. In To The Lighthouse, Time was still a stumbling-block; & it was relegated, unfairly but very beautifully, to a chapter all by itself called Time Passes. She was aware that in the first ? 250 pages, it hadn't passed. The Waves solved the problem in a different way, the very carefully selected, very exquisitely divided series of successive Views, stripped of everything but the minds of the people.

This business – to most of us so simple – of lots of things happening *together* seems to have tormented her terrifically sensitive mind. She cdn't rise to them *all*. An extreme case of the child leaving Peter Pan & hardly believing that the buses have gone on down Piccadilly just the same.

You remember in A Room of One's Own: 'she looked out on the Orchestral Strand: and it was clear, only too clear, that no one there had recently been reading Antony & Cleopatra' (quoting from memory: but I think 'orchestral' is right). – Well, I think B. the A. picked up all *this* thread in a most interesting way. Time – once again one must somehow get a whole historical sweep in, to give the reality of England on a summer day: & the Pageant idea allows the 'real' & the 'historic' to interpenetrate: you remember when the real cows do their part in the incidental effects. And it ends with the fierce almost Swiftian last Act when the players come rushing on with bits of cracked mirror, "Last Act: ourselves". And then the whole medley of confused impressions – near madness if you let it go too far – which a very sensitive mind receives every minute of the day. That's wonderfully given now & then: in fact, as I said, it's nearly mad. And I think in a sense she was nearly mad when she became as sensitive as that: mad with Hamlet's madness. And – is this worth adding? – like Shakespeare's folk who are 'on the border line' obsessed occasionally with sex: Lear, Hamlet & Ophelia etc. I won't stress this, which may be rot: but there was a touch or two about rape in this book which wasn't quite V.W's fastidious aristocratic style.

'Yes, yes' you say, if you've read as far, 'but what about bills, & the lady who only speaks in poetry, & the rather footling love-story?' I know: I can't quite get that into focus: there are always bits in V.W. I definitely don't understand. But Miss La Trobe is an old friend: the Artist side of V.W. – whose whole life is an effort to "get it right" & "get it across", with her pregnant failures, & furies at the Ox-like British Public and her rare gleams of success: cp. Lily, & Orlando as eternal author of The Oak Tree. Orlando again gives one a parallel to the slightly tiresome Isa. The sensitive cultivated mind, so soaked in other peoples' words & The Hundred Best Books (oh, classical head masters beware!) that everything they see or think suggests a quotation: in V.W. an exquisitely appropriate one (& if she can't think of one, like W. Scott she makes one up!) cp. – from a different angle – Bernard in The Waves. I really mustn't go on any longer. I won't apologise to you, Betty, for hurling all this at you. Dont take it seriously or acknowledge it. But as soon as I began to write, I knew it had to come: & one thing I'm sure of – you wont give it a disdainful glance & say 'Highbrow!'

V.W. is more to my taste on Sun. evening than Smollett or even The Queen broadcasting to America.

Yours ever
JTC

Mrs LeFanu
at Downton Castle
Downton-on-the-Rock
Shropshire

About the Art of Knowing the Young Men

A parody published in the *Oxford Magazine* on 31 May 1962.

Now with regard to the knowing of the youths by the dons, as Aristotle might put it, let us begin by saying that this is from of old an activity characteristic in theory of most universities, but in fact especially of Oxford and Cambridge; for at many universities, not only in far countries but in our own, the teachers on the one hand live not in colleges but at a distance from the youths (and without proximity it is hard to know men), and on the other hand the number itself of the youths now stretches out towards the infinite, and a tutor cannot know according to friendship more than a limited number, though the famous Phryne was said to have had a thousand followers but not according to friendship.

And since every activity must have its proper end, let us posit that the end of knowing the young men is, by understanding their minds and dispositions, to train them better. It being therefore the virtue of a trainer to train well, he will strive to know those whom he trains; and also through his knowing the youths it will happen that the youths will come to know him (and if he is good, good; if not, not) though perhaps they will not know him in the same way or with equal accuracy, like the young man who believed his tutor to be an aged bachelor until by chance he met his grandson at the Bump Supper.

Knowing the youths therefore being a university activity with a view to training them better, it will take more forms in particular than admit of accurate description, owing to the great diversity of mankind, and even more now than formerly, in as much as once both teachers and taught had the same sort of education among the well-to-do, but now many of both kinds - and in my opinion rightly - are children of stonemasons or clerks or it may be of confectioners.

But in general let us distinguish several ways of this kind of knowing, on the one hand by chance and on the other hand of set purpose. Chance-meetings may depend on the situation of college-rooms, Chapel seating or, according to the old proverb, a Nod in the Quad; which meetings the youth indeed supposes to be more a matter of chance than they really are, but for the tutor they reveal the youth's character and can lay a foundation for friendship. And this is true even if a man is not the youth's appointed teacher, for our grandfathers have often said that when young they knew the tutors irrespective of the special study of each, telling how such men would first accost them not even knowing their names, and soon would see much of them not only in Term, but would study with them on holidays, teaching also as a side-issue to fish or to scale mountains. But nowadays many tutors know only their own pupils, and if they do recognize any others by sight, they do not know them as is necessary with a view to friendship, nor when, nor where.

Among meetings of set purpose we must include tutorial instruction which could be called a mercenary meeting (the man being hired for this very purpose) and I deal with it in another part of my treatise; but also all forms of deliberate entertainment whether the tutor be host or guest. As to watching the youths at sport, for the tutor at least, this is of set purpose especially in winter, but of chance as regards the youth, and so it may be termed a mixed sort of meeting. Not but what it can contribute no little towards a tutor's knowledge of the youth of what kind he is, as was proved by the young man who being rather slow at French was very fast at football, of whom his tutor prophesied a low result indeed in examinations, but high success in after life, guessing both rightly; for the youth becoming a Minister of the Crown was able to benefit his college and especially his old tutor as having not judged him solely on his learning.

Now as to entertainments and social meetings, there are in the first place the four chief meals of the day; but we will pass over the breakfast-party though this was formerly popular, since compared to our ancestors we are more surly early. After luncheon they will not linger long because probably at least one will leave for the palaestra or the river and the rest will follow, except on Sundays; just as after tea many will attend their tutors, and on Sundays there will be Chapel whose bell even if it is no longer a summons to pray is at least a signal to disperse. Dinner parties may stretch out to midnight, or even beyond if the men live in, and such parties are best kept for those with whom the tutor is well acquainted, so that he can end the party at will, without incurring a charge of boorishness. At all such gatherings if limited in number, the don can talk to each by himself and remember his name at least for a little time, but in squashes for twenty or thirty he will run the risk of confusing Callias with Callicles, which will be forgiven if he does it once, but not thrice, though if he does it nine times, as happened in the case of the Professor of Palaeontology, it may be reckoned both laughable and delightful. Moreover in squashes the don and his wife will not so much hold conversation as make it, and he will say the same things to different youths, or even to the same youths, escaping his own notice so doing, but not theirs.

Better than these are College Societies, attended sometimes by twenty youths in a room designed for two; here if the don can be present on a fair pretext, he can learn much, and more by keeping silent than if he speaks himself, but though he is placed in the more comfortable of the two chairs (the rest meanwhile reclining on the floor) he should leave fairly early, praying that the youths will continue to argue till a late hour about the Gods, the nature of Justice and the chance of Immortality.

Best of all is when the youths come in to the man's room unasked, for the mere pleasure of his society, but probably this happens to only a few dons owing to a gift of nature or a certain divine chance.

There remains over a quantity of questions about these things – for example, whom especially it behoves to know the youths and how and when; for the Chaplain indeed will know all a little, but the good most; while the Dean knows all fairly well, but the wicked first; whereas the professor is not bound to know any one person, his crimes or his merits, but only the mysteries of his own particular wisdom, though for this very reason he can gain the confidence of some better than the rest of the teachers. For the present however, about the knowing of the young men, its true end and its proper methods, let this much have been said.

Dogberry's Local Defence Force – 1940

Westminster School was evacuated to Lancing when war began in 1939: JTC and several of his staff joined the improvised 'Local Defence Volunteers' before the Home Guard was officially organised.

Good neighbour Carleton, an thou hast not a pretty wit, an' thou hast not the prick on't as well as any man in Illyria, call me not Scholemaster – in sooth, no sooner did I clap eyes on this Master Wainwright than I thought "twill be the mercy of God' quoth I to neighbour Pumphrey that was sitting nigh – "twill be the mercy of God if this old sparker prove not a damp squib: for has he not a nose as blunt as a broken pen' – 'an' that he hath' quoth Pumphrey. 'An' hath a' not', quoth I, 'a wild roving glance, and a great viol da gambo voice' quoth I, 'like a Parson at Martinmas when he hath colic?'

Welladay, whether it was the summer drowse, or whether it was yon sherris sack, good neighbour Carleton, I fell asleep incontinent; and on a sudden Master Pumphrey gave me a great nudge, and quotha, ''Tis time to go Sir John'. So we went our ways: and I was fain to question friend Pumphrey what the Ancient had said while I lay asleep.

'Oh', said he 'he told every man of us we were on the King's business and we should wear the King's livery, only there be no liveries for us; we must keep a sharp look out at midnight, but above all we must show no lights; for we should always know these plaguey parapet-men in the dark, for they were clad in green with zeppelins to fasten their doublets withal, and steel helmets atop, while our men wore no helmets, but perchance they would anon: and even so the foe might wear no helmets to make us mistake them: so you will always know them' he said. And if they gave not back the password, we must shoot them dead, by'r Lady; and then bear them off to good Sergeant Williams of the Watch, but above all to keep them with us all the night, with our bayonets to their rumps, only we had no bayonets.

And we must circle them round on every side, above all keeping close together, because there would be such din in the air a man could scarce whisper to his neighbour: so if we fell apart we must e'en hollo'. So I thanked neighbour Pumphrey for that he had made all clear, and bade him good night.

Apologia

A letter in verse form addressed to the Secretary of the Athenaeum during the latter part of the war, after another member had complained – also in verse form – about being disturbed at night in an underground shelter provided for fire-watchers when off duty.

Dear Mr Secretary
I blush with shame
That all through me your bunks should lose their name
For comfort, safety, undisturbed repose
And every boon that every member knows
He need but raise a casual eye to see 'em

Provided *gratis* at The Athenaeum.
Hear but one plea – if I may make so bold.
'The solemn tongue of midnight' scarce had tolled,
When I descending from my lofty attic
Girt up my loins to leap – all acrobatic,
Up to the perch – I quote your own kind tongue –
'Reserved for those still active, and still young'.
Mark now my words: at that still hour so dread
The bunk below lay all unvisited;
There was the pillow vacant, virgin, neat;
No stertorous form disturbed the unruffled sheet.
Day broke, and rousing from my slumbers chain
Lightly I leapt to find the floor again.
Ah! What was this, recumbent vague and vast
That, all unknown to me, ere night had passed
Snatching some hectic moments of repose,
Now heaved its bulk to meet my trembling toes?
A man! I knew it by the muffled curse.
I fled, lest after bad should follow worse.
Guilty, at breakfast time I scanned the throng:
Who the celebrity had suffered wrong?
A Judge, a General? Prelate, Priest, or Peer?
No face looked more than commonly austere.
Little I dreamt 'neath Hills's[1] glance serene
Lurked outraged dignity and secret spleen.
My plea is made; but, in the name of Pity,
Let not our brawlings vex your great Committee.
On me alone be laid the due disgrace:
The tribe of teachers are a touchy race.
Note, Fellow members – and none more than I –
That sleeping Hills, like dogs, are better left to lie.

[1] The offended member!

To Arthur Norrington, Knight, 1968

How rarely now the courtiers who compile
A New Year's Honours List can raise a smile -
Smile not of irony that notes the name
Of some determined devotee of Fame,
Nor yet a smile of pity apt to grace
M.P's too sensitive to stand the pace,
Promoted sadly to Another Place;
Rather the smile for one we loved and knew -
Kindly, clear-headed, humorous and true,
Pillar of Oxford, unafraid to scan
Wider horizons - yet a 'College Man';
Ready of speech to charm a Gaudy dinner,
To curb a colleague, or to chide a sinner.
Books were his business once, and still his pleasure,
He positively *reads* them in his leisure!
No donnish pedant he; sure 'some divinity'
(See Hamlet) 'shaped his end' - to reign at Trinity.
Wise dons! rewarded in their shrewd selection;
There's not a soul regretted that Election.
Nought see we in the record here to deprecate or cancel or
Regret - the very model of an up-to-date Vice Chancellor.
So let us greet Sir Arthur in due style
And title - not without a lurking smile
To hear he earns the knightly accolade
'For contributions to the Export Trade'!
Go on and prosper that 'Sir Arthur' hight:
Thus Oxford will acclaim its latest Knight.
Here among friends pray take this tribute from us,
But still remain our one and only THOMAS.

SELECTED WRITINGS

Part IV · On Religion and Christianity

How should the Bible be read?

A radio talk of the late 1940s

There can be no single answer to the question. The Bible is bound in a single volume, but in no other sense is it a single book. It is a library, as various as if you bound together historical chronicles, ballads and a bit of Milton with a collection of sermons, letters and lyrics, and some ancient laws about health and naturalization. Under this variety lies the great unity expressed by the one word, God. The more you study the Bible the more you grasp the unity, but if you don't appreciate the variety first, you may go to the Bible making the wrong pictures and asking the wrong questions. The Bible is more than a library in itself: for most of us it is a separate literature, a literature extending in time further than from Alfred to the present day, and in space from Babylon to Rome.

If one asks, 'Why read the Bible at all?' the answer is that, even for those to whom religion means little, the Bible is unique in its beauty and wisdom, and its experience of the hearts of men. The man who does not know the Bible is like a man who has never seen the sea.

The task of reading the Bible is not made easier by having the whole presented in tiny print, peppered with small numbers and letters, and cut up in into thousands of verses. Some religious people still think it almost irreverent to read the Scriptures without this familiar paraphernalia: it is more irreverent to ignore them altogether, as most people do nowadays. To the student, references are indispensable: for the plain man, who would like to take up his Bible again, it is better to start with some more easily legible edition such as is provided by 'The World's Classics' or 'The Bible as Literature'.

Whatever the edition, read it aloud. All poetry, and indeed almost all literature except sheer information, should be read aloud.

For the greater passages of the Prophets – 'Arise, shine, for thy light is come and the glory of the Lord is risen upon thee' – the mere printed words are no more than a musical score which will not come to life for most of us until it is sounded. We are re-entering the age of the spoken word; the radio, itself as great a landmark in the history of civilization as the invention of printing, is bringing the sound of words back to its rightful place. Reading the Bible aloud, to yourself or to a family audience, doubles the beauty of the language; and the tongue is less tempted than the eye to 'skip'.

But unless you know your way about a Bible, some guidance is good, to begin with. Read, say, the story of Joseph, or the story of David and Absalom 'extensively', at a sitting. Whatever the 'moral' may be, such stories have the grandeur and simplicity of great literature, and these things also come of God. In a film-ridden, press-ridden world they 'disinfect the soul'. As for intensive reading, the trouble to-day is that few people read anything 'intensively'. Only children, with instinctive good sense, will read the same story, or hear it read, over and over again. To them it is not a mere story: it is a part of their experience as real as Nanny or the cat.

So with Bible-reading: its purpose is not just to read, but to make its thoughts the warp and woof of one's own life, like a friendship: 'to hear them, read, mark, learn and *inwardly digest*', like the food by which we grow. Professor Burkitt, incidentally, used to maintain that those familiar words should run 'to hear them read' - read by someone else: reading to yourself was not a common skill when that collect was composed.

To this 'intensive' reading there need be no limit. Take some familiar passage, like the parable of the Prodigal Son: study it with any commentaries you can find, ancient or modern; with the help, too, that the painters can give you. No one who has seen the picture of the forgiving father in the Rembrandt print could ever forget it. Then, when it is becoming too familiar, read it in a different language or a different English version. New Versions give one a shock, but they make one think. This is especially true of St. Paul's Epistles: 'let him that sheweth mercy do it with cheerfulness', says St. Paul. Moffat has 'the sick-visitor should be cheerful'. The Authorised Version suffers probably from more mistranslation in the Old Testament than in the New: but its total effect is more misleading in the New than in the Old. Much of the Old Testament is archaic or poetical in tone, and is fairly represented by elaborate Tudor English. The New Testament, and particularly the Gospels, is not. The language of Jesus is the simple idiom of everyday. 'He began talking to them': that has not the same implication in our ears as 'he spake'.

For the Old Testament the Revised Version is the best: it avoids the errors of the A.V., but does not, like one modern version, render 'God saw that it was good' by 'God saw that the result was satisfactory'!

The final reward of 'intensive' reading is to have it by heart. There the words will remain, ready to flash out with a power to console or exhort that no other words can give. Readers of Prothero's 'The Psalms in Human Life' will recall how the Psalmist all through the centuries has 'spoken to men's condition'. When they rejoiced over a great deliverance, or were waiting for the executioner; when they were besieged in the Indian Mutiny, or dying lonely in Africa, the Psalmist had the right words. 'He had been there before', as Scott Holland used to say.

There are, in conclusion, two classes of Bible-reader in particular to consider. First, those - a dwindling company - who have never given up the practice of their fathers and grandfathers, and read the Bible straight through chapter by chapter. Fine lives of duty and devotion have been based on that habit, but it has its dangers especially if we want to transmit a love of the Bible to the younger generation. The old tradition assumed that all the Bible was literally true, and that all parts of it were of equal spiritual value. Most of us believe neither of those things to-day.

The Bible represents a developing search for God through many stages of primitive outgrown religion: for the student all these stages fall into place when he grasps the whole, and his discovery of the grand climax in Jesus of Nazareth is the more precious for the way the student has come. But we can no longer take a text from the early history of Israel and act on it as a law for to-day. Thence come witch-hunting and persecution. There are more people who hold such a view of the Bible than one would suppose until one has spoken about these subjects on the wireless. They are treating the Bible as an idol: they think of the living, expanding spirit of Religion as a thing fixed and static. But that spirit cannot be imprisoned in a book any more than it could in a molten image. Lessing said that if an angel came one night and offered him in one hand Truth and in the other hand the search for Truth and bade him choose, he would choose the search.

Secondly, there are those who have already from conscientious teachers the 'latest views' about the authenticity of the Scriptures: they have in schoolboy phrase 'done' the Bible, and perhaps have gained a Distinction in the Higher Certificate for their pains. They have read anything worth reading in it, they feel, and now they can put it aside together with other books of school and childhood. In truth, they are giving up the Bible at the very point where it might mean most to them. They will find difficulties there and inconsistencies: two accounts of the Creation in *Genesis*, two accounts apparently of Noah's Flood: history from one angle in *Kings*, and the same history from another angle in *Chronicles*. But these things make the study of the Old Testament more worth while, not less: the greater the variety on the surface, the more impressive is the fundamental unity – the idea of God. Similarly in the New Testament, the three first evangelists give differing accounts of the same event: few people realize, until they have tried it, what a fascinating game it is, putting it at its lowest, to compare and investigate the differences. In the words of Jesus Himself there are many apparent contradictions to be reconciled: He said 'My peace I leave with you', and He also said 'I come not to bring peace, but a sword'. The realization of such differences and what they imply marks, not the moment at which to give up study of the Bible, but the moment at which to begin all over again.

The Greatest of These

Four talks broadcast on the 'Forces Programme' on consecutive Sundays in April 1942, the first Sunday being Easter Day.

1. The Greeks had no word for it

The question was asked a year or two ago in a competition what the competitors thought were the most important, most far-reaching two minutes in the history of the world.

There were many interesting answers: the moment when Columbus sighted America, the moment at Waterloo when

Wellington gave the general order to advance, and so on. What would you say if you were asked that question this afternoon? I know what my answer would be. The moment very early in the morning in that cold starlit garden when Jesus turned him about and said 'Mary' and she cried 'Master'. For at that moment the news was out – the greatest news in history, the news that Jesus wasn't dead after all, the news that changed eleven frightened and despairing men into eleven brave leaders, the news that turned the world upside down: the old news – that yet must be learned anew by everyone who wants to understand the greatest force in men's lives, either then or now. That's how I see it. What would *you* say? Some would agree. Others would say: 'That's all a fable, a fairy-story. Men don't rise from the dead. The age of miracles is past: and I doubt if it ever existed.' All right: but even so you can't get away from the historical effects of that great moment of the first Easter Day, even if you disbelieve in the fact. The day before – yesterday, so to speak – no men could have felt more disappointed and disillusioned than those followers of Jesus. From to-day – Easter Day – onwards, they were utterly new men, feeling there was nothing they couldn't tackle and couldn't achieve: but even they would hardly have dared to imagine the effects they did achieve – they and their followers.

What was the new thing that began to run its glorious course in the world that first Easter morning? Christianity? Well, not Christianity with the outward signs as we know them to-day. A Church with a tower? Those early Christians met in private houses or in dark basements to escape from persecution. Bishops, Priests and Deacons? It was many years before *they* were fully organized. The Gospels? They weren't written yet. All these came later as the result of a New Spirit: a Spirit – that intangible something, that is yet more important than anything you can touch or see: the spirit of a ship, we say, or a regiment: what the soul is to the body. What was this new Spirit? You can put it in one short word. Love. A very simple word: a word used every day by infants, schoolboys, Bishops, crooners (too much by crooners, for me!): and a very difficult word just because it is used in so many senses: I love strawberries, I love my sweetheart, I love my daughter, I love God. The Christian word for Love was a new word for a new thing: a new word for a new thing. That's very important to remember. The Greeks were a clever race, and a wise race: perhaps the cleverest race there has ever been, with the richest and most expressive language in the world. They had words for love, of course: the love of a man for a maid: another for love of friends: another for nice quiet family affection. But they hadn't a word for Christian love. No one before Jesus knew that there could be such a thing: so there wasn't a word for it, any more than there was a word 'aeroplane' before men began to fly.

It was a new word then: and it's a great pity we use for this wonderful new thing a word which has to do duty for so much besides. The new word in Greek was Agapè. A new word for a new thing, and it has to be learnt in a new and different way. Other kinds of love come natural to a man: love of food, love of a mate, love of comrades; we share those with the animals. But this other sort of love – agapè – is utterly new: and it's not natural to man.

In my own case anyhow, it was a long time before I realized just how new a thing it was. When I was a boy I had to listen to sermons about being good and kind and loving, and I used to think 'Oh yes, I know all about that: it's easy to understand. The real difficulty is to *do* it. Why go on talking about it?' But I was quite wrong: I hadn't even, as they say, 'got the idea.' Once you have got it – even in a rather misty way – it's as new a thing as, say, Radio was. What would our fathers have said if they'd been told thirty years ago that they could hear half a dozen different voices from hundreds of miles away in their own room by switching a knob? But that's true: and it has made an immense difference to our lives. So will this new idea of agapè. Once we 'get' it and let it work, we shall begin to hear voices we never heard before. People we were ignorant of will come into our lives. People we disliked will be able to teach us things worth learning. The routine of our lives, the 'one damned thing after another,' will suddenly begin to look different and to feel different because we shall see it against a wide new background.

It's this new thing I want to talk about for the next three Sundays. I'm not a professional preacher, but there's an old saying that everyone has one sermon in him, one thing worth saying that may help other people. I looked round at my life – and I was very clear that this thing agapè has been the biggest, deepest, newest force in my own life: and I want to share it with you.

It's as well, to begin with, to get one or two wrong ideas about love *out* of one's head. People say 'Why tell us we *ought* to love our neighbours? One can't love to order. One either does or doesn't love the person, and there's an end of it.' I've said that myself: but it shows one hasn't begun to understand what love means. It's true you can't *like* to order. But liking is not loving. Love is not even a very strong degree of liking. You like a person – why? Because he amuses you: because he gives you a good time: because he shares your interests. In liking, there's always an element of 'getting something out of it' – a feeling of pleasure for yourself. A *feeling*.

Now love isn't primarily a feeling at all: it's a matter quite as much of will as of feeling. It's a determination to help where help is needed: to help and to share. A determination so strong that it simply swamps all feelings of like or dislike.

If you saw a man lying by the roadside, just run down by a car that hadn't stopped, you wouldn't turn him carefully over with your toe to see if he was nice to know, before you helped him. You would go to it straight away. 'Well,' you say 'there's nothing peculiar in that: that's just common decency.' Yes, but wait a minute: it's only regarded as common decency because our own countrymen have been living on Christian standards, and unconsciously breathing a Christian air for centuries. There are countries to-day where persons of a high caste would be forbidden by their Religion – yes, actually by their Religion – to touch a man in such a plight for fear of being made unclean. It isn't really quite such a universal and obvious duty as you might imagine. The natural man in us doesn't want to help the fellow who had been run over: our natural man shrinks from a nasty messy body covered with blood. Most of us would have to bring some constraint on ourselves to touch it at all. But we should know we ought to. That's the first faint beginnings of something that deserves to be called Love. A hard thing often: against the grain: against our natural feelings it may be (though of course it needn't be). But how very different from the quiet comfortable feeling of liking and being liked! Different too – utterly different – from the eager possessive feeling of sex love.

Christian love isn't that sort of Love: and it isn't liking. And we can do it 'to order.' Whose order, I wonder.

It was a long time before I began to see an answer to *that* question. Meantime I had got my new idea: my new Radio Set, so to speak, and I was keen to try it out. It led me much further afield than I ever expected it would: and I heard new voices. Voices from the Home Station; voices from Foreign Stations that at first I could not understand: urgent private messages, S.O.S. calls. They had been in the air all the time: but until I had begun to use my new idea I hadn't heard them.

Next Sunday, I want to tell you something more of these experiments. Till then, goodbye.

2. Loving people you can't bear

I was saying last Sunday that the big thing which happened in the world on the first Easter Day was the first appearance of Love: Love in the Christian sense of the term – a new thing for which there had never yet been a word, even in the rich language of the Greeks. So a new word had to be found: among the early Christians that word was agapè; agapè was something utterly different from family affection, from sex love or from the feeling that we call *liking*. Agapè, we said, wasn't primarily a feeling: it begins from the Will, not from feelings. Sex love wants to possess: agapè wants to share. Liking expects to 'get something out of it': agapè expects to give. You mustn't misunderstand me: both in sex love and in liking there may well be elements of Christian Love. But to see agapè at its clearest we must – as in a chemical experiment – isolate it, and detach it from other elements, to study it unmixed and pure.

Obviously to differentiate liking from loving, we ought to consider the possibility of loving people you don't like, people you 'can't bear' as the saying goes.

This is an unfamiliar experience for most people, and not an easy one, especially if one has spent one's life keeping clear of people whom you 'can't bear': not thinking much about them at all, or, if you do, only with criticism or resentment in your heart.

But there seems to me no doubt that this is the first step if one wants to understand and experience this great new Power at its purest and most effective. Here then is something one can start straight away; this evening; next Wednesday; any time. I imagine that everybody in his heart recognizes someone he 'can't bear': someone who irritates you, seems to you selfish, silly, conceited or lazy. Certainly the fragments of talk to be heard on 'buses or trains would lead one to suppose so. Well, there's your chance. There's the field for your experiment, perhaps your first experiment, in agapè. Who is it? The extravagant woman three doors down the road: the grumbler in the daily morning train to London: the platoon sergeant: the clumsy charwoman with no manners: one of your brothers- or sisters-in-law? You've thought of someone: good. 'Well, now' you say 'What on earth am I expected to do about it? Go up to them with a forced smile, saying "I think you're one of the nicest people I know",' though you know, and they know, that you don't and can't feel anything of the sort? No: that's not the way. Right at the start one's falling into the mistake of treating it as a question of *feeling*. To begin with, think very straight and steadily about your own feelings. Why does this person irritate me? Because, say, they're always telling stories about themselves and their own affairs? Is that another way of saying that they prevent me from telling my favourite stories? Do I really dislike them because they hinder my vanity? That doesn't sound quite such a good reason for annoyance, does it! Suppose this time I don't begin with the determination to tell my story which is continually frustrated by their chatter; but suppose I give up all idea of telling my story and really throw myself into theirs, leading them on and asking them questions. See how that works. Or take the grumbler in the train. What does anyone know of him or his personal life? Large general grumbles about the Government or the Railways usually mean that there is something wrong much nearer home. Suppose you listen to him for a change, instead of giving him a glare and then shutting him out with the *Daily Telegraph* between you. It is in these simple, absurdly simple, ways that agapè can and must begin.

I've tried it myself, and the first thing I found was this: it's no good waiting until you meet the person and then resolving to try agapè. It begins long before, in the mind: when you're alone, walking to the station, listening – or half listening – to the Radio, cleaning your teeth at night. Does that sound ridiculous? Why, I've found myself cleaning my teeth with special ferocity some nights, because I was still hurt and sore about something that had been said to me during the day! Those are the moments when hatred starts. They're fearfully important, those casual minutes of routine or leisure. And if you surrender them to hatred, agapè can't have a chance. Your experiment will fail. It has to start in the mind. Think steadily and impartially about the person: the moment the feeling appears that you 'can't bear' them, resist it or, better, replace it with another thought.

Having got as far as that, then, in my own experience, something else happens. You begin to find that the person in question is becoming much more tolerable when you meet him. This isn't just another way of saying that you're being much nicer to him. I shouldn't dwell too much on that side of the thing. It has an awkward way of spoiling much of what you're trying to do: and it will make you a prig. (The nearest Bible equivalent for 'prig' is Pharisee.) No it isn't only *you*. Even before you begin conversation, they seem readier to sympathize more, and to boast or to grumble less. If that is so, good: the experiment is working, or beginning to work. There's a very long way to go yet. For, after a bit, you discover something else as well. There spring up all round you more and more fields for agapè. It never lets you rest, this great new power you have let into your life. Your early irritations have dropped away and died; even turned into friendships, perhaps, with liking as well as loving in them. But there are new demands round the corner. New demands and responsibilities: a new sense of success, and equally surely – if you are at all on the right lines – a new sense of failure.

Thus far, I found, one could be carried by common sense and reasonable interest in other men's lives. But there came a conflict. On the one hand, the recognition that there were some people who, do what you may, simply won't respond: people who seem to see through your efforts and snub you all the more. 'Hard-boiled' people. And on the other hand there's the conviction that agapè is enormously worth while, that it is the secret of a happy effective life, and that unless it goes on spreading it dies. Only, in your case, it really seems to have gone as far as it can go. There's the conflict: and men will differ in the way they meet it. I can only speak of my way. This conflict was the thing which started me saying prayers again, after I'd given it up for years. Very selfish doubting sort of prayers: but real prayers. Just things like this, 'O God, whoever you are, O God who – we're told – was revealed in Jesus, give me more Love, more agapè. Make the little love I've got wider and, stronger and more patient. Thank you for letting me see that it's the greatest thing in the world, and please pour more of it into me, and more, and more.'

More did come. And something came besides. The understanding that all along it had not been anything generated by me, but a force coming from outside. The right picture of it wasn't a dynamo inside me which I had to keep up to so many revolutions a minute and which couldn't generate more than so much power a day: but the right picture was of a pipe or channel connected with a vast water-main, whose power had nothing to do with me: and my job was to keep the pipe from getting blocked or furred.

I will add this much before I end to-day. There may be some people who, while they would in general admit the importance of agapè, grew suspicious at the introduction of God in what seemed to them an arbitrary and rather childish way. I understand their feeling. It is never a strictly logical step to fall on your knees and pray, and I can only speak of it as it happened to me. But surely, for most of us, the birth - or re-birth - of the idea of God in our minds does not come as the end of an argument. Many men, who do not normally pray, fall to prayer at times of great anxiety or great gratitude. If you want a thing deeply enough - as one *ought* to want agapè - prayer is man's natural re-action, and you don't get rid of the power of prayer or the reality of God by talking about wish-fulfilment or auto-suggestion. However I was myself still a long way from the Christian position. There were further discoveries to make, which I will speak of next Sunday.

3. Loving people who can't bear you

I had learned a little of the secret of loving people I 'couldn't bear'. Now came a new challenge: loving people who 'couldn't bear' me.

It is remarkable how deeply most of us shrink from even the idea that we are thoroughly disliked by others. Indeed it is often only when agapè, with its increase of our sincerity and courage, enters our comfortable civilized lives that we are first aware of the humbling fact that there *are* people who dislike and despise us, and will only hide their feelings as long as we are fairly passive and keep out of their way. (But there need be nothing wrong in being disliked: it may be a compliment. It is often a far worse fate - rightly viewed - to be liked by everybody.) The world will go along with you and applaud you for some virtues: but in others, and sometimes in agapè, it will not. We must be ready for that.

One remembers Mr Gladstone's fearless befriending of the women of the streets - pure and splendid instance of agapè - and how he was howled at even by some of his admirers. In truth, there is something in the humility and sincerity generated by agapè which rouses real hatred in hearts of a different kind. Men glibly quote 'We needs must love the highest when we see it'. But that is not the impression we get when we read the Gospel. Jesus speaking of some of the Jews said 'But now they have seen and hated both me and my father'. One remembers the words of Iago, in Shakespeare's *Othello*, where he says of the charming and lovable Cassio 'He hath a daily beauty in his life which makes mine ugly'.

Nowhere is the newness of agapè more apparent than in this demand that we should love those who hate us. It is far harder, in my experience, than loving those we hate. Indeed until Jesus came, such a standard was never considered possible, or even desirable, for a man. The proper standard of virtue among the ancient Greeks never went further than 'being a joy to your friends and a bitter grief to your enemies'. And I don't think it would be possible for struggling and imperfect Christians even to attempt this further step - it certainly wouldn't have been for me - without the discovery I was speaking of last Sunday that agapè did not ultimately depend on one's self but came from outside. At this stage it is all giving and no getting: feelings not merely count for nothing but must be resolutely ignored: for our feelings are being deliberately wounded by those who hate us.

To look back again for a moment over the course I had come, I had found, you remember, that the conviction of the worth of agapè and the increasing difficulty of exercising it had set up a conflict, which had started me once again in the practice of prayer to God. So now this further demand to use agapè to those who 'can't bear' one took me another step on: it sent me to the Gospels.

There was the first, the supreme, the only perfect example of someone loving those who hated him. I read the whole story anew: I read it, in those days, largely as an unbeliever might read it: sceptical of all miracles, very doubtful about the resurrection, and thinking that Good Friday was probably the end of the true historical Jesus. But, even on that interpretation, what a story! The greatest story in the world. Something to which this earth had never seen a parallel.

I read on, through the Ministry, on to that Upper Room and the mystical Last Supper, on to the shadowy garden and the swords and staves glinting through the olive trees, the mockery of a trial, the torture, as hands and feet were nailed to the wood. What did he say then, as the nails went through, when the very most that *we* could muster would be fierce defiant courage? He said: 'Father forgive them for they know not what they do.' That was tremendous: the words were unique in history. Think what you like of miracles, of the supernatural, here was something you couldn't explain in merely human terms. In a word, the search for agapè had brought me first to God: and now to Jesus. That discovery can be the beginning of a long voyage to anyone who makes it, and different pilgrims set out along different paths though they all meet at the end. But my main concern was still with agapè: how to bring more and more of my life under its power.

Why had I, in my life, absolutely none of this attitude to those who disliked me, those who 'couldn't bear' me? What happened when I met them? I felt angry that I wasn't appreciated: I felt in some cases frightened, and that made me false to myself in order to cover up what they didn't like. Yes, that was one thing: I hadn't enough confidence in anything, outside my own self-esteem, to back it against their disapproval and dislike. Less vanity and more confidence was needed: more trust: what the New Testament calls 'faith'. If I did suffer from their hatred, all the natural man in me had always wanted to hit back, to make them feel a little of what they made me feel, or else, more likely because more practicable, to hit someone else: to bully the office boy because the senior partner had bullied me: in fact, to 'hand it on'. Jesus had been the victim of bullying, injustice, mockery, desertion and torture: he had not handed it on. It had come to rest in his heart, even though the heart might break. Here then was something else about agapè: it was a 'non-conductor'. How difficult! How much harder than anything I had ever attempted. 'Hard, but oh the glory of the winning, were it won.'

The first attempts no doubt would be wretched: like one's first efforts at a new game, clumsy, ineffective, ridiculous. But it didn't just depend on me: I mustn't forget that earlier discovery. I was only a pipe, a channel: and I must keep it clear. Down to prayers again, more fervent this time and less doubting, and with more thought of Jesus than of me.

Even so, the old difficulties remained, indeed still remain, and seemingly harder than ever. One was this – after each effort towards agapè in personal relations, there always lurked behind the door the suggestion 'Well done: that was really Christian of you. What are they saying of you at the moment? "What a delightful person he is: so sympathetic, so forgiving!"' A devilish suggestion, that: the enemy right inside the citadel. If you yield to it, you're on the way to becoming the sort of person whom of all others Jesus seemed to rebuke most sternly – the spiritually conceited. You're guilty of using this great power just as a dodge to get round people and gain a little reputation on the way. Very soon the power will dry up in you altogether and you'll be left the man – or woman – with the kindly smile and the cooing voice and nothing behind it. The person who has done more than any other to discredit Christian Love. 'Salt that has lost its savour' Jesus called such people, and it was fit only for the dunghill. '*Salt* that had lost its savour': that was worth pondering. Not 'honey that had lost its sweetness'. There should be something salty, astringent and antiseptic about real love. If love is a passionate determination to help others to make the most of themselves, it cannot always be sweet and sympathetic. It must sometimes be stern, demanding obedience, earning unpopularity, clear-sighted and uncompromising. It was about at this point that something else occured to me: very obvious on every page of the Gospels, but I had overlooked it. Agapè is not only the right attitude of man to man: it is also the eternal attitude of God to man. In the next talk, which will be the last, I must try to say more of that.

4. The working-model

Even at that point, I could hardly have called myself a Christian. But then I read the great story again, and again; and I began to see it more and more as the *one* model – the working-model – of agapè in action in the world. The word itself occurred more rarely than I expected: the story was of a life inspired *by* love, not an exposition, or a treatise *on* love.

It had been my intention to say something of two great passages in the New Testament which for me threw a searchlight on the true meaning of love. One was St Paul's famous chapter – 1. Corinthians, chapter xiii: one can't know that chapter too well: to prevent the mere words from sounding stale in one's ear, try reading it in a different translation, Moffatt or Weymouth, or in a foreign language. And the other was that mysterious and very moving passage in the last chapter of St John's Gospel, where, in the half-light of dawn by the lakeside the risen Jesus asks Peter the same question thrice: 'Peter, do you love me? Do you love me with agapè?' And Peter can only falter: 'I . . . I'm fond of you, Master,' using *phileo*, the lower word for love. And then the third time Jesus comes to Peter's level and seems to say 'well, are you even fond of me?' Whichever it is, the duty of the disciple is the same; 'do my work: spread my message: feed my sheep'. But I will content myself with brief mention of these two passages, hoping you will ponder them for yourselves, because I understand that it is the practical application of agapè which listeners wish to hear more of. Now, in that very wish, there may lurk a misconception. Agapè is not – and never can be – a *dodge* for getting on more comfortably with difficult people. If you treat it as that, and no more than that, first you may begin to feel pleased with yourself over it – a fatal state of mind, as I said last Sunday: and secondly, even as a dodge, it will soon fail. If you think of it as a dodge, its motive power – its centre of gravity, so to say – will remain inside you; and the secret of a strong and happy life is to get your centre of gravity outside yourself – in an absorbing job, in the welfare of another, in a great cause. Many people know that, from one experience at least which happens to most of us: I mean, 'falling in love' in the ordinary sense of the phrase. Our whole centre of gravity is, for a time, not in us, but in the beloved. And *how* it increases our energy! How easily we find time to write long letters to her, or to him, almost every day! How much more attractive our everyday neighbours suddenly seem to our eyes, when we are in love. That's the *kind* of state – only more permanent – that we must regard as possible in our pursuit of agapè. How? Well, Christianity has its answer. It tells us that the ultimate object of our love must be God.

I don't want, for a moment, to minimise the difficulty of even understanding what is meant by our feeling love for God. Agapè, we had said, meant sympathy, forbearance: usually with awkward people. In what sense can you possibly apply that to our feelings for God? For years that was a standing puzzle to me, and I didn't attempt to solve it. I can't offer you a neat solution now: better and wiser men than I could do so, I expect, though I often think religious books don't face the question quite squarely.

But let us start like this: not from our dealings with God, but His dealings with us. According to Christians, if we want to know God's attitude to men, we shall find it in the character of Jesus of Nazareth. That isn't simply a dogma of Christianity: it follows from our feelings towards Jesus Himself and our reliance on His words. If we trust His teaching and admire His way of life – even as a purely human figure, to begin with – we shall be inclined to believe what He tells us. Now, the absolute core and centre of His message to men is that God's attitude to us is that of a loving father to His family. Such a familiar idea, often sentimentalized. But let us try to think of it freshly, we who have children of our own.

A father: who wants us to be happy, wants us to make the most of what we have inherited from him, wants us to grow up fully, learning from our follies and our sufferings as well as from our successes, wanting us above all to be free. Jesus didn't merely teach that as God's messenger: He lived it, as God's incarnation. Why do you think He went about with the profiteers and the harlots, to the great scandal of the respectable and the great prejudice of His own success? Because He *liked* them? On the contrary, He seems to have been as much alive as any of us would be, to the attractive personality of the centurion and the charm of the enthusiastic rich young ruler. No, He didn't like the outcasts: He loved them, because they needed help and He could give it.

That is agapè: the eternal relation of God to man: and this – as far as we can achieve it – must be our relation to our fellow-men. It's the one condition that the great Father of the family makes about His own love: 'you can't be fully a member of the family if you refuse to get on with Jack and Dick and Mary. If their shortcomings pain you, surely you can see they pain me far more.'

So we learn to say – every day – forgive me my faults, Father, just in so far as I try to forgive Jack and Dick and Mary.

But now to return to our original question. What is our attitude to this Father to be?

'Agapè,' says Christianity. At any rate, it can be nothing lower than that. That is the thing in us least unworthy of God. Any of our other qualities, which we're secretly so proud of, our cleverness, our charm, our powers of organization – look rather trivial when viewed through the clear eyes of Jesus. Agapè then, it must be. That's the answer. But what about our difficulty, that we can't speak of showing patience and forbearance in our dealings with God? That objection doesn't show that the answer's wrong: only that our original conception of agapè wasn't nearly wide enough. In truth, agapè, as I now began to realize, wasn't *only* the showing of sympathy and tolerance and so on. It was also the receiving it. And for some – independent, self-confident people – that's very difficult: for them it's so hard to say thank you, 'to be beholden' to anyone. But it's an essential part of real agapè: and it's often the one thing lacking in a strong benevolent character to turn him into a Christian. That's one answer to the question, 'how can we show agapè *to* God?' And another, of course, is this. When we try to show love to our neighbours, we're appealing to them as members of the family. The part which *we* inherit from our Father calls to the part which *they* inherit from Him. It is *with* Him in them that we make contact. What clumsy words! As always, the Gospel says it far better. 'Forasmuch as ye did it unto one of these, ye did it unto me.'

Christianity came into the world with Jesus as a new thing, and the world had to learn it. It is new to each one of us: each of us must learn it. To the majority, then as now, it seemed unpractical, a matter of trusting in people against the evidence, of hoping for the best in them. But Christians dared to say that trust and hope were not the feeble deceptive guides the Greek philosophers supposed them to be. When other virtues waned, they stood firm. But there was a greater still. 'Now there are left standing faith, hope, love, these three: but the greatest of these is love.'

Good-bye. Good-bye means 'God be with you.' And God means love.

Christian Worship

'The Layman's View of Worship', a sermon preached at the University Church of St Mary the Virgin, Oxford, on Sunday evening, 13 February 1955, when JTC was Principal of Jesus College.

Like most of you, I imagine, I was brought up as a Christian: I had to learn my Catechism, was taken to Church, was confirmed. At Oxford I could have called myself some kind of Christian; at any rate, not an atheist. The Gospels seemed to set before one the highest standard that man could conceive, in the character of Christ. One wondered how far some parts were literally true – Bethlehem, Lazarus, above all the Resurrection. Anyhow, the character of Christ was infinitely attractive, wise, noble. And my chief reason for belief in God – a beneficent God – was that Christ, the most effective figure in the history of the world, based his whole life on God. Surely *He* could not have been utterly mistaken and deluded. For me Christ came first and clearest, and God was a shadowy mystery in the background. Still, if one wanted to follow Christ, if one wanted to let something Christlike shine through one – it was not merely a question of moral effort. Even at twenty I saw that: to make one's religion primarily a matter of self-improvement would soon turn one into a first-rate prig. There was more than morality in the Christian religion. One must – to take Christ at his word – try for a glimpse of that mysterious Being, God, whom Christ spoke of with such wonderful confidence: in fact one must 'SEE God'. 'Blessed are the pure in heart' said the Gospel 'for they shall *see God*'. I knew quite well what being pure-in-heart meant, and I knew that I was not. I tried, in obedience not only to Christ but to all the great teachers, Buddha, Plato, to be more pure in heart. I made great efforts to control my imagination, to be more single-eyed, hoping thus to get nearer to 'seeing God'. Alas! I did not, to any appreciable degree. Meantime religion was by no means one's only interest: there were friendships and one's Schools; there was the fun of the moment, and the secret ambitions for one's life. A limited amount of religion seemed quite enough to go on with – a general interest in the subject, private prayer not quite as regular as it might have been, and communions not nearly as regular as they might have been.

And what about Worship? That meant to me what was officially called Divine Worship – Mattins at 11.0, School Chapel, in the Army Church Parade, and of course Communion – which somehow stood apart.

I have sketched the background of my deficient brand of Christianity to let you see how little room there was for Worship; and indeed Worship in the sense of churchgoing seemed to me then quite the least inspiring and least important part of one's religious life. I found the service boring. 'What good can one get from them' I would say after a Sunday Service, with warlike Psalms, even more warlike First Lesson, sentimental hymns and a mediocre sermon. I tended less and less to attend church: that was during my last year at Oxford.

And then I began to earn my living as a schoolmaster at an ancient Boarding School, quite ready to criticize the services as I had when a schoolboy myself. What has this to do with religion, I would say: compulsory attendance, hearty exhortations from the pulpit and rollicking hymns?

I came to change that attitude pretty soon, not because I experienced 'Conversion', or because the services altered their character perceptibly. I think it was because, enjoying my job at that school, I soon felt a deep interest in the people round me, boys and masters – people so different, so delightful, so infuriating, and yet all of them serving the society with the gifts they had. I came suddenly to see how self-centered had been that critical 'clever' approach. I had been standing on the brink of the pool making smart remarks about the swimmers. Now I had to dive in. It was harder to swim than I had thought. All that had little directly to do with religion. But my heart was saying 'join in: do what is required of you, though you may do it clumsily; shift the centre of gravity away from self'. At Oxford I fear that I had done only the things I was good at. A dreadful doubt sprang up: did my various virtues, such as they were, come from a desire to stand well in my own eyes? Had I been looking at my best self in a mirror? The subtlety in the temptation to take that attitude is that it seems to work so well: the world approves of it. But it was not religion: it was certainly not 'mine eyes are ever looking unto the Lord'. Whatever one meant by 'the Lord', he was not the figure at the back of the looking-glass. No: shift the centre of gravity: throw one's self into the job. But even then 'they' were looking at you: and you inevitably watched your step. You couldn't help knowing that your progress was being observed, discussed. Was one tied and bound to this selfconsciousness, as long as one remained on the level of human contacts? It seemed to me that one was. You could of course drop off the plateau, as it were; drown yourself in lower animal satisfactions and get self-abandonment in that way. Right for animals; wrong for men, and bringing weakness and regrets in its train. One needed no parson to tell one that. Shakespeare knew it: 'an expense of spirit in a waste of shame' he called such pleasures. But self-abandonment was the objective: if one must not go to the lower level, what about the higher? I began to attempt it, and I soon found that 'attempt' was the wrong word. Worship, it seemed to me, must mean – among much else – the spontaneous recognition of worth ('worth-ship') in something, or in someone, other. That depended not on effort, but on one's own unforced state of mind and heart. To me it came in two moods principally: one when I felt peculiarly unworthy, peculiarly far from what I knew a man might make of himself. The other mood was quite different: it was the mood of feeling thankful and happy: grateful for success, for praise well-earned and – important this – for the success of others. In these two moods one could for the moment slough off self: in the first – 'O God, I have failed again: alone, I cannot do what I would. Breathe on me, breath of God, fill me with life anew'. And the second – irrational, uncritical, but very real – 'O God, how glorious: youth, strength, success: a weakness conquered. Non nobis, Domine'. (The Psalmist incidentally knows all about those two moods.) But even here the mind so easily turned away from God to self: self-disgust is not always repentance: it can be a form of vanity: if you cannot be the chief saint then you will place yourself in the picture by being the chief sinner. And thanksgiving can quickly become a variation on the theme of 'well done, me!'

It was just at this point that I remembered that other note of worship, Community. If you acknowledge your wretchedness, or praise God for his goodness, only at your own bedside, the prayers easily run to egoism: but in company with five hundred others, it was different. This praying and singing together made it positively difficult to concentrate on one's own failures and successes. What, in fact, did fill one's mind and one's heart? Not, of course, noble and uplifting aspirations towards God all the time. Even during the best kind of worship there were daydreams and irrelevancies in the shadow of self; and every now and then one would be caught up, simply as a member of the whole company. Caught up: one could not say more than that because at the moment one took no notice of one's own re-actions. But later one could reflect on them, and slowly one could begin to form what I suppose could be called a layman's view of Worship.

One thing was evident, especially at a school where the range of age and intellect was wide: worship can touch the congregation as a whole in a way that few sermons can. The preacher must ask himself 'am I speaking to the Upper Vth, or the Lower Vth, or the IIIrd?' But words of pure worship, still more a symbolic act of worship, as at the Communion, can have a profound significance at very different levels: stupid boy and clever boy, master and servant, professor and peasant – all can find in a united act of worship something that satisfies each of them personally.

But worship in that sense needs practice and it needs humility: it has taken me years to arrive even at such a view as I hold to-day. I stress that word 'view'; what sort of view? It was not like the view you have of a picture, or a theory, or even of another man's character – something that stood before you, and waited to be examined. It was more like the view the walker has of a mountain-peak – seen by glimpses through the mists, cut off at times by spurs or gorges, appearing suddenly at unexpected angles to the main route, so that often one asks 'is that my peak? or is there another behind it in the clouds?' – that was the kind of view I began to have. By then I at least had my feet on a path, and to-day I still have much of the journey to make. But here I must abridge my experience, and put down for you, in brief, some convictions which took me years to realize more fully.

First, this link between Worship and the sense of community grew stronger. The stronger the sense of fellowship in your secular life together, the more vivid the sense of worship in the church. That was why worship in a school seemed to have more reality: you were already such a close-knit society, and in Chapel you saw the love and unity of the society on its Godward side.

(Conversely, how difficult to find the basis of a worshipping congregation in a modern suburban town where you may not even be on speaking terms with your next-door neighbour!) No doubt the advanced Christian can feel a true sense of worship in private prayer; for me, at such times, petition and repentance come easily, but not 'adoration'. I expect one should cultivate, even in solitude, a sense of 'the whole company of heaven', dead as well as living: but in this region I would not presume to offer advice. One form of true worship, however, we can all practice, alone or with others, Thanksgiving. It has the marks of true worship. It lifts the mind away from self: it keeps one humble; it 'disinfects the soul of egoism' (Abbé Bremond), provided that it is genuine gratitude to God and not self-congratulation.

A second conviction was this: worship is only one element in religion, though a vital one. One cannot expect to preserve for long this special sense of the greatness, yet nearness, of God. A sad mistake to suppose the only moments of true religion are the moments of rapture! There must be time for study of God's word; time for honest grappling with the deep fundamental mysteries – the Incarnation, the Atonement – grappling perhaps for years without finding ultimate certainty to rest in. There must be time for petition and intercession, and time, above all, for practice of Christian conduct in the tasks of every day. The sense of worship, like the spirit of God, bloweth where it listeth; we cannot command it. But we can prepare for it; we can open the windows and we must not be too proud and independent to make use of set forms. Set forms have their danger – formalism, monotony. But they have at least two great merits. First, they prevent one's worship becoming shapeless, subjective, sentimental. Secondly – and this is surely true of our own Anglican liturgy – they give to one's acts of worship a regularity, a pattern and a rhythm: they tie it to the procession of the seasons: 'seedtime and harvest, summer and winter, day and night' (as we heard in the Lesson this evening). Worship is an art, and in acquiring any art that is worth learning, regularity is three-quarters of the battle. The liturgy we have inherited, as our set form of worship, represents the progress of the natural year, not just because that is a beautiful idea, but because it was the patterns of man's work. It serves to remind us that work and worship still go together, though many of us no longer labour in the fields. It was one of the bad legacies of Puritanism that the one day set apart for worship was the day on which essentially you did no work. It suggests a divorce between work and worship, to the impoverishment of both. If you reply that the idea descends not so much from the Puritans as from the story of Creation in the Book of Genesis, I would boldly say that here the New Testament develops and corrects the Old. Genesis represents work as the curse of Adam: in the Gospels – well, look up the word 'Work' in a Concordance to St John's Gospel, and you will see what I mean.

With thoughts like these I was travelling some way from my first conception of worship as the momentary self-forgetful burst of praise or penitence in company with others. Self-forgetful – that was still the operative word: self-forgetful, self-abandoning, not only in Church, but outside it. I remembered two wise words of William Temple's (who used to speak so memorably in this very place). One was 'The stronger a man's religion is, the more secular it can afford to be'. Could the spirit of worship, I wondered, extend into the tasks of every day? And the second was this: 'Religious experience is the *whole* experience of a religious man'. The whole experience? What? His holidays, his jokes, his income tax? William Temple did not merely preach that; he lived it. Now I am not saying that the spirit of Worship, even for an advanced Christian, can extend thus far: certainly not for me. But our secular activities must not be packed away into a trunk labelled 'not wanted in Church'. We should look at them now and again in the light of what we say and feel in our moments of worship. If we sing with exultation on Sunday morning 'Praise the Lord, O my soul, and forget not all his benefits', and spend the rest of Sunday round the fire criticizing authority and complaining of the weather, then there is something wrong with our worship. I freely acknowledge that there are simple human difficulties which stand in the way of this ideal. The standard set before us in the words of worship is so high and so pure that it is hard, with sincerity, to apply such aspirations to our own lives. But at least we can each light our own candles at that great blaze of fire, and do our best to keep the candles burning. Nor, of course, does all worship carry with it a personal reference to the worshipper; much of it – and here temperaments differ in their capacity – more nearly resembles our response to the natural beauty of mountain scenery or to a great work of art. We have what an Oxford teacher has called 'The Vision of Greatness'; we feel that 'it is good for us to have been here'. And the effect on our lives is all the greater for being largely unconscious. And further, there is this great difference between a glimpse of God in worship, and our view of a mountain or a picture. If we can trust the experience of Christians down the centuries, what we worship is no static beauty: for the Christian the picture steps forth from the frame; the mountain reaches down a hand to help the climber.

We *can*, then, do our daily work consciously or unconsciously in the light of the vision that we are granted in Worship. Can we go further? Can we say, in any way intelligible to the normal layman who is only moderately religious, that for a Christian his 'work is his worship?' I find that very difficult, myself. I have read such statements in little books about Religion and I have heard it from the pulpit. But still I do not find it easy to regard any part of my daily routine work as worship. Some of you may well understand this better than I do, and I may learn something from you in our discussion afterwards.

And yet, pondering on the matter, one sees how parts of some man's work could have the marks of worship. Some great piece of architecture, say, undertaken with passionate intensity and forgetfulness of cost or labour, to perpetuate a memory or to enshrine an ideal – like the Taj Mahal or a medieval cathedral: some great achievement of the spirit like Handel's Messiah: did he not say that Heaven seemed opening before him as he composed it? Yes, there are great works, which are also acts of worship. But, oh, dear! – how far away from the office and the counting-house; from dictating letters and teaching students. I have a very long way to go before my own daily routine bears any resemblance to worship. Is it really possible for a day-to-day human life to bear the marks of worship? One would say not, perhaps. But wait a moment.

I said earlier that our own liturgy was tied to a pattern, a cycle – the pattern of the year and its seasons. Equally it is tied to another annual cycle – the life and death and resurrection of Jesus Christ. The Coming, the Birth, the Wise Men at Epiphany, the Temptation and Passion in Lent, Easter, Ascension, Pentecost: that makes the first half of the Christian Year, and the second half expounds to us the Teaching of the Master. That life stands to us as the symbol, the perfect symbol, of many things – of courage and constancy, of truth, of love, of redemption. Is it fanciful to see in it, as a whole, an act of worship to God the Father? There is a hard text in St Paul which one always associates with funerals, because it occurs in the Funeral Lesson 1 Cor. xv: 'then cometh the end when Christ, having subdued all rule and authority and power, shall have delivered up his kingdom to God the Father'. What that suggests to me – as I warned you, I am no theologian – is the picture of a Christ who, his work on earth and his work on heaven completed by his redeeming power, takes the whole achievement and casts it, in an act of worship, before the throne of his father: 'Your world, Sir, all present, and redeemed'.

These are high matters: too high for a layman you may be thinking, and the layman would agree. But I have tried to speak to you as simply and sincerely as I can about one man's path up the lower slopes of the mount called Worship. To all of us who keep at it there come glimpses of the peaks, and my prayer for you would be that such glimpses may come more clearly and more frequently to you than they have so far to me.

And so to sum up what I know to be an uninstructed talk on the development of a sense of worship: – Worship is Godward not manward. It must be self-forgetful, self-abandoning, mostly in company with others, so that we look towards them rather than at ourselves and then *with* them to God. Thus come the true moments of worship: but they will not last. That is the experience of far better Christians than most of us are likely to be: hence the vital importance of regularity. If we are regular in worship, we shall detect the rhythm and the pattern that underlie our annual forms of prayer and praise. This serves to sustain us in our dull and barren times, but let us remember that some worship which has little appeal to us personally may be the word of life to others in the congregation. And finally the patterns of worship, which Christians are taught to follow, link us up with the year-long work of man, and supremely with the redemptive work of God revealed in the life and teaching and death and resurrection of Jesus Christ our Lord.

There are many ways in which Christians can and should express their Christian faith: prayer, works of mercy, good conduct. Prayer *can* be self-regarding; works of mercy *can* be ostentatious; good conduct *can* be self-righteous. Worship at its best can lead us, and with us our fellow-Christians, more surely than any other way, into the presence of God Himself.

The Humanity of Jesus

Six addresses broadcast in the series 'Lift up your Hearts' at 7.50 a.m. during the mornings of a single week, 27 October to 1 November 1947.

Monday: The Humanity of Jesus

'Very God and Very Man' – that is what the Christian Creed says about Jesus of Nazareth: 'really and truly both human and divine' – that is the way we might put it to-day. Many people do not believe that he *was* 'really and truly divine': 'Just a very good and wonderful man' they say, 'nothing more than that.' Very well: let us assume that for the moment. The point I want to make in these talks is that the merely human character of Jesus is immensely worth thinking about; the great majority of people never think about it at all. It need have nothing to do with 'being a Christian' – at first. I would say that never to study the character of Jesus of Nazareth is to miss a vital part of one's education. Even assuming that the whole thing came to an end on Good Friday, even so, it's an astonishing story of an astonishing personality. This carpenter's son, with no money, no 'influential backing,' no organized force behind him, and dying a criminal's death at the age of just over thirty! And yet he has had a far deeper and more permanent effect on the world – your life and mine, than most other 'great men,' whom we study in history, choose whom you like – Julius Caesar, Napoleon, Isaac Newton, Shakespeare. The nearest equivalent to him, in the range and permanence of his effect you would find in one of his own professed followers, like John Wesley.

You may not end up your study of this character – Jesus of Nazareth – by becoming a Christian: but I am convinced that no one can be the worse for such direction of his thoughts. Most of the famous atheists and agnostics have studied his character with the deepest care, and whatever hard things they have found to say about Christians, Churches and Priests, I can't think of one who did not feel respect for the character of Jesus.

And if you are already a Christian, well, I can't believe there's anything wrong or irreverent in concentrating, for a time, your mind and imagination on Jesus as he must have appeared to the crowds in Palestine and to his own chosen followers. After all, the disciples did not begin by thinking he was divine. In treating Jesus this week as a purely human figure, we shall surely be seeing him as his disciples saw him. When Jesus asked that fateful question, 'Who do you think I am?' and Peter blurted out, 'Christ, the Son of God' – by that time we are far on with the story, only a short time before the Passion: and Jesus himself seems to treat this confession as a great and momentous secret. Till then He had been, in men's eyes, a marvellous teacher – original (his hearers said of him, 'never man spake like this man'), wise (Peter had cried, 'To whom else can we turn? You have the words of eternal life'), and yet simple ('the common people heard him gladly'), and immensely brave – which many teachers and philosophers are not. So, for the next four mornings I want to take these human – apparently quite human – qualities of Jesus one by one, his originality, his wisdom, his simplicity and his courage, and to see what we can make of them. Of course there are other qualities quite as much worth studying: his gift as a teacher for instance – which interests me particularly as a schoolmaster – his poetry, even his humour. But this week I must keep to those I have chosen: Originality, Wisdom, Simplicity and Courage.

Above all remember that Jesus appeared to his contemporaries as a vital tireless man: dismiss from your minds for the moment the suffering exhausted Jesus of so many pictures and stained-glass windows. That at any rate is not the whole truth about him. 'He came that we might have life and have it in abundance.' He was himself abundantly alive.

Tuesday: The Originality of Jesus

I was saying yesterday that this week I wanted to think of Jesus of Nazareth as a purely human character. Christians believe he was more than that: but they think of Jesus as Perfect Man as well as Perfect God, and a perfect man has qualities of his own:

he has more character than the rest of us, not less: and this morning I will speak of his originality. It is always difficult to get back to the first impression that a great man makes on his contemporaries: to strip off the veneration that has grown round him, to see again the startling, shocking, even revolutionary qualities in him. This is especially true of Jesus: listen to him on the hill-side when he was speaking to his own chosen followers, but overheard no doubt by the casual passers-by, as Hyde Park speakers are to-day. How did his speaking sound to them? Very strange stuff some of it. Their Scriptures had told them that prosperity was a sign of God's favour: it told them to love their neighbours and hate the ungodly – 'hate them right sore even as though they were mine enemy', so said the Psalmist. Very right and proper too. But this man was saying you should love your enemies. What could one make of that? And he said it was very hard for a rich man to be a member of God's Kingdom: as hard as getting a camel through a needle's eye, as hard, we might say, as pushing an elephant through a turnstile. They had remembered that: it made them smile. But it was strange unpractical stuff. If the rich and respectable weren't to be looked up to, if they weren't the happy ones, who were? Well, Jesus would answer that one. He gave a list of the people he would call truly happy (the word rendered 'blessed' in the Gospels nearly means happy): they were the peacemakers, the forgiving, the pure in heart. Well, may be. But besides them, the poor and the sorrowing. The poor and the sorrowing! Did you ever hear such topsy-turvy ideas? And the casual listeners passed on. Some thought it rather beautiful: but to most it seemed unpractical dreaming. People thought so then, and they think so still. But why, if it was unpractical and absurd, has it lasted so long? It's not difficult to *say* something startling and original. But unless there is wisdom behind it, it won't live much longer than last week's Sunday newspaper. There was a profound wisdom behind those words of Jesus. Many of the best and greatest men that we know have built their lives on them and found them not to fail. And I believe there is something in the heart of most of us, which responds to those startling words, which knows they are proved true by experience and by common sense.

Notice that Jesus rarely lays down direct orders, saying, 'you must' or 'you ought.' More often he says, 'if you do so and so, you'll find that so and so follows. Try and see.' How few of us have ever tried! We have let familiarity blunt and dim the originality of Jesus' words: we miss that. And at the same time, they are so unlike the wisdom of the world that we don't believe in them even enough to try and put them into practice. To Christians, of course, the words come with a divine sanction. Some may even think it irreverent to discuss them from the angle of common-sense and experience, to see their deep practical wisdom. Such sacred words are too sacred to discuss, they feel: well, the danger is that they soon become too sacred to think about either! One's religion must come out into the open and stand the test of everyday language and everyday living. It musn't be kept as a respectable extra like a Sunday suit! Christian living goes far beyond the highest common sense: but there is a point where Christianity and common sense coincide.

Wednesday: The Wisdom of Jesus

Jesus's teaching is familiar to us to-day – little as we act up to it. But it sounded strangely original then to the first people who heard it. So original that many deemed it then – as many do to-day – downright impossible and absurd. I believe that such teaching shows not only the originality of Jesus, but his true wisdom. It really and truly is the foundation for a happy life. 'Love your enemies.' Jesus never said there were no such people as enemies: people who 'can't bear' us and whom we 'can't bear'. It may be our duty, both as Christians and as loyal citizens, to oppose them. But you can oppose a man in firmness and ultimately in love. What *good* ever came of hatred? It is the most barren of human feelings, and ends by damaging the hater more than the hated. Do we doubt the wisdom of this word of Jesus in 1947, after two World Wars? Isn't the force of facts simply driving us to see that hate and suspicion even of former enemies leads only to death, and that love and co-operation is not merely the best way, but the only way of life?

And then – 'how hardly shall a rich man enter the Kingdom of God'. For those who *are* Christians and believe in God, great wealth has always tended to chain a man down to earth. It need not. Some rich men sit loosely to their wealth: they use it as a trust from God and they would be quite contented without it. These are they whom Jesus meant, I think, by 'the poor in spirit'.

Nevertheless for the Christian, riches are always a temptation to separate one's self from God and from the majority of one's fellow men. But even for non-Christians, even for those who want the wisest guidance through life from the wisest teachers – isn't it true that great riches do not of themselves bring happiness? Don't the obviously rich often look irritable, competitive, and a prey to worry? – anxious only to keep their place in the world? Isn't it the simplest truth and the truest wisdom that riches buy pleasures but cannot buy happiness?

And then the most difficult and startling saying of all perhaps – 'blessed are the sorrowing'. But is sorrow after all the worst that can befall a man? If you have sinned – and we all sin – are you better or worse if you sorrow for it? If your son has gone astray, wouldn't you pray that he might feel sorrow for what he has done? Wouldn't that be the first step to reconciliation and happiness? Would it not be much worse if he was incapable of sorrow? Or take, not sorrow for sin, but sorrow in bereavement. You have lost, suppose, a loved one in the war. If you were offered by some miracle complete relief from your sorrow together with forgetfulness of the loss – would you choose the relief? Would you not be happier sorrowing and remembering? Jesus of Nazareth was the first to stir such thoughts: that was his originality. And they are as true to-day as they were then. That was his wisdom.

Thursday: The Simplicity of Jesus

Even to those who do not profess Christianity, Jesus remains among the very greatest of 'wise men'; that would be admitted by the atheist, the Mahometan or the follower of Gandhi. He is ignored not by the non-Christian but by the fool. But in one respect he is markedly different from most wise men: his teaching was very simple to understand. Most wise men that have revolutionized our thoughts about the world have felt bound to give their message in difficult new words to express their difficult new ideas; and philosophers dispute to-day over the meaning of these words, that are almost technical terms.

On the simplest plane the teachings of Jesus can be comprehended by a child: you could give it all, so to speak, in words of not more than two syllables. It was concrete: not abstract and remote. It often took the form of stories. 'The lilies of the field toil not neither do they spin, and yet I say unto you, Solomon in all his glory was not arrayed like one of these.' 'The rains descended and the floods came and beat upon that house, and it fell and great was the fall of it.' 'Let not your heart be troubled, neither let it be afraid.' Apart from the beauty of such words, consider their majestic simplicity. The thoughts which they convey are so profound, so fertile, that wise men through the centuries have not exhausted their meaning in a life-time: yet the words themselves are as simple as the stories told us in childhood.

This great simplicity leads naturally to two further thoughts: the first to be appreciated by anyone who reads the Gospel story, whether he be a Christian or not. Such teaching, unlike most philosophy, can reach the heart of every man and woman: the flowers of the field, the lost coin, the straying sheep – it needs no elaborate education to understand such things. Such teaching reaches a circle a thousand times wider than Plato could ever reach. And, secondly, to Christians the supreme simplicity of Christ's words suggests a teacher so utterly confident of his message, so brimming with the spirit of the Gospel, that everything he saw around him – the simplest things of every day, were to him pictures of the power and love of God: the lilies, the sparrows, the grass of the field, the signs of the weather, the children at play in the market place, and at last the bread and the wine: – nothing was too humble or too simple to be an illustration of the great good news he came to bring.

Other teachers and wise men have been original and arresting: the wisdom of many of them has been given to the mass of men in easier and more popular form because in the original it is too difficult. But herein lies the secret of Jesus's teaching, herein is the universal quality of his appeal – I mean its simplicity. No one can be too simple to understand the good news of Jesus of Nazareth: most of us, I suppose, are not simple enough. 'Except ye become as little children, ye shall in no wise enter into the Kingdom of Heaven.'

Here, then, are three qualities that marked Jesus the teacher: his originality, his wisdom and his simplicity. But Jesus, even taking him as a man among men, was distinguished not merely by what he said, but also by what he was. Every schoolmaster knows that the power of a good life is greater than the power of any number of good lessons.

Friday: The Courage of Jesus

What a teacher *is* matters, in the long run, even more than what he says, and to-day I would consider the courage of Jesus.

Two things first about courage in general: the greatest kind of courage is not simply fearlessness but the conquest of fear and weakness and secondly, the rarest sort of courage is hidden courage: not the bravery of bravado that strikes attitudes and makes a parade of itself, but the bravery which has so mastered fear in obedience to duty that no one suspects how great the bravery was. The courage of Jesus was, in both respects, of this kind. The point is worth making, because many people, especially perhaps boys and young men, were brought up to think only of the gentle Jesus, the man of meekness and of sorrows, with the kind face of the stained-glass window. They forget, or never realize, the stern tireless formidable side of his character. And for this reason, they think of Christ's followers as rather 'sissy' people. 'Do you go to Church?' I've often asked boys, 'Well, no, sir: not now. I used to. My sister does, and, of course, my mother.' You see: Christianity is a very nice thing for women and children.

We are thinking this week of Jesus primarily as a human personality: one danger of regarding him as wholly super-human is that we forget the very real human weakness and temptation which surely he, like every other man, had to conquer. We know of his temptation in the wilderness: but I do not think that was the only one. The devil left him, we hear, for a season: he attacked again. And who can forget Jesus' words in the garden of Gethsemane: 'Father, if it be possible, let this cup pass from me: nevertheless not as I will, but as Thou wilt'? He knew what it was to shrink from pain, and surely he knew what it was, for the moment, to lose hope and faith. As he hung upon the Cross he quoted the terrible words from the Psalm: 'My God, My God, why have you deserted me?' That Psalm finishes on a note of confidence, and no doubt Jesus himself sounded that note before the end. But for the moment he knew the blackness of despair. And yet he went through with it: he drank the cup to the last drop in calm cold courage: in weariness, and in physical torture, among mockers and traitors, and false witnesses, he keeps the same self-control and dignity. A few days before it all began 'he set his face to go up to Jerusalem': he could guess what was in store for him. He understood the arguments against such a bold step: 'Master, surely you won't go back to Jerusalem *now*, of all times: you are walking straight into the trap. Remember the value of a life like yours – if not to yourself, then to us and to the world. Wait till the storm blows over.' Nevertheless, he set his face to go up to Jerusalem. And in the days that followed never had he seemed calmer or more supremely master of himself. His thought was all for them, not for his own life. 'Having loved his own, he loved them to the end.' No sign of fear, not even of fierce defiance, which would be the best that most of us could hope to muster among that wild mob shouting for our blood.

There was courage, if you like. And as they nailed him to the cross, what was it he said? 'Father forgive them, for they know not what they do.' Perhaps the most impressive words even in the New Testament. There is courage in them: but there is a quality too beyond even the highest courage, and in my last talk, to-morrow, I must try to say something of it.

Saturday: The Love of Jesus

Courage was a quality that mankind had long known and praised. It rings like a trumpet through the pages of Homer, and the history of the early world: and Jesus showed it in abundant measure. But here was something new: men had died bravely before Jesus of Nazareth. But not one had died praying to God for the forgiveness of his executioners. And this brings me to the last and greatest of his qualities – the mainspring and foundation of his whole life – Love, as evident all through his Ministry in Galilee as in his death on Calvary. It was a new thing in the world, and it needed a new word: the Greeks called it Agapè. Loving, in this sense, is a widely different thing from liking: Love is not really a feeling at all. It is a settled direction of the will to help where help is most needed – a will so strong that 'like' and 'dislike' cease to matter. That was why Jesus associated most with the unpopular and the down-and-outs, the tax collectors and the harlots. He did not, I think, especially *like* them: he liked the sort of people we should have liked – the open-hearted Roman centurion, the charming enthusiastic young ruler. But they did not need his help the most.

Now the real test of such love as this is whether you can have it for those you don't naturally like, and – sharpest test of all –

for those who don't like you. This love is so far beyond the range of most of us that, without the assurance of Jesus, we should not have known even its possibility: we know it now, hard though it is; and remember that even the effort to love, in this sense, is in itself a true form of love. This great force of love was behind all that Jesus taught and did and was: but men cannot attain to it by their own unaided strength. That is the record of the Gospel, and the witness of the innumerable Company of Christians – those 'Saints' through the ages whom we commemorate to-day – All Saints' Day.

Ah! you will say – but I thought you were assuming in these talks that Jesus was just a human figure. Yes, I was: but here, confronted by this over-mastering love, I throw away my assumption. It *is* possible to read much of the Ministry of Jesus Christ, and even the earlier part of the Passion, and still assume that he was a human personality – though it means ignoring some essential features and his own words. But when you reach that prayer for forgiveness for the soldiers as they nailed him to the Cross, then – I give it as my personal experience: it was those words that 'converted' me to the truth of Christianity – then, you lift your eyes from the page, and you ask yourself the crucial question: *Was* this man even as other men are? Or is the old story the tremendous truth after all, that God came down from Heaven to take his place at man's side and, in the strength of love, to suffer the worst that hate could inflict? I stand with the centurion who had watched that Crucifixion and as the end drew near, cried out, 'Truly this man was the Son of God.' Perhaps you don't: but I would ask you to study Jesus first as a man and to see whither your study will lead you.